THE
EVERYTHING
Superfoods
Book

Dear Reader,

As a nutritional counselor, I meet people every day who have transformed their health and lives by simply adding the highest quality foods to their diet. So it is with great pleasure that I introduce you to my favorite, most healthful foods. I wrote this book so you can fully understand the importance of giving your body what it needs to stay strong and healthy. This transformational magic comes in the form of nutrient-dense foods such as whole grains, vegetables, fruits, and proteins. These are the building blocks that will give you beautiful skin and hair; strong nails, energy, and vitality, with a mental sense of joy and well-being. It is that simple. Feed your body the best foods, treat your body with the love and respect it deserves, and your life will be transformed for the better.

I created each chapter's recipes as a basic introduction to the twenty Superfoods. Consequently, they are simple and easy to make, but delicious and satisfying to eat. Naturally, feel free to adjust the recipes' seasonings to suit your taste, but don't miss out on combining several recipes into a full and hearty meal.

With Warm Regards,

Delia Quigley, C.N.C.

Welcome to the EVERYTHING Series!

These handy, accessible books give you all you need to tackle a difficult project, gain a new hobby, comprehend a fascinating topic, prepare for an exam, or even brush up on something you learned back in school but have since forgotten.

You can choose to read an *Everything*® book from cover to cover or just pick out the information you want from our four useful boxes: e-questions, e-facts, e-alerts, e-ssentials. We give you everything you need to know on the subject, but throw in a lot of fun stuff along the way, too.

We now have more than 400 *Everything*® books in print, spanning such wide-ranging categories as weddings, pregnancy, cooking, music instruction, foreign language, crafts, pets, New Age, and so much more. When you're done reading them all, you can finally say you know *Everything*®!

QUESTION?
Answers to common questions

FACTS
Important snippets of information

ALERTS!
Urgent warnings

ESSENTIALS
Quick handy tips

DIRECTOR OF INNOVATION Paula Munier

MANAGING EDITOR, EVERYTHING SERIES Lisa Laing

COPY CHIEF Casey Ebert

ACQUISITIONS EDITOR Brielle Matson

DEVELOPMENT EDITOR Brett Palana-Shanahan

EDITORIAL ASSISTANT Hillary Thompson

Visit the entire Everything® series at *www.everything.com*

THE
EVERYTHING®
SUPERFOODS
BOOK

Discover what to eat to look younger,
live longer, and enjoy life to the fullest

Delia Quigley, C.N.C.

with Brierley E. Wright, R.D.

Avon, Massachusetts

An Everything® Series Book.
Everything® and everything.com® are registered trademarks of F+W Publications, Inc.

Published by Adams Media, an F+W Publications Company
57 Littlefield Street, Avon, MA 02322. U.S.A.
www.adamsmedia.com

ISBN 10: 1-59869-682-3
ISBN 13: 978-1-59869-682-0

Printed in the United States of America.

J I H G F E D C B A

Library of Congress Cataloging-in-Publication Data
is available from the publisher.

This publication is designed to provide accurate and authoritative information with regard to the subject matter covered. It is sold with the understanding that the publisher is not engaged in rendering legal, accounting, or other professional advice. If legal advice or other expert assistance is required, the services of a competent professional person should be sought.
—From a *Declaration of Principles* jointly adopted by a Committee of the American Bar Association and a Committee of Publishers and Associations

Many of the designations used by manufacturers and sellers to distinguish their products are claimed as trademarks. Where those designations appear in this book and Adams Media was aware of a trademark claim, the designations have been printed with initial capital letters.

This book is available at quantity discounts for bulk purchases.
For information, please call 1-800-289-0963.

Dedication

To all local community farmers who strive to grow quality organic food, keeping in balance with nature and with a deep respect for the earth. It is your efforts that will preserve our health and the future of our planet.

Acknowledgments

A big thank-you goes to my agent, Jacky Sach, for her support and consideration in guiding me to write this book.

To my Body Rejuvenation Cleanse teachers, Denise Kay, Susan Jalbert, Salina Hornak, Lois Burmester, Yvonne Douglas, and Alice Smith, for your delicious recipe inspirations and ideas.

Also, my thanks to Kerry Smith and Brielle Matson for all your help.

Contents

Top Ten Reasons for Eating Superfoods

1. Each Superfood listed contributes significant vitamins, minerals, and other nutrients to support the proper functions of your body.

2. Numerous international scientific studies confirm that Superfoods should be a part of your diet on a daily and weekly basis.

3. The vitamins and minerals contained in Superfoods are more easily absorbed and assimilated by the body than any supplements.

4. The twenty Superfoods listed are natural, whole foods that have helped human beings evolve on this planet over thousands and thousands of years.

5. The high amounts of antioxidants in Superfoods protect your body from damage caused by free radicals in the environment.

6. Superfoods can be eaten for everyday nutritional support and they can be used medicinally to help cleanse, heal, and rejuvenate the body.

7. People who eat Superfoods harvested from the sea have been shown to have fewer problems from mineral depletion and tend to live longer, healthier lives.

8. The Superfood garlic has been called the natural antibiotic for its powerful antibacterial, antifungal, and antiviral properties.

9. Superfoods provide the basic, essential carbohydrates, protein, and quality fats needed in your daily diet.

10. All the Superfoods have been recommended by the U.S. Dietary Guidelines for achieving and maintaining optimal health.

Introduction

▶ IF ALL THE scientific, nutritional, and medical reports are to be believed, the health of America is in serious jeopardy. No doubt you've read about the high rates of obesity, heart disease, and cancer affecting not only adults, but young children and teenagers as well. There is no longer any doubt that what you eat affects the state of your health. The difficult part is taking those first few steps toward doing something about it. Most people want to do better for themselves and their family, but feel trapped in an endless loop of cravings, weight gain, and depression. Perhaps you've lost a few pounds trying the latest fad diet, only to regain twice as much as you lost, leaving you feeling frustrated and defeated.

Take a moment to consider that some of the worst foods for you to eat are probably the ones you eat on a daily basis: French fries, donuts, potato chips, corn chips, soda pop, snack cakes, candy, granola bars, fast-food burgers, fat-free cookies, bagels, pretzels, pizza, ice cream, processed cheese, bacon, coffee drinks, and white bread.

Feel right at home with that list? Well, if you've picked up this book, then you've taken your first step toward changing your health and life for the better. If you were to replace just one of those "worst foods" each day with one of the Superfoods listed in this book, you would be taking twenty steps toward significantly improving your diet. Think about it: By reading one chapter at a time, and implementing the knowledge you gain, you can successfully cleanse, purify, renew, rejuvenate, and rebuild your body on a cellular level. That is the power of eating a Superfoods diet made up of whole grains, vegetables, fruit, nuts, seeds, beans, and quality animal protein.

Now, eating a whole-foods diet that includes the twenty Superfoods in this book is not a new phenomenon. Actually, these are the same foods that people from cultures worldwide have been consuming since humans first appeared on this planet. These same foods strengthened our ancestors' immune systems to adapt to harsh climates and conditions, fine tuned their RNA/DNA, and fed their brains so we could evolve as an intelligent species making conscious decisions. No other species on earth has the capacity to think, understand, and make choices the way humans can, and it was all possible because the earth provided us with the foods we needed to make this growth and transformation possible.

In this book, you will find detailed information concerning the history of each food, its nutrient content, healing powers, tips for cooking, and most importantly, delicious recipes to include in your daily menu plans. These are basic recipes created with your quick, no-time-for-cooking lifestyle in mind. Once you have familiarized yourself with these recipes, experimented with them for meals, and adjusted the seasonings to suit your taste buds, they will fall right into your daily diet routine. Think of it as a culinary adventure, a journey that can only lead to better health, optimal weight, a strong immune system, and a vital, energetic, disease-free you. No pill or fad diet can provide what eating the twenty Superfoods will once you introduce them into your life.

More than anything, enjoy the experience of change and renewal this book will open up for you. As a wise and ancient philosopher once wrote, "The journey of a thousand miles begins with the first step." Superfoods gives you the first twenty steps, so let's begin!

CHAPTER 1

The Nutrition of Superfoods

Many of the scientific food studies concerning what Americans eat should be taken with a grain of salt, as they can be based on a manufacturer's need to sell product. This research can also be influenced by who is funding the study and what they hope to gain from a positive outcome. However, the overwhelming evidence of research points to the benefits of eating specific whole foods for optimal health and well-being. This chapter introduces twenty Superfoods that will help you sustain a balanced internal ecology, a strong digestive system, and ultimately, a long and healthy life.

What Are Superfoods?

Superfoods are particular types of food containing high amounts of phyto-nutrients, necessary for the proper function of the body. Individually, they provide important health benefits, but taken as a whole they become a major defense against the ravages of free radicals, environmental toxins, and heavy-metal contamination. You can find numerous articles on the benefits of foods considered to be "super," and it seems everyone has their favorites; but for the most part the twenty foods detailed in this book can almost unanimously be found on all the Superfood lists.

The Familiar and Not-So-Familiar

The majority of these Superfoods should not appear unusual; as a matter of fact, most of you probably eat them on a daily basis. Take apples for instance, a favorite snack loaded with antioxidants that can be eaten plain or with a smear of nut butter, or transformed into an apple crumb pie. Blueberries, on any list of favorites, are low in fat and high in fiber and easy to use in smoothies or smothered in another Superfood, probiotic-rich yogurt. Perfect for your digestive system, a plain, tart yogurt can be puréed with the powerful cruciferous super vegetable, broccoli, for a healthy soup or vegetable dip. Quinoa may be new to most of you, coming only recently from the mountains of Peru, but its high protein content makes it a must-have on your shopping list. And not many people can live without their chocolate—the darker the healthier, so go ahead and find out why you can enjoy a bite of decadence.

Land and Sea Vegetables

This Superfoods list would not be complete without both land and sea vegetables. The oceans provide an amazing storehouse of mineral-rich foods to rival the most nutrient dense land produce; dulse, arame, hijiki, and kombu are proving themselves to be effective in weight-loss studies and preventing osteoporosis, so check out the recipe pairing them with garlic, known for centuries to be a cure-all for whatever might ail you.

South of the border they know how to appreciate the healthy fats in avocado. These are the "good" fats you want to include in your diet, because when you balance them with a few sprigs of the blood-cleansing parsley, everything flows along nicely. Add wild salmon to the menu and you have the ideal source of omega-3 fatty acids, essential fats your body needs for clear beautiful skin, shiny hair, and a well-functioning brain. Beans, a vegetarian source of protein, provide you with nutrients and fiber, and there is a wide variety to choose from. Kale, on the other hand, is a powerful cancer-fighting vegetable, easy to prepare and delicious with sautéed garlic.

Rounding Out the Top Twenty

Meanwhile, you can sip your antioxidants in green tea and support your prostate and bones with a handful of pumpkin seeds for a snack. You can always add the tea and seeds to a blender with mineral-rich chlorella, spirulina, blue-green algae, or wheat-grass juice, some frozen blueberries, and sweetener of choice for a quick and healthy smoothie.

FACT

Former Surgeon General C. Everett Koop claims that, out of 2.1 million deaths a year in the United States, 1.6 million are related to poor nutrition. This can be easily remedied by eating a diet of whole grains, fruit, vegetables, beans, legumes, nuts, seeds, and lean animal protein and eliminating junk-food snacks.

Wondering what to eat for breakfast? Look no further than a bowl of "the mother of all grains," whole oats cooked overnight in the crockpot and served warm the next morning with a few tablespoons of walnuts. For lunch, a powerhouse salad of cooked sweet potatoes, high in vitamin A, and cooked kale, topped with toasted walnuts and tossed with an apple cider vinaigrette, allows for easy digestion and assimilation of nutrients.

The Nutrition and Science of Superfoods

The understanding of our nutritional needs based on the quality of food intake has been a slow scientific process from which we are constantly and continuously learning. When fast foods were first introduced to the American public, they were thought to be an antidote to our increasingly busy lifestyles. Now, some fifty years later, you see the results of this way of thinking. Along with a processed, fast-food diet, came a host of other unhealthy habits: Serving sizes increased, while at the same time, people became less active. More refined carbohydrates were consumed with higher amounts of hydrogenated oils used to prepare them. The intake of omega-3 fatty acids declined, as refined-sugar consumption increased. Fruits and vegetables became a small side dish and pasteurized, homogenized dairy products such as milk, cheese, and ice cream were consumed in overabundance. American diets became more refined and processed with fewer varieties of foods eaten.

In the same amount of time, scientific research has repeatedly shown that eating a balanced whole-foods diet, made up of a variety of foods including the twenty Superfoods, will lower rates of obesity, diabetes, heart disease, and cancer. The facts speak for themselves, and people are beginning to take notice.

Eating Habits

According to studies concerning America's eating habits, people tend to rotate ten meals over and over in the course of a week. Unfortunately, many of those meals are from processed or packaged foods, supplemented with eating out in fast-food restaurants and pizza parlors. If this sounds like you, then your body is not receiving the necessary nutrients needed to sustain health. This way of eating only promotes obesity, diabetes, and degenerative disease. The beauty of incorporating the Superfoods into your weekly meal plan ensures that you're eating the highest-quality whole foods that meet your nutritional needs. Go ahead and rotate ten meals a week—just make them with the foods on the Superfoods list.

ALERT!

The 1997 edition of the *Food Composition Handbook* showed a 25–50 percent decline in the vitamin and mineral content of land foods since 1975. What this decline shows is a steady deterioration in soil, air, and water quality, as well as a reduced seed vitality that is depleting minerals and other inorganic compounds from our food.

With the slow deterioration of our food supply due to poor-quality soil, use of toxic pesticides and herbicides, genetic engineering of plants, and a host of chemicals used to preserve, color, and flavor stimulate and addict your senses; coming back to the essential basics of whole foods is a good move. Superfoods provide essential vitamins, minerals, trace minerals, phytonutrients, antioxidants, proteins, carbohydrates, and good fats necessary to help meet your daily nutritional needs, and they are delicious to eat as well.

Eating for Optimal Health

Most foods contain a combination of two groups that you will want to include when planning your food menu: *macronutrients*, so called because the body needs more of them; and *micronutrients*, nutrients required in only small amounts—these include vitamins and minerals.

Macronutrients include carbohydrates, fats, and proteins, which are the foods your body uses for energy and growth. When planning your menu or snack, try to include each of the macronutrients to ensure well-balanced meals.

Carbohydrates

Carbohydrates include all starches and sugars and are the body's main source of energy. Each gram of carbohydrate provides four calories. Most foods contain carbohydrates. The main sugar in food is sucrose, which is everyday white or brown sugar. Other sugars include lactose (found in milk) and fructose (found in most fruits and many vegetables). Starches are a more complex form of carbohydrate; they are more filling and contain more nutrients than foods with lots of sugars, fats, or oils. Foods containing starches include beans, breads, cereals, pastas, and potatoes.

Fats

Fats pack a lot of energy. Each gram of fat provides nine calories. There are three kinds of fat: saturated, monounsaturated, and polyunsaturated.

Animal, coconut oils, and dairy fats, which remain solid at room temperature, are saturated fats. Unsaturated fats include vegetable fat and oils; they remain liquid at room temperature.

Proteins

Protein provides energy at four calories per gram, but they are more important as the body's building materials. Muscle, skin, bone, and hair are made up largely of proteins. In addition, every cell contains proteins called enzymes, which facilitate chemical reactions in the body; cells could not function without these enzymes. The body uses proteins to make antibodies, or disease-fighting chemicals, and certain hormones such as insulin, which serve as chemical messengers in the body. (Other hormones, such as the female hormone estrogen, are not made from proteins.) Meat, poultry, fish, dairy products, eggs, cereals, legumes, and nuts are all good sources of protein.

The USDA Food Pyramid

The USDA has created a food pyramid as a guide for balancing your diet with proper foods (see *www.mypyramid.gov*). One way to look at this is from a caloric level, based on 2,000 calories a day. This is equivalent to 6 ounces of whole grains, 2½ cups of vegetables, 2 cups of fruit, 3 cups of milk products, 5½ ounces animal protein and beans, 6 teaspoons of quality oil, and 267 discretionary calories.

To break it down further, your day could look like this:

- **5–7 servings of whole grains** = 1 slice of bread, ½ cup of cereal, ½ cup of whole grains, ½ cup of pasta, 1 tortilla
- **3–5 servings of fruit** = 1 apple or pear, 8 ounces of fresh fruit juice, 2 tablespoons raisins, 2 dates
- **1–3 servings of dairy or nondairy foods** = 8 ounces low-fat milk, 4 ounces of yogurt, 8 ounces of rice or hemp milk
- **1–2 servings of animal protein** = 4 ounces skinless chicken breast, 1 egg, 4 ounces wild salmon, or 3 ounces lean red meat

- **1–3 servings vegetarian protein** = ½ cup beans, 4 ounces soy tempeh, 1 cup cooked lentils
- **1–2 servings of nuts, seeds, avocado, extra-virgin olive oil, flaxseed oil** = 2 tablespoons daily
- **Vegetables** are always unlimited, with a minimum of 5 servings a day.
- **Alcohol** consumption is 1–3 drinks per week for women and 2–8 drinks for men.
- **Recreational foods** such as chocolate, butter, honey, or other sweets should be limited to 132–512 calories per day depending on your age and body weight.

This is a great list to copy and refer to daily as you learn how to create and balance your meals.

QUESTION?

How much should you eat from each food group on a daily basis?
Contrary to restaurant serving sizes, you don't need to eat much for optimal health, you only need to eat the most nutrient-dense foods for your body to be satisfied. The amount of food you need to consume also depends on your age, sex, and level of physical activity.

A Typical Day

The nutritional information provided by the USDA Pyramid is a good place to begin putting together some sample menus and create a full day of meals, snacks, and drinks. At first it may seem a bit overwhelming as you learn how many grams of protein, carbohydrates, and fats you and your family need, but little by little it will all come together for you. Here's an example of what you might eat in a day, on a whole-foods diet, based on standard portion sizes. Feel free to adjust the portions to suit your body type and lifestyle.

- **Upon rising:** Have a cup of herbal tea or fresh lemon juice in water to prepare your digestive system for the day. Keep coffee consumption to 1 cup in the morning.
- **Breakfast:** Have ½ cup of oatmeal (not instant) or soft cooked grains, or make a 1–2 egg omelet with cooked kale and a slice of whole-grain bread.
- **Mid-morning snack:** 1 medium apple with ½ cup of plain yogurt and a sprinkle of cinnamon, or make a smoothie using yogurt, 1 table-spoon of green foods, ground flax meal, and hemp-seed protein powder.
- **Lunch:** Make this the main meal of your day, with 4 ounces of animal protein, cooked broccoli or other land and sea vegetables, and fresh green salad with olive oil and apple-cider vinaigrette.
- **Afternoon snack:** ½–1 apple with 1 tablespoon of peanut or almond butter.
- **Dinner:** Vegetable bean or lentil soup with quinoa, grilled salmon with cooked-vegetable salad of broccoli, kale, and sweet potatoes tossed with olive oil and balsamic vinegar and topped with a table-spoon of toasted pumpkin seeds, and whole-grain bread with 1 tea-spoon of nut or seed butter.

ESSENTIAL

To balance your daily intake of food, you need to eat a calorie range of no less than 1,200–2,200 calories made up of 20–25 percent protein, 50–55 percent carbohydrates (with the emphasis on vegetables and fruit), and 20–30 percent good, quality fats.

Try to finish eating by 7:30 P.M. to give your body 2–3 hours to fully digest dinner before bedtime. Going to bed on a full or partially full stomach can interfere with your sleep, and leave you groggy in the morning. Many people find that they won't be hungry come time to "break fast," because the body is still trying to digest the meal from the night before.

How Vitamins Help

Vitamins are essential for life, and you get them from the foods you eat as well as in supplemental form. Often times, the food you buy has traveled thousands of miles to sit on your grocery-store shelves for days or even weeks, depleting many of the vitamins these foods once contained. For example, according to the *Pocket Atlas of Nutrition*, by Hans Konrad Biesalski and Peter Grimm, even normal food storage can cause a loss of vitamin C. Vitamins are necessary for the growth of cells, to help your body systems function properly, and provide energy and vitality.

FACT

There are six nutrients essential for energy, proper functioning of the organs, and cell growth: carbohydrates, proteins, fats, vitamins, minerals, and water. These nutrients are utilized by the body through the digestive process, which simplifies the nutrients via enzymatic actions that break the nutrients down into smaller chemical fragments. These then enter the bloodstream to be utilized by the body.

The list of nutrients found in the twenty Superfoods is astounding, and when added to your daily diet, will leave you feeling energized, alert, and satisfied, with fewer cravings and addictions. This is because they supply your body with the essential vitamins it needs. For example, vitamin A is a fat-soluble vitamin that actually needs good fats and minerals to be properly absorbed. In its beta carotene form, it neutralizes free radicals through its antioxidant properties. Numerous studies have shown that when included in the diet, it can prevent bad cholesterol (LDL) from clogging the heart and coronary blood vessels. This is in addition to its ability to inhibit abnormal cell growth, strengthen the immune system, and aid in fortifying your body's cellular functions. That's a lot of things that don't happen if there's no vitamin A taken in from your food.

List of Vitamins

It is essential that you get all the vitamins from your food; they work together in a synergistic way, so that if one is missing, your whole system is off. You should familiarize yourself with the vitamins you and your children need on a daily basis for optimal health.

The following list of vitamins are what you will get from a well-balanced diet, based on the USDA Food Pyramid:

- Vitamin A
- Vitamin C
- Vitamin E: alpha tocopheryl, beta, delta, and gamma
- Vitamin D (cholecalciferol)
- B Vitamins: thiamine (B1), riboflavin (B2), niacin (B3), pyridoxine (B6), folate (B9), cyanocobalamin (B12), pantothenic acid, and biotin
- Vitamin K (phylloquinone)
- Choline

Each one of these nutrients helps balance the others, working together like a well-trained team. When your energy is low or your immune system is weakened, you may be missing certain vitamins from your diet. This is why it is so important to eat a diet high in nutrient-rich foods.

ALERT!

Whenever you take more water-soluble vitamins than you need, small amounts are stored in body tissue—particularly the liver—but most of the excess is excreted in the urine. Because water-soluble vitamins are not stored in the body in appreciable amounts and are depleted from the body so quickly, it is important to get your B vitamin from food sources or to replenish these important vitamins with a quality supplement.

Minerals Can Help, Too

In addition to vitamins, your body also needs the essential minerals to help in the assimilation of the vitamins. Minerals are a miracle in themselves, and your body utilizes over eighty minerals to help accelerate the billions of chemical reactions taking place in your body every day. There are minerals to regulate the utilization of certain vitamins and others to help metabolize proteins, carbohydrates, and fats. Some become actual components of your bones, cartilage, fingernails, and toenails, contributing to their hardness and strength.

Nutritionally, minerals are grouped into two categories: bulk or essential minerals, also called macrominerals, and trace minerals or microminerals. Macrominerals, such as calcium and magnesium, are needed by the body in larger amounts. Although only minute quantities of trace minerals are needed, they are nevertheless important for good health. Microminerals include boron, chromium, iron, zinc, and many others.

If you are not getting all of your minerals from food or are having trouble absorbing the minerals into your system, you can experience energy loss, premature aging, diminished sense of taste, sight, and hearing, and symptoms of degenerative diseases such as osteoporosis, heart disease, and cancer. This is all the more reason to include the vitamin- and mineral-rich Superfoods in your daily diet.

Important Plant Nutrients

Another nutrient you will find in the twenty Superfoods are *bioflavonoids,* a group of naturally occurring plant compounds that act primarily as plant pigments and antioxidants. They cover a wide range of biological activities, most notably their powerful antioxidant properties. Bioflavonoids work with other antioxidants to offer a system of protection for your body. The health-promoting effects of bioflavonoids include better eyesight, improved cardiovascular health, increased capillary strength, improved structure of connective tissues and appearance of skin, and a stronger immune system. Bioflavonoids also offer the health-promoting effect of lowering the risk of some diseases, such as atherosclerosis, cancer, arthritis, and gastrointestinal disorders. The therapeutic applications include treating a variety of diseases and disorders, including coronary heart disease, allergies, inflammation, hemorrhoids, respiratory diseases, viral infections, some types of cancers, and peptic ulcers.

Do You Need Food Supplements?

Your best source for all essential nutrients are nutrient-dense foods. If you feel your diet is lacking nutrient-dense foods, you may want to take a whole-foods supplement to support your daily diet. This will help balance out any deficiencies in the processed foods you are eating, as well as help with poor eating habits as you gradually improve the quality of foods you prepare.

CHAPTER 2

Apples Fight Free Radicals

Apples have long been a symbol of good health and well-being. As long ago as the Middle Ages, there was an English phrase that went, "To eat an apple before going to bed, will make the doctor beg his bread." Later, that same saying became, "An apple a day keeps the doctor away." In this chapter, you will come to appreciate the fruit Americans have grown up eating, as you learn about its antioxidant properties and how eating an apple a day can keep you healthy, wealthy, and wise.

What Makes Them Super

With only 95 calories in an average-sized apple, they are the perfect low-calorie, low-fat snack, and can be used in a smoothie or as a quick dessert. Apples pack a whole lot of nutritional benefits as a source of antioxidants, including polyphenols, flavonoids, and vitamin C. They are a good source of fiber and potassium, which have been shown to lower your risk for heart disease and help prevent cancer. The super ingredient in this Superfood is the antioxidant capacity of its skin. Apple skin, otherwise known as apple peel, provides 2–6 times more antioxidant activity than the flesh of the apple. In particular, the skin, more than most other fruits and vegetables, contains quercetin, proven to prevent unstable oxygen molecules—or free radicals—from damaging your cells. Free-radical damage can lead to heart disease, type 2 diabetes, and cancer.

Along with being high in antioxidants, apples are fat free and loaded with both the soluble and insoluble fibers that support your digestive system. One apple provides 15 percent of the recommended daily dose of fiber for adults. They are perfect for snacking due to their complex carbohydrates, which give your body a longer, more even energy boost compared to high-sugar junk foods. Another super boost in apples is boron, an essential trace element vitally important in calcium and magnesium function and bone metabolism.

ALERT!

Soluble fiber lowers cholesterol and regulates the body's use of sugar, while insoluble fiber helps to prevent constipation. To obtain the full nutritional benefits of this amazing fruit, make sure you get all of the fiber possible by eating the skin.

The History of Apples

Let's go back to the Garden of Eden, where the Bible says that Eve handed Adam a forbidden apple from the Tree of Knowledge. From this auspicious moment, apples have been associated with temptation, fertility, sexuality, health, and virility to name but a few. Later, the Greeks mythologized apples in the story of how Gaia (Mother Earth) gave Zeus and his bride, Hera, a golden apple tree on their wedding day. This golden tree was guarded by the serpent Ladon, much like the serpent of temptation mentioned in the Bible, who was known to play with man's weakness for love, greed, and possession. Legend holds that the apple's connection with all that is romantic and intimate gave it a place at the end of a meal. Apples were considered the ideal dessert food: sweet; delicious; an aid to digestion; and very possibly an aphrodisiac, despite the troubles that might follow.

Roman Times

Around 100 B.C., the Roman poet Horace wrote that the perfect meal in Italy begins with eggs and ends with apples. This followed on the heels of Romans adopting apples from the Greeks and creating their own orchards. It was from this point that the Romans carried their apple seeds to the farthest reaches of their empire, including Europe and the British Isles. To honor this most highly regarded fruit, they created the deity, Pomona, goddess of all fruit-bearing trees.

FACT

Legend has it that the famous Greek physician, Hippocrates, who lived around 200 A.D., would prescribe sweet apples be eaten after meals to aid in the assimilation and digestion of rich foods, and when needed, sour apples be eaten to relieve constipation.

The American Apple

Somewhere around 1629, John Endicott, one of the early governors of the Massachusetts Bay Colony, is said to have brought the first apple trees to America. Over time, cultivated varieties of apples gradually spread out from the Atlantic coast and headed west. The apple seeds were probably given in trade to the Native Americans, who planted them in their villages.

Then there was John Chapman, who came to be known as Johnny Appleseed. He would travel across the American countryside carrying apple seeds, planting them wherever he went. His travels and deeds became legend, and the seeds he planted grew into orchards of apple trees where there hadn't been any before.

Apple's Nutrient Content

Today, America is the number one apple grower in the world, producing a wide and varied assortment of apples. Each variety has its own unique skin color, and these come with a number of differences in the chemical makeup of the skin itself. This is because the phytonutrient content varies in concentration and types of polyphenols present in the apple skin. A prime example is the Fuji apple, which has the highest total of polyphenols and total flavonoid content of any apple. This is why you should eat a wide variety of apples to ensure that a balance of all of these antioxidant agents is maintained.

FACT

Polyphenol is a broad class of antioxidants including flavonoids and catechins. Catechins are a type of flavonoid contained in the skin of apples. Catechins are very strong antioxidants, 25–100 times more powerful than vitamins A, C, E, and beta carotene at combating harmful free radicals and protecting fragile DNA.

The nutritional content of one medium apple contains:

CALORIES	95	NIACIN	0.1 mg
WATER	115.8 g	PANTOTHENIC ACID	0.08 mg
CARBOHYDRATES	21.1 g	SODIUM	1 mg
PROTEIN	0.3 g	CALCIUM	10 mg
FAT	0.5 g	MAGNESIUM	6 mg
DIETARY FIBER	2.8 g	ZINC	0.05 mg
VITAMIN A	74 IU	MANGANESE	0.06 mg

VITAMIN C	8 mg	POTASSIUM	159 mg
VITAMIN B1	0.02 mg	PHOSPHORUS	10 mg
VITAMIN B2	0.02 mg	IRON	0.25 mg
VITAMIN B6	0.07 mg	COPPER	0.06 mg
FOLATE	4 mg		

One large apple can have up to 2.8 grams of fiber, which is 20 percent of the minimum amount of daily fiber intake, as listed by the daily values (DV). Diets that are high in fiber have been correlated with a reduced risk of developing heart disease. Apples not only provide you with a healthy snack for your heart, but have also been linked to the prevention of lung cancer, improved lung function, and the prevention of type 2 diabetes.

The Healing Properties of Apples

Eating an apple a day can be a powerful key to preventing breast cancer, according to a Cornell University study. Conducting the first-ever research on the direct effects of apples on breast cancer, this study, led by Dr. Rui Hai Liu, Cornell Associate Professor of Food Science, found that the incidence of tumor was reduced considerably in rats fed the human equivalent of 1–6 apples a day over a twenty-four-week period. The Cornell University food scientists have also discovered the substances in apple skin, called phytochemicals, provide a big boost of antioxidant and anticancer benefits. In an article published in the journal *Nature*, Dr. Liu and his colleagues credited the phytochemicals in fresh apples with inhibiting human liver and colon cancer cell growth.

Antioxidants help prevent cancer by ridding the body of cell-damaging free radicals and inhibiting the production of reactive substances that could damage normal cells. The *Journal of Agricultural and Food Chemistry* lists apples as one of the top fifty foods for total antioxidant capacity.

The Cornell University food studies have consistently proven that it is the additive and synergistic effects of the phytochemicals present in fruits and vegetables that are responsible for their potent antioxidant and anticancer activities. Their findings suggest that people may gain significant health benefits by consuming more fruits and vegetables and whole-grain foods than in consuming expensive dietary supplements, which do not contain the same array of balanced, complex components.

The polyphenol compounds, flavonoids, and antioxidants found in apples have been found to contribute to the prevention or healing of quite a number of diseases and health conditions over the centuries. These include:

- **Cholera:** Apples inhibit the effects of the cholera toxin.
- **COPD:** Chronic obstructive pulmonary disease leaves its victims gasping for breath. Dutch scientists found that the flavonoid and catechin class of food compounds in apples could improve symptoms in COPD patients.
- **Bladder cancer:** Apples were listed as an important source of dietary flavonoids responsible for the antimutagenicity associated with foods and beverages that protect the mucosal cells in the bladder.
- **Lung cancer:** Based on studies done at the University of Hawaii's Cancer Research Center of Hawaii in Honolulu, the flavonoid quercetin found in apples may help protect against certain forms of lung cancer.
- **Stroke:** Apples were a major source of the flavonoid quercetin used in a twenty-eight-year study by Finnish researchers with the conclusion that, "The results suggest that the intake of apples is related to a decreased risk of thrombotic stroke."
- **Heart disease:** According to both Finnish and Dutch researchers, catechins, a member of the flavonoid family found in apples, may reduce the risk of ischemic heart-disease mortality.
- **Cholesterol:** A diet that includes apples on a daily basis can help lower blood cholesterol levels due to pectin, apples' soluble fiber.

With all of this positive research pointing to the benefits of eating apples, you should include them in your meals for breakfast, lunch, dinner, or as a quick snack. They travel well, are loved by children as well as adults, and are available all year round. What other fresh, natural food do you know that can boast all of these attributes?

FACT

In 1999, food scientists at the University of California at Davis studying the composition of apple juice found that both fresh apple and commercial apple juices inhibited copper-catalyzed LDL oxidation. They concluded that because of the in-vitro antioxidant activity of apples, the fruit and its juice should be included in a healthy human diet.

Apples and Aging

Americans are a people who refuse to grow old, yet we know that aging is inevitable, and that getting old can be delayed by eating a diet high in antioxidant foods such as apples. According to the U.S. Department of Agriculture's Jean Mayer Human Nutrition Research Center on Aging, based at Tufts University in Boston, Massachusetts, the consumption of diets high in antioxidants has a direct correlation to the reduction in aging-related mental and physical degeneration. Scientists at the UCLA Center for Human Nutrition in Los Angeles, California, stated in the November 2001 *Journal of Nutrition* that "red and purple foods contain anthocyanins, which are powerful antioxidants found in red apples, grapes, berries, and wine."

Apples are not only good for your brain, they can also have a significant effect on how well your skin ages. Along with a diet high in vegetables, legumes, olive oil, fruits (particularly apples), and tea, Australian researchers concluded a study showing that skin wrinkling in older people of various ethnic backgrounds due to sun overexposure may be reduced by including apples as part of a balanced whole foods diet.

The Benefits of Apple Cider Vinegar

A folk remedy of high and pure repute, apple cider vinegar was mentioned by the Greek physician Hippocrates as a healing elixir and energizing tonic. His recommendation to take 1–2 teaspoons of raw apple cider vinegar and 1–2 teaspoons raw honey mixed in 8 ounces of water has been passed down over thousands of years right to the present day, where it is touted by many alternative healers as being beneficial for all parts of the body.

Apple cider vinegar is made from freshly pressed apple juice that is first fermented into a hard apple cider and then fermented once again into apple cider vinegar. This process allows for the vinegar to retain all the nutritional value of the apples, and provides the added benefit of powerful enzymes created during the fermentation process.

ALERT!

When purchasing apple cider vinegar, look for brands that are raw, unpasteurized, and unfiltered. You want vinegar to contain what is called the mother, a natural sediment found in the bottom of the vinegar bottle. This ensures that this unfiltered product retains all its nutritional and healing benefits.

Some of the health benefits associated with apple cider vinegar are as diverse as helping with weight loss to preventing ticks and fleas on your animals. You can use it to make salad dressings, homemade mayonnaise, and tomato ketchup, and even as a nontoxic household cleanser, deodorizer, and disinfectant.

Buying and Storage Tips

In the orchards, apples are first tested for the level of maturity with a starch-iodine test. This indicates ripeness by providing the level of sugar present in the apple. Once it is determined that the apples are ripe, the ones intended for fresh eating are harvested by hand. Before they are sent to the retail stores, they are shipped to packing houses to be graded and packed. Some apples may be sprayed with a thin coating of edible wax to improve their appearance and increase their shelf life. If, on the other hand, apples are to be kept for any length of time, they are immediately placed in storage bins after harvesting and cooled quickly. The two most frequent storage methods used to keep apples at their best for long periods of time are cold storage and controlled atmosphere storage. A third method, known as low oxygen storage, is a modified version of the controlled atmosphere technique.

ALERT!

The ethylene gas produced by apples as they mature can damage leafy greens and other vegetables when stored together. On the other hand, this same ethylene can help speed the ripening of pears, bananas, peaches, and plums by placing an apple in a paper bag with the unripe fruit.

When shopping for apples, pick ones that are firm, of good color, and free of soft and bruised spots. Store your apples in the crisper of the refrigerator to slow ripening and maintain crispness, as they tend to go soft ten times faster at room temperature. Avoid storing bruised or moldy apples with fresh apples to prevent them all from going bad.

SERVES 8

440 calories
16 g fat
74 g carbohydrates
5 g protein
44 g sugars
7 g fiber

INGREDIENTS

5 large red apples
½ cup raisins
½ cup apple juice
Juice of 1 lemon
¼ cup maple syrup
1 teaspoon cinnamon powder
2 cups raw oats (not instant)
½ cup walnuts
¼ teaspoon sea salt
1 teaspoon vanilla extract
⅓ cup vegetable oil
⅔ cup maple syrup

Quick Apple Crisp

There is nothing like the taste of maple syrup, apples, and cinnamon heated together and baked—an American classic the whole family will enjoy. Serve warm with a scoop of vanilla ice cream or by itself. Delicious!

1. Preheat oven to 350°F.

2. Peel, core, and slice the apples. Layer in a 9" × 12" baking pan with the raisins.

3. In a small bowl, whisk together the apple juice, lemon juice, ¼ cup maple syrup, and cinnamon; pour over the apples.

4. To make the topping, process the oats in a food processor until almost flour consistency.

5. Add the walnuts and sea salt to the oats; pulse to lightly chop. Pour the mixture into a large bowl.

6. In a medium-size bowl, whisk together the vanilla extract, oil, and ⅔ cup maple syrup.

7. Pour the liquid mixture over the oats; use a wooden spoon to combine. You may need to use your hands to mix well enough to coat the oats and walnuts.

8. When done, spoon the mixture over the top of the apples. Bake 30 minutes, or until apples are tender and topping is a golden brown.

9. Allow to cool slightly before serving.

Maple Syrup

Maple syrup is made from the sap of the sugar black or red maple tree. The tree is first tapped (pierced), which allows the sap to run out freely. The clear, tasteless sap is then boiled down to evaporate the water, giving it the characteristic maple flavor and amber color, with a sugar content of 60 percent.

Apple, Ginger, and Carrot Salad

For a sweet salad use red apples, but for something more tart, to help balance out the carrots and cranberries, use the green Granny Smith variety of apple.

1. Core and chop the apples into bite-size pieces. Place in a medium-size bowl; toss with lemon juice.

2. Peel and grate the carrots; add to the apples along with the cranberries and walnut halves.

3. On the fine setting, grate a 2-inch piece of fresh ginger and squeeze or press to extract the juice.

4. In a small bowl, whisk together the oil, ginger juice, balsamic vinegar, and plum vinegar; pour over the apple salad. Toss to mix well; serve on a bed of fresh spinach or arugula leaves.

Golden Balsamic Vinegar
Golden Balsamic Vinegar is pure, fresh, and fruity, with a delicately balanced aroma similar to Chardonnay. When buying, look for authentic Golden Balsamic Vinegar (Aceto Balsamico Naturale) from the Modena district in central Italy, and produced from Trebbiano grapes picked late in the season at the peak of residual sugar.

SERVES 4

280 calories
18 g fat
31 g carbohydrates
2 g protein
22 g sugars
4 g fiber

INGREDIENTS
2 apples
Juice of ½ lemon
2 large carrots
¼ cup dried cranberries
12 walnut halves
¼ cup extra-virgin olive oil
1 teaspoon fresh ginger juice
¼ cup golden balsamic vinegar
1 teaspoon ume plum vinegar

CHAPTER 3

Blueberries to the Rescue

Hard to imagine that with all the foods in the plant kingdom, the tiny blueberry is a top choice for beneficial health. A superstar of Superfoods, the blueberry is loaded with more antioxidants than any other fruit or vegetable! Research scientists have taken to testing it for all kinds of health conditions, and it keeps responding to the challenge in positive ways. In this chapter, you will come to love blueberries for what they can do for you and your family's health, while enjoying them in delicious, easy-to-make recipes.

What Makes Them Super

The first thing to point out is that, although blueberries are loaded with taste and antioxidants, they are also low in calories and high in fiber. This makes them the perfect food for dieters and anyone looking for a nutritious snack. One cup of blueberries provides you with the equivalent antioxidant content of five servings of carrots, broccoli, squash, and apples. What this means for your health is a lower risk of heart disease; vibrant, firm skin; and a boost in brain power.

Blueberries Versus Red Wine

Red wine has been touted in the media for having a beneficial effect on your heart because of the same antioxidants that blueberries contain. However, a recent study found that blueberries have 38 percent more of these antioxidants than red wine. The report, published in the *Journal of Agriculture and Food Chemistry*, showed that:

- 4 ounces of white wine contained .47 mmol of antioxidants
- 4 ounces of red wine contained 2.04 mmol of antioxidants
- 4 ounces of blueberry wine contained 2.42 mmol of protective antioxidants

Mmol stands for millimole, a very common unit of an amount or substance equal to 0.001 mole. Moles measure the actual number of atoms or molecules in an object.

For those of you who abstain from drinking wine due to the alcohol content, eat more blueberries and you'll be getting plenty of heart-healthy protection.

FACT

Thus far, antioxidants seem to have the most conclusive role in the prevention and delaying of such diseases as cancer and heart disease, as well as the aging process. However, more long-term studies on human beings still need to be conducted.

Blueberries' Antioxidant Force

The primary force behind blueberries' super power is the phytonutrient anthocyanin, a particular type of flavonoid—the one that gives blueberries that deep blue pigment. The anthocyanin family of flavonoids is responsible for a long list of health benefits that are integral to how your body functions properly. Take, for example, the way these flavonoids work with the collagen matrix, the ground substance of all your body's tissues. Your bones are made up of proteins, minerals (calcium and phosphate), water, and matrix, which is the scaffolding for your bones. The most abundant protein in your body is collagen, which is needed to form bone, cartilage, skin, and tendons. Ninety percent of the matrix proteins are collagen. The anthocyanin flavonoid in blueberries is crucial for the support and stabilization of the collagen matrix.

With so many health benefits available in blueberries, a summary list of these qualities include:

- Improving the integrity of support structures in the veins and entire vascular system
- Enhancing the effects of vitamin C
- Preventing free-radical damage
- Improving capillary integrity
- Stabilizing the collagen matrix
- Inhibiting enzymes from cleaving the collagen matrix
- Directly cross linking with collagen fibers to form a more stable collagen matrix

These antioxidant benefits of anthocyanin are thought to protect your body against the damaging effects of free radicals and the chronic diseases associated with the aging process. Based on data from the USDA Human Nutrition Research Center on Aging, blueberries are among the fruits with the highest antioxidant activity. Using a test called ORAC (Oxygen Radical Absorbance Capacity), researchers have shown that a serving of fresh blueberries provides more antioxidant activity than many other fresh fruits and vegetables.

The History of Blueberries

Blueberries are grown in thirty-five states and are one of the few fruits native to North America. The Native American tribes would use the leaves, roots, and berries for medicinal purposes. They also taught the Pilgrims how to use the indigo-blue skin and juice as a fabric dye and a spice rub to season meat. In the late 1700s, Captain James Cook noted in his journals how the cows loved eating from the blueberry shrub; and so it received its Latin name, *Vaccinium*, from the Latin root word *vacca*, which means "cow."

Early American folk remedies used blueberry tea to help women relax during childbirth. They also took the leaves from the blueberry bush to make a blood purifier that was good for the kidneys, and extracted the blueberry juice to help with coughs and other respiratory conditions.

Modern Blueberry Production

Today, the most common variety of blueberry sold in the supermarkets are the "highbush" or "cultivated" blueberries, which grow on tree-sized shrubs that can get as high as fifteen feet tall. The "lowbush," or wild blueberries, grow on small, ankle-high shrubs (only about one foot tall) and are about one-third the size of the cultivated blueberries. The wild blueberries are preferred by people who like the tangy, complex flavor of sweet and sour. The wild blueberries are from a different species than cultivated blueberries, but are part of the same plant family.

Known as the "Caviar of Maine," wild blueberries grow all over the state and some think they are tastier than the domesticated variety. In 1822, after centuries of blueberries being picked by hand, Abijah Tabbutt, a Maine farmer, invented the blueberry rake and made the berry a crop that could be harvested and sold on such a broad scale it became the state berry.

Meanwhile, thousands of miles across the country, Oregon grows twenty varieties of blueberries, each one with its own unique characteristics, including size, flavor, and harvest season. Blueberries are classified by a variety of sizes, from small—approximately 90–250 berries per cup—to extra large—less than 90 berries per cup.

Blueberries' Nutrient Content

Besides containing high amounts of the antioxidant flavonoids anthocyanins, as well as phenolics, blueberries are also a good source of vitamins, minerals, dietary fiber, and are very low in fat and sodium. In just half a cup of blueberries you get 2 grams of fiber, equal to a slice of whole grain bread. The nutrient content of blueberries is a dieter's dream come true.

FACT

According to *Health Magazine,* blueberries are a particularly rich source of antioxidants called anthocyanins (also contained in apples, grapes, blackberries, radishes, and red cabbage). Several studies suggest anthocyanins help prevent heart attacks by discouraging blood clots from forming. They also appear to improve night vision and to slow macular degeneration by strengthening tiny blood vessels in the back of the eye.

Based on the guidelines for getting your five or more servings a day of fruits and vegetables, one serving of fresh blueberries would be ½ cup, one serving of 100 percent blueberry juice is ¾ cup, and one serving of dried blueberries is ¼ cup. The nutritional content of 1 cup of fresh blueberries includes:

CALORIES	84	MAGNESIUM	9 mg
PROTEIN	1.10 g	PHOSPHORUS	18 mg
FAT	0.49	POTASSIUM	114 mg
CARBOHYDRATE	21.45 g	VITAMIN C	14.4
FIBER	3.6 g	VITAMIN A	80 IU
CALCIUM	9 mg	VITAMIN K	28.6 mcg
IRON	0.41 mg		

A serving of blueberries can be a topping for your morning cereal, cooked into a sweet cobbler, or eaten by the spoonful, and still provide the nutrients you need.

THE EVERYTHING SUPERFOODS BOOK

For those of you interested in just how much sugar blueberries contain, here are the percentages based on 1 cup (148 g) of fresh blueberries:

- Sucrose: 1 percent
- Glucose: 49 percent
- Fructose: 50 percent

ESSENTIAL

It is not always easy to decipher the abbreviations of certain nutrient measurements in books and magazines. For your information, when reading a nutrient chart, here are a few common abbreviations and their meanings: g = grams, mg = milligrams, kcal = kilocalorie, IU = International Units, mcg = micrograms, mmol=millimole.

Healing Properties of Blueberries

Researchers at Rutgers University in New Jersey have identified compounds in blueberries, called proanthocyanidins, that promote urinary tract health and reduce the risk of infection by preventing bacteria from adhering to the cells that line the walls of the urinary tract. Rutgers scientist Amy Howell, Ph.D., explains that blueberries, like cranberries, contain these compounds that prevent the bacteria responsible for urinary tract infections from attaching to the bladder wall.

In a *Newsweek* article from June 17, 2002, neuroscientist James Joseph, of Tufts University, made it clear that when it comes to brain protection, there's nothing quite like blueberries, which he calls the "brain berry." Dr. Joseph attributes the blueberry's health benefits to its antioxidant and anti-inflammatory compounds, and sees its potential for reversing short-term memory loss and forestalling many other effects of aging.

By eating only half a cup of fresh or frozen blueberries a day, you can receive their antioxidant protection and benefit from their antiaging properties. When out of season, buy them frozen to have in a smoothie or mixed with yogurt and walnuts as a delicious snack.

In a study on reversing memory loss, the *Wall Street Journal* reported that aging rodents fed several different fruits behaved more like their younger

30

counterparts when given blueberries to eat. The blueberries had a stronger impact on their mental functions than any of the other fruits tested.

Much of that credit goes to the beautiful blue-black color of the berry. According to the 5 A Day: The Color Way for Better Health Program, blue and purple foods can significantly lower your risk of getting certain cancers, help protect urinary tract health, improve memory function, and counter the effects of aging. Even the American Institute for Cancer Research recommends eating blueberries because they are "one of the best sources of antioxidants, substances that can slow the aging process and reduce cell damage that can lead to cancer."

QUESTION?

What is the 5 A Day: The Color Way for Better Health Program?
The Produce for Better Health Foundation has created a program to encourage children, adults, and the elderly to eat a colorful variety of fruits and vegetables that provide a wide range of nutrients important for good health. It has been implemented around the country, including the Public Health Department of Washington State.

What you get from eating blueberries are the many health-promoting benefits, which can include:

- Strengthening blood vessels
- Clearing arteries
- Improved vision
- More antioxidants for disease protection
- Enhanced memory
- Help for urinary tract infections
- Reversal of age-related physical and mental deterioration
- Promotes weight control

The Journal of Food Science reported in 2000 on a University of Illinois study by Mary Ann Lila Smith, Ph.D., that looked at a particular flavonoid that inhibits an enzyme involved in promoting cancer. Of the fruits tested, wild blueberries showed the greatest anti-cancer activity.

Buying and Storage Tips

When buying blueberries, make sure they are firm and deep indigo blue with a silvery bloom. Make sure there is no mold on them, and avoid containers with shriveled or mushy berries. At home, you can keep them refrigerated in a moisture-proof container for up to five days. Only when you are ready to eat the berries should you rinse them well under water; this prevents mold from growing on the damp skin.

During the summer months when blueberries are abundant, buy enough to freeze. To freeze blueberries, simply pour them fresh onto a baking sheet (do not wash first) and place them in the freezer. When frozen, transfer them to plastic freezer bags and store in the freezer.

Cooking with Blueberries

Blueberries can be used in recipes or just eaten plain. They are wonderful in baked goods, jams, pies, pancakes, salads, or, best of all, with a simple dollop of plain sheep's yogurt. Fresh or frozen berries can be used in baked goods, but frozen berries will discolor the batter. To prevent this blue "bleeding," roll the blueberries lightly in flour before adding them to the batter. It will help to know a few tried-and-true tips about cooking with fresh or frozen blueberries:

- When making blueberry muffins, the blueberries should be the final ingredient you add, just before you pour the batter into the muffin pans.
- Avoid overmixing blueberries in batter, as it may break the fragile berries and release their color.
- Fresh, frozen, or dried blueberries can be used in muffins, cakes, pancakes, and waffles.
- Use only fresh blueberries for topping cold cereals, baking fruit pies, and making fruit salads.
- Tossing blueberries in flour before adding them to cake batter keeps them from sinking to the bottom of the pan.
- When using frozen blueberries in cake batter, increase baking time by forty minutes.

You can enjoy eating blueberries all year long by keeping a supply of frozen berries in your freezer. In addition to baking, you can use blueberries to make a quick sauce for desserts and ice cream. To do so, heat frozen blueberries in a saucepan with a little juice or water and thicken with some cornstarch or arrowroot powder. No matter what your culinary experience, you will find blueberries are easy and virtually foolproof to use in recipes.

SERVES 8

180 calories
8 g fat
22 g carbohydrates
6 g protein
7 g sugar
4 g fiber

INGREDIENTS

Crepes
4 eggs
1 cup soy or rice milk
½ cup water
½ teaspoon sea salt
1 cup spelt flour
3 tablespoons melted ghee

Apple-Blueberry Filling
1 apple
1 pear
Pinch of stevia powder
2 tablespoons xylitol
1 cup water
2 cups blueberries
1 tablespoon kudzu powder

Crepes with Blueberry Sauce

This crepe recipe can be used with the roasted vegetables and walnut parsley sauce in Chapter 22, or with other cooked vegetables and topped with grated Romano cheese.

Crepe

1. Combine all crepe ingredients in a blender; purée until smooth. Scrape sides and purée until everything is combined. Place in fridge for 2 hours, or overnight.

2. Heat a crepe pan; spray with oil. When hot, pour ¼ cup batter onto a 10" pan (2 tablespoons for a 7" pan); swirl around to cover the bottom. Cook until browned on bottom, about 1 minute.

3. Loosen the crepe with a spatula or knife; flip with your fingers. Cook the second side for about 30 seconds.

4. Stack the crepes to keep them warm; cover with a clean cloth towel.

Filling

1. Peel and core the apple and pear; slice and place in a heavy saucepan with sweetener and ½ cup water.

2. Add the blueberries; bring mixture to a simmer; cook until fruit is tender, about 10 minutes.

3. Dissolve the kudzu powder in the remaining water; add to the fruit while cooking. Stir until liquid thickens. Remove from heat and set aside.

4. Lay out a crepe on a plate; spoon some of the fruit mixture onto one half of the crepe. Fold the crepe over; sprinkle the top with some xylitol and/or cinnamon.

Herbal Sweetener

Stevia is an herbal sweetener used by diabetics and dieters and actually helps to balance blood sugar levels The herb *stevia rebaudiana* is a member of the South American daisy family. It is 300 times sweeter than regular sugar, contains no calories, and is heat-stable. Finally, a great alternative to refined and artificial sweeteners!

Blueberry Waffle Cakes

Nondairy milks such as rice, oat, almond, or soy milk will work well with baked goods. They are equivalent to a 2% dairy milk in consistency.

1. Toss the blueberries in the 2 tablespoons of spelt flour; set aside.

2. Combine remaining ingredients (except syrup) in a blender; purée until smooth.

3. Pour batter into a bowl; gently stir in blueberries.

4. Pour ¼–⅓ cup batter onto heated waffle iron; cook until steam diminishes, about 1–2 minutes.

5. Remove to a plate; top with yogurt, agave syrup, and fresh blueberries.

Blueberry Cooking Time

Remember when using fresh blueberries in batter to increase the cooking time. For the waffle recipe, wait an extra 1–2 minutes after the steam diminishes before removing the waffle. You may have to experiment with time depending on the size and temperature of your waffle iron.

MAKES 12 (4-INCH) PANCAKES OR WAFFLES

Nutritional stats per pancake or waffle:
90 calories
1.5 g fat
16 g carbohydrates
4 g protein
1 g sugar
3 g fiber

INGREDIENTS
1 cup fresh or frozen blueberries
2 tablespoons spelt flour
2 cups spelt flour
1½ teaspoons baking soda
½ teaspoon salt
1 cup soy or rice milk (you may need to use a little more or less)
1 egg
1 tablespoon agave syrup
Fresh blueberries for garnish
Plain yogurt for garnish

CHAPTER 4

Broccoli Helps Prevent Cancer

Broccoli is one of the bestselling vegetables in the United States; adored by many, yet disliked by others. It is usually one of the few vegetable side dishes available on restaurant menus, and is found on most crudités party platters. In this chapter, you will come to understand this vegetable that most people take for granted. Once you know how beneficial for your health broccoli can be, you will want to make it a regular part of your diet.

What Makes It Super

What has elevated this cruciferous vegetable to the status of Superfood is its powerhouse of nutrients, which have been proven to boost your immune system, protect against cancer, lower your incidence of cataracts, build strong bones, and protect your heart from disease. Because of its many components, broccoli provides a wide range of tastes and textures, from soft and flowery (the floret) to fibrous and crunchy (the stem and stalk). It is the sulfur compounds that are released while cooking that turn many people away, but don't let that keep you from experiencing a delightful dish of lightly steamed broccoli tossed with sautéed garlic and olive oil.

One of the ten most-popular vegetables eaten in the United States, broccoli comes third in the amount of polyphenols it provides, with only beets and red onions containing more per serving. Broccoli is classified as *Brassica oleracea italica*, whose other members include cauliflower, kale, cabbage, collards, turnips, rutabagas, Brussels sprouts, and Chinese cabbage. The *Brassica* vegetables all share a common feature—a four-petaled flower bearing a resemblance to the Greek cross, which explains why they are known as crucifers, or cruciferous vegetables.

FACT

Phytonutrients work as antioxidants to disarm free radicals before they can damage DNA, cell membranes, and fat-containing molecules such as cholesterol. The phytonutrient compounds in broccoli, however, works at such a deep level that they actually signal your genes to increase production of enzymes involved in the detoxification process through which your body eliminates harmful compounds.

In 1992, Dr. Paul Talalay, a researcher at Johns Hopkins University, announced the discovery of the phytonutrient sulforaphane, a compound found in broccoli that prevented the development of tumors by 60 percent in one study group and reduced the size of tumors that did develop in another group by 75 percent. In 1997, building on this research, Dr. Talalay and his research team found that broccoli also contains indole-3-carbinol, a compound that helps deactivate a potent estrogen metabolite

(4-hydroxyestrone) that promotes tumor growth, especially in estrogen-sensitive breast cells. Indole-3-carbinol has been shown to suppress not only breast-tumor cell growth, but also the movement of cancerous cells to other parts of the body.

Broccoli Sprout Research

Later research carried out by the Johns Hopkins research team focused on broccoli sprouts, which contain a concentrated form of the sulfur-containing phytonutrients found in broccoli, called sulfurophane glucosinolate (SGS). In his groundbreaking work with broccoli sprouts, Dr. Talalay found that three-day-old broccoli sprouts consistently contained 20–50 times the amount of chemo-protective compounds found in mature broccoli heads, thereby offering a simple, dietary means of chemically reducing cancer risk. These super sprouts boost enzymes in the body, while detoxifying potential carcinogens. By including a healthy serving of broccoli sprouts in your salad or sandwich, you can receive these powerful phytonutrients and support your overall health.

The antioxidants found in broccoli sprouts may help prevent several types of cancer, heart disease, macular degeneration, and stomach ulcers, and may also help reduce cholesterol levels.

ALERT!

Researchers estimate that broccoli sprouts provide 10–100 times the power of mature broccoli to neutralize carcinogens. A sprinkling of broccoli sprouts in your salad or on your sandwich can do more than even a couple of spears of broccoli. Children who dislike the taste of broccoli often enjoy the milder flavor of the sprouts, and they will get even more nutritional benefits.

How much cooked broccoli would you need to eat to get the same benefits you would get from eating broccoli sprouts? According to research from Johns Hopkins School of Medicine, you would need to eat at least 1¼ pounds of cooked broccoli to get the same amount of protection you would from eating just 1 ounce of broccoli sprouts.

Growing Broccoli Sprouts

In less than a week, you can easily grow broccoli sprouts in your kitchen. A tablespoon of broccoli seeds will produce about 1 cup of sprouts. Start with ¼ cup of seeds to supply you with a good week's worth of sprouts. To begin, rinse the seeds and place in a sprouting or canning jar, cover with water, and let soak 8–10 hours or overnight. With the sprouting lid in place or using a piece of cheesecloth secured to the top of the jar, drain and rinse the seeds, then drain again. Keep the jar on your counter out of direct sunlight, inverted in a bowl so no water accumulates and creates mold. Rinse and drain the seeds at least twice a day. After a few days, you will notice tiny yellow leaves that will turn green after about a day. At this time, you can place the sprouts in a large bowl and fill with cool water. Agitate the water to loosen the seed hulls from the sprout; they will float to the top. Remove as many of the seed hulls as possible. Drain the sprouts and let them dry completely. Store the sprouts in a covered container and refrigerate. They will keep for two weeks in the refrigerator, but for maximum benefit, eat them before that.

The History of Broccoli

The cultivation of broccoli is said to have originated in Calabria, Italy. The word *broccoli* comes from the Latin word *bracchium*, which means "strong arm" or "branch." The famous Roman chef of the day, Apicius, a beloved cookbook author of ancient Rome, prepared broccoli by first boiling it and then bruising it "with a mixture of cumin and coriander seeds, chopped onion plus a few drops of oil and sun-made wine." Over time, the Romans developed recipes preparing broccoli with all sorts of creamy sauces, some cooked with wine and others flavored simply with olive oil, garlic, and herbs.

In 1775, John Randolph wrote a description of broccoli in *A Treatise on Gardening by a Citizen of Virginia:* "The stems will eat like asparagus, and the heads like cauliflower."

Catherine de Medici, a daughter of the powerful Florentine banking family, married Henry II in the sixteenth century and was instrumental in introducing broccoli to French gardeners and the French cuisine of the time. From there, the vegetable spread throughout Europe. Broccoli was first brought to North America in the 1700s, to be cultivated in the gardens of Virginia.

One Virginia farmer who planted broccoli on his estate was Thomas Jefferson, often called the "farmer president," an avid gardener and collector of new fruit and vegetable seeds. On May 27, 1767, he recorded in his journal that he had planted broccoli, along with radishes, lettuce, and cauliflower. However, broccoli would not receive the attention it deserved until the 1920s, when two brothers from Messina, Italy, Stephano and Andrea D'Arrigo, came to the United States, bringing along their broccoli seeds. Today, broccoli is revered around the world for its distinctive flavor and ability to adapt to any style of cuisine.

Broccoli's Nutrient Content

Despite the fact that broccoli has been grown in the United States for the past 200 years, it is only in the last twenty-five years that the American public has recognized its benefits and embraced it fully. In 1 cup of steamed broccoli, you receive almost 44 calories, along with vitamin A, vitamin C, potassium, folate, iron, and fiber. One ounce of broccoli contains 11 mg of calcium along with vitamin A in the form of beta carotene, indole-3-carbinol, and phytochemicals called glucosinolates, which your body metabolizes into powerful anticarcinogens called isothiocyanates.

QUESTION?

What is so important about folic acid?
Folate (the plant form of folic acid) is known as vitamin B9, and is required for DNA synthesis and cell growth. It is important for red blood cell formation, energy production, and the formation of amino acids. Broccoli is so rich in folates that a single cup of raw, chopped broccoli provides more than 50 milligrams of this vitamin.

One cup of steamed broccoli contains the following nutrients:

CALORIES	31	POTASSIUM	288 mg
VITAMIN C	81.2 mg	PHOSPHORUS	60 mg
VITAMIN K	92.5 mcg	MAGNESIUM	19 mg
VITAMIN A	567 IU	PROTEIN	2.57 g
FOLATE	57 mcg	IRON	.66 mg
DIETARY FIBER	2.4 g	CALCIUM	43 mg

Along with all the vitamin and mineral support that broccoli provides, it also contains the carotenoid antioxidants lutein and zeaxanthin, which, along with vitamin C, are highly beneficial for the lens and retina of the eye, to the point of protecting your eyes from any free-radical damage that ultraviolet light can cause.

Healing Properties of Broccoli

One of the most significant contributions broccoli can make to your health is as an anti-cancer agent. The naturally occurring component of the brassica family of vegetables, including broccoli, cabbage, and Brussels sprouts, indole-3-carbinol (I3C), has been recognized as a promising anti-cancer agent against certain reproductive tumor cells, as well as prostate, colorectal, and lung cancer, even when compared to consuming a diet high in other vegetables.

FACT

One study showed that eating two servings a day of cruciferous vegetables, including ½ cup of broccoli, may result in as much as a 50 percent reduction in the risk of certain types of cancers such as cancers of the lung, stomach, colon, and rectum.

While scientists continue to do valuable research into the causes of cancer, they have come to realize that it may be easier to prevent cancer than to cure it. Eating a whole-foods diet containing broccoli, as well as the other Superfoods listed in this book, can nourish your body on a cellular level, helping to strengthen your immune system, fight disease, and keep you healthy. Scientific research has shown that almost 30 percent of all cancers are related to the quality of food that you eat, and that a diet lacking in cruciferous vegetables can play a major role in whether you develop cancer or not.

According to a study published in *Cancer Research,* broccoli and tomatoes are a powerful team in preventing prostate cancer. John Erdman, Professor of Food Science and Human Nutrition at the University of Illinois, found that when tomatoes and broccoli are eaten together, there is an additive effect due to the different bioactive compounds in each food working on different anti-cancer pathways.

Those cancer-preventing sulfur compounds are also the reason broccoli and other cruciferous vegetables have such a strong, and for some, unappealing odor; the sometimes-bitter taste and smell of these vegetables protects them from insects and animals. Many people have difficulty digesting raw broccoli due to the high fiber and sulfur content of the vegetable. This can cause gas and bloating in the gastrointestinal tract, which can lead to an embarrassing release of rather toxic-smelling fumes. Rather than eliminate these all-important cancer-fighting vegetables from your diet, make sure to cook them before eating.

Buying and Storage Tips

Despite broccoli being listed as one of America's most popular vegetables, we're still not eating enough of it. Instead, most people consider iceberg lettuce and French fries sufficient vegetables to keep them healthy, missing out on the nutrients broccoli can provide.

Broccoli is in season October through May, yet can be found in super-markets all year long. Naturally, broccoli is at its most nutritious when grown without chemicals in your home garden or purchased from a local organic farmer, yet frozen organic broccoli also contains a high level of valuable nutrients.

When buying broccoli fresh, look for the young plant, as the older broccoli can be tough and can also have a strong odor. There are an assortment of new broccoli varieties available in your food market in colors varying from a rich sage green to deep forest green and even shades of purple. Look for the most deeply colored florets, since these contain the most phytonutrients. You can also explore the tastes of other family members, such as broccolini, a combination of broccoli and kale, or broccoflower, a combination of broccoli and cauliflower. Both provide a one-two punch of anti-cancer phytonutrients. A few tips to remember when shopping for and storing broccoli:

- Look for tight, deeply colored, and dense florets, or flowers.
- The smaller the head, the better the flavor.
- Yellowing florets are signs that the broccoli is past its prime.
- Leaves on the stalks should be firm and fresh looking; wilted leaves are a sign of old broccoli.
- Do not discard the leaves, as they are also rich in nutrients; instead, wash and cook them along with the florets.
- Broccoli will keep in the fridge crisper for up to seven days.
- Never wash the broccoli before storing, as it can develop mold when damp.

Although it might cost a few cents more, organically grown broccoli has been shown to be higher in phytonutrients than chemically sprayed, conventionally grown varieties.

Cooking with Broccoli

Before cooking, make sure to wash the broccoli well, allowing it to soak in cold water to remove any sand or loose dirt. Cut off and discard the lower part of the stalk, then peel the remaining stalk using a paring knife or a vegetable peeler. (The stalk is the sweetest part of the broccoli plant.) Slice on the diagonal and cook along with the florets. Steaming broccoli or simmering it in very little water is the best way to cook it. Keep the heat low and simmer gently, as boiled broccoli can lose more than 50 percent of its vitamin C.

Tips for Serving Broccoli

Broccoli is one of the most versatile vegetables when it comes to cooking. You can't go wrong when preparing broccoli in any of the following ways:

- Sauté broccoli florets, sliced garlic, and chopped onion in olive oil and add to your favorite breakfast omelet; serve with grilled tomatoes.
- Simmer chopped broccoli florets and stalk in vegetable stock until just tender, then purée in a blender with a dash of milk, cream, or silken tofu. Salt and pepper to taste.
- Serve a salad of lightly steamed broccoli florets with a bowl of fresh tomato soup as a delicious cancer-preventive lunch.
- Steam broccoli florets, add to tomato sauce, and layer with cheese across the top of a pizza crust.
- Sauté broccoli florets in olive oil with other vegetables, such as onions, carrots, and mushrooms, and add to pasta sauce; serve with whole-wheat pasta or brown rice.
- For a quick snack, serve lightly steamed broccoli florets and sliced carrots and celery sticks with hummus dip and whole grain crackers.

Broccoli teams well with other vegetables when used in stir-fry, casseroles, soups, and even stews. You can serve it as a simple vegetable side dish complementing your protein entrée or steamed and tossed in a salad as a quick meal. Regardless of how you prepare broccoli, it will be a super-healthy addition to your family's diet.

SERVES 8

120 calories
4 g fat
16 g carbohydrates
9 g protein
5 g sugar
6 g fiber

INGREDIENTS

½ onion, chopped
2 cloves garlic, minced
1 tablespoon extra-virgin olive oil
½ cup fresh parsley, minced
6 cups chicken or vegetable stock
2 heads of broccoli
3 tablespoons white or yellow miso
1 (12-ounce) package silken tofu
Sea salt, to taste
Freshly ground white pepper, to taste

Cream of Broccoli Soup

Silken tofu makes an excellent substitute for dairy cream or milk in this simple, tasty soup. Top with toasted pine nuts for that extra crunchy flavor.

1. Cut the florets off the broccoli stems; peel and chop.

2. In a large heavy saucepan, sauté the onion and garlic in oil until just tender; add half the parsley, setting the rest aside to use as garnish.

3. Add the stock and broccoli; bring to a boil; reduce heat and simmer until broccoli is tender, about 15 minutes.

4. Remove a small amount of broth to a bowl; dissolve the miso. Return to the soup pot; remove pot from heat.

5. Crumble silken tofu into broth; use a hand wand mixer to purée until smooth. An alternative is to ladle the soup into a blender in batches and purée until smooth.

6. Add salt and pepper to taste; serve either warm or chilled, topped with toasted pine nuts and minced parsley.

Two Kinds of Tofu

Basic tofu is made by crushing dried soybeans with water, extracting the liquid to produce soy milk. This soy milk is then boiled, and a coagulant such as a natural food acid or a salt is added to produce curds. The resultant solid mass is then cut and packaged for sale.

Broccoli and Tomatoes in Anchovy Sauce

The broccoli and tomatoes can be tossed with the sauce and served as a side dish or the whole thing can be combined with cooked angel-hair pasta and served with a fresh green salad and a hunk of country whole-grain bread.

1. In a mortar and pestle or food processor, combine the oil, garlic, anchovies, and parsley; process to a loose paste. Add more oil as needed for consistency.

2. Steam or water sauté the broccoli until just tender. Remove from the heat; place in a medium-size bowl.

3. Quarter and chop tomatoes; add to the broccoli.

4. Spoon anchovy sauce into the broccoli and tomatoes; toss gently to coat.

5. Sprinkle with Romano cheese, add salt as desired, and serve.

What Does Water Sauté Mean?

When you want a quick, fat-free way to cook vegetables, while still retaining flavor and nutrients, a water sauté is the way to go. Simply pour 1–2 inches of water into a skillet, add the chopped vegetables, cover, and bring to a low simmer. Cook until the vegetables are just tender, then cool under running water and set aside until ready to use.

SERVES 4

260 calories
21 g fat
12 g carbohydrates
8 g protein
2 g sugars
5 g fiber

INGREDIENTS
⅓ cup extra-virgin olive oil
3 cloves garlic
6 anchovy fillets or 2 tablespoons anchovy paste
½ cup fresh parsley, stems removed
1 pound broccoli florets
2 large, ripe tomatoes
½ cup grated Romano cheese
Sea salt, to taste

CHAPTER 5

Quinoa: The Mother Grain

With a nickname like "the Mother Grain," you can imagine just how beneficial quinoa can be for your body. In this chapter, you will learn all about this tough little "grain," including its nutritional content, how it came to North America, and how quick and easy it is to include in a wide variety of recipes. Quinoa is an excellent vegetarian protein source to add to your family's diet.

What Makes It Super

Quinoa, pronounced "keen-wah," is really a nutrient-rich seed used for thousands of years to sustain the diet of the South American Inca people. Although referred to as a grain, technically, quinoa is classified as a pseudocereal, a vegetable plant food from the *Chenopodium quinoa* species of the goosefoot family, the same botanical family as spinach, beets, and Swiss chard. The leaves of the quinoa plant can be cooked and eaten like spinach. It is known to grow at high altitudes, under extremely harsh conditions, thriving in poor soil with little rainfall and freezing temperatures. This makes one hearty little "grain" with more protein, iron, and unsaturated fats but fewer carbohydrates than any real grain on the market. Considered a complete protein, quinoa provides ten essential amino acids and is packed with minerals, B vitamins, and fiber.

Once known as "the gold of the Incas," the nutritional value of quinoa was recognized by ancient Incan warriors as a way to build strength and increase stamina. When cooked, quinoa's hard coating becomes soft yet crunchy, with a grain-like texture and a delicious nutty flavor. Quick and easy to prepare, this complete protein includes all nine essential amino acids, which makes it an excellent choice for vegetarians, vegans, and the rest of the population. Lifting quinoa to the status of a Superfood is extra high amounts of the amino acid lysine, which is essential for tissue growth and repair. In addition, quinoa is a very good source of manganese, as well as magnesium, iron, copper, and phosphorus.

QUESTION?

What is quinoa?
An annual herb, *Chenopodium quinoa*, is an edible seed of the goosefoot species of plant native to the Andes. The high-protein dried fruits and seeds are used as a food staple, which can also be ground into a flour.

For such a small herb, quinoa provides a whole lot of nutrients that can be especially beneficial for persons suffering from migraine headaches, diabetes, atherosclerosis, and other debilitating health issues.

The History of Quinoa

Born and raised in the Andes, quinoa has a long and distinguished history in South America. It has been cultivated in the Andean highlands since 5000 B.C., and the Quechua language of the Inca translates quinoa as *chisiya mama* or "mother grain." It was so highly regarded that quinoa came to be revered as a sacred food. On long marches to do battle, the Incan armies would eat a mixture of quinoa and fat called "war balls," which would sustain their strength and give them stamina. Historians have attributed the success of the Incan empire, in part, to its ability to feed not only its own population, but those of conquered tribes as well. Through wise cultivation, storage, and distribution of indigenous plants, including quinoa, the Inca were able to sustain their growing empire.

Arrival of the Spanish

The arrival of the Spanish conquerors changed all that. Farmers were sent into the gold mines of Peru and Bolivia, and nonnative crops were introduced for Spanish consumption, thus altering centuries of agricultural patterns. The Spanish sought to decimate the Inca Indians and their culture by destroying their quinoa growing fields. They even made it illegal for the Indians to grow quinoa, punishing offenders with a sentence of death. This all but extinguished the cultivation of the sacred mother grain of South America.

Present-Day Quinoa

In the 1980s, quinoa seeds were brought to America and cultivated in Colorado. Due to its ability to adapt to cold, dry climates, and with a seed processing similar to rice, quinoa is now grown in New Mexico, California, Colorado, and Canada. It is readily available in natural-foods stores in both bulk and packaged form, used by thousands of health-conscious individuals for both its high fiber and its protein content. Good news for individuals with wheat and gluten allergies: Quinoa is an excellent replacement for processed forms of wheat such as couscous and bulgur wheat. It can easily be used in traditional Middle Eastern recipes such as tabouli and couscous salad. From the highlands of Peru to your dinner plate, quinoa has made an amazing and successful journey, bringing only the best in health-promoting benefits.

Quinoa's Nutrient Content

For the ancient inhabitants of South America, quinoa was used to replace animal protein in their diets. The nutritional value of quinoa is superior to traditional cereal grains, and studies have shown it to be similar to milk in protein content. Calcium and iron are significantly higher in quinoa than in rice, maize, wheat, or oats, with many varieties of quinoa containing saponins, a bitter substance in the plant's seed coat that keeps away birds and insects.

ALERT!

Saponins function as antinutrients, and are not normally absorbed from the gut, but have been known to induce small-intestine damage or reduce intestinal absorption of nutrients in some people. Before cooking with quinoa, place the grain in a strainer and rinse well under running water. Soaking grains for 4–8 hours in water before cooking helps make them easier to digest.

A sampling of the nutritional benefits for ¼ cup uncooked quinoa contains:

CALORIES	158.95	PHOSPHORUS	174.25 mg
PROTEIN	5.57 g	POTASSIUM	314.50 mg
CARBOHYDRATES	29.28 g	FOLATE	20.83 mcg
FIBER	2.51 g	CALCIUM	25.50 mg
FAT	2.47 g	IRON	3.93 mg
MAGNESIUM	89.25 mg		

It is also important to note that as a good source of insoluble and soluble fiber, quinoa helps your bowels function properly, staving off gastrointestinal problems such as constipation, diverticulitis, Crohn's disease, Irritable Bowel Syndrome, colitis, and colon cancer.

High in Magnesium

Quinoa is also an excellent source of magnesium, an extremely important mineral essential for a number of biological processes to occur in your body. Magnesium:

- Aids in your body's absorption of calcium
- Plays a key role in the strength and formation of bones and teeth
- Is vital for maintaining a healthy heart
- Helps stabilize the rhythm of your heart
- Helps prevent abnormal blood clotting in your heart
- Aids in maintaining healthy blood-pressure levels
- Can significantly lower the chance of heart attacks and strokes
- Can aid in the recovery from a heart attack or stroke
- Helps maintain proper muscle function by keeping them properly relaxed

By including quinoa in your regular diet, you are supporting your body's ability to function properly, maintaining a healthy heart, strong bones, and normal blood-pressure levels.

FACT

The FDA permits the claim that by eating quinoa and other foods that contain at least 51 percent whole grains by weight and that are low in fat, saturated fat, and cholesterol, you may lower your risk for heart disease and certain cancers. Research now also suggests regular consumption of whole grains reduces your risk of developing type 2 diabetes.

Strong In Iron

A common health issue for close to 18 million Americans is iron-deficiency anemia, a condition that occurs when your blood lacks the proper amount of iron. Iron creates healthy red blood cells that can carry oxygen to all of your body's tissues, creating energy and a healthy glow to your skin. Iron-deficiency anemia is most often found in women, with symptoms ranging from pale skin to feeling fatigued much of the time. Anemia can also cause headaches, stomach disorders, restless-leg syndrome, and a loss of sex drive. Not supplementing your diet with iron-rich foods can increase your risk of developing anemia, but with 2.8 milligrams of iron per one-cup serving, quinoa can save the day.

Iron-rich quinoa, plus the essential minerals copper and zinc, help you develop strong bones, teeth, and muscles; sharpen your senses; and build strong blood. When it comes to getting the nutrients you need, eating quinoa is like hitting the mother lode.

Healing Properties of Quinoa

With those high doses of fiber, quinoa can now do battle with high cholesterol, heart disease, and stroke. In fact, one study determined that for every extra 10 grams of fiber consumed a day, women lowered their risk of heart disease by 19 percent. Along with providing a healthy dose of fiber, quinoa is also low in unsaturated fat, which actually helps lower cholesterol levels. It is when there is too much cholesterol in your blood that you can develop clogged arteries, high blood pressure, heart disease, or stroke.

Quinoa Protects Your Eyes

The polyunsaturated fats in quinoa also work to protect your eyes, according to the Australian Blue Mountain Eye Study. These fats, in combination with the protein found in quinoa, can help protect your eyes from developing cataracts. In the study, people who ate the most protein, about 99 grams a day, were only half as likely as those who ate the least amount of protein to develop a nuclear cataract. With a nuclear cataract, light has trouble passing through the center of your eye's lens. Meanwhile, those who ate the most polyunsaturated fat, about 17 grams a day, were 30 percent less likely to get a cortical cataract, which affects the outer lens.

High in Protein

Being a complete protein makes quinoa an excellent source of the B vitamins, especially folate, another essential nutrient needed for the formation and development of new and normal body tissue. Your body cannot make folate, so it must be obtained from foods and supplements. The other B vitamin quinoa provides is riboflavin or B2, which is necessary for the proper production of cellular energy in your body. By improving the energy metabolism within the brain and muscle cells, B2 may help reduce the frequency of migraine attacks.

The key issue is that quinoa provides a vegetarian form of protein without the high levels of saturated fat and cholesterol that eating eggs and meat would provide. This combination of protein and high amounts of potassium and magnesium content help lower your blood pressure and strengthen your heart.

FACT

For a complete protein, add some beans or legumes when serving quinoa. Getting enough protein in your diet will provide you with a consistent flow of energy and build new body tissue, while repairing any old tissue that has been damaged. Eat a balance of protein, carbohydrates, and fats to get all of the nutrients your body needs to function.

Buying and Storage Tips

Quinoa is still relatively unknown to many consumers and may not be readily available in your local supermarkets. You will have a better time finding it in a health-food store, either prepackaged or located in the bulk bins next to the other grains.

ALERT!

When purchasing quinoa or other grains from the bulk bins, check to see that there is no sign of moisture or grain bugs. Buy from stores with a quick turnover of product to ensure freshness.

Store quinoa in an airtight container, such as a mason jar, along with a dried bay leaf to discourage grain bugs from finding a home. Quinoa will keep for about a month left out on the shelf, 3–6 months when stored in the refrigerator, and up to a year in the freezer. Buy just what you need and make it a regular part of your weekly diet, which is easy to do because it cooks in half the time of other grains.

Cooking Quinoa

Always make sure to rinse quinoa before cooking, to remove the bitter compound saponin, which acts as a natural deterrent to birds. This coating is generally removed by soaking or rinsing prior to cooking; but most quinoa sold commercially has already been processed to remove this coating. Nonetheless, it still needs a good rinsing. Although it may appear to be a tiny grain, it tends to expand, and 1 cup of quinoa can feed six to eight people. After rinsing, combine quinoa in a saucepan with water and sea salt, cover, bring to a boil, and simmer until all the water has been absorbed, about twenty minutes. The ratio of water to grain is 2 cups water to 1 cup quinoa, which gives a fluffy texture good for cold salads, stir-fries, or wraps. Adding more water makes a thick, sticky mixture that can be used for making grain burgers or in wraps with other ingredients.

Preparation Ideas

Once you familiarize yourself with quinoa's light, nutty taste and easy preparation, you will want to use it in all manner of ways, including:

- Toss cooked quinoa with chopped green onion, grated carrot, and currants in a lemon olive-oil vinaigrette.
- Cooked quinoa can be used to make moist cakes and cookies.
- Quinoa flour is an excellent gluten-free substitute for many of your favorite baking recipes.
- Use quinoa in place of bulgur wheat to make tabouli salad.
- Quinoa is delicious as a cold salad mixed with chopped apple, walnuts, raisins, celery, lemon juice, and cinnamon.
- Add some curry powder to yogurt and mix it into cooked quinoa, broccoli, and grilled chicken pieces.

- Quinoa is a great addition to soup or stew recipes.
- Add cooked quinoa to your favorite pancake recipe for moist, nutritious cakes.

As you can see, the ideas for cooking with quinoa go on and on. It can replace your other grains in favorite recipes without any problem, and the light nutty taste only adds to the flavor. Try the two easy-to-make recipes presented in this chapter as a great introduction to this versatile grain. Your whole family will be happy you did.

SERVES 4–6

200 calories
11 g fat
22 g carbohydrates
4 g protein
0 g sugar
2 g fiber

INGREDIENTS
1 cup quinoa
2 cups water or vegetable stock
½ teaspoon sea salt
½ medium onion
6 cloves garlic
¼ cup extra-virgin olive oil

Quinoa with Sautéed Garlic

This is the type of recipe that can become a staple in your kitchen. Quick, easy, and a very delicious way to prepare any type of grain. Of course, anything tastes great tossed with olive oil and garlic!

1. Place the quinoa in a metal strainer; rinse well under running water. Drain; add to a heavy saucepan with water or stock and sea salt.

2. Chop onion; add to quinoa.

3. Cover and bring to a boil over medium-high heat; reduce heat and simmer until all water has been absorbed, about 15–20 minutes.

4. Meanwhile, slice the garlic lengthwise along the clove and set aside.

5. Heat oil in a small skillet; sauté garlic until just crisp, but not yet brown. Remove from heat.

6. When quinoa is done, pour garlic and oil over quinoa; toss gently. Serve as a side dish or top with stir-fried beans and vegetables for a main dish.

A Gluten Substitute

For gluten-intolerant individuals, quinoa is a good substitute for gluten-based grains such as couscous, a refined wheat product that also cooks quickly and is found in many Middle Eastern recipes. Quinoa is available in grain, flour, bread, and pasta form in many natural-foods stores.

Quinoa Breakfast Congee

Congee is a porridge traditionally made with rice, and is primarily eaten as a breakfast food. It can be fed to individuals who are unable to chew due to illness or poor digestion. Congee takes a long time to cook, so it can be made in a rice cooker or slow cooker and cooked overnight.

1. Soak hijiki in hot water for 10 minutes. Drain and set aside.

2. Chop onion and set aside.

3. Before going to bed, plug in a 1.5-quart slow cooker and add quinoa, rice, hijiki, onion, sea salt, and water. Set the temperature on low and cook overnight. (You can also use a rice cooker if it has a setting for "congee," as some do.)

4. In the morning, toast the pumpkin seeds in a dry skillet and set aside.

5. Stir the congee; spoon into individual serving bowls. Top with the pumpkin seeds and serve with cooked greens such as kale, spinach, or broccoli.

Quinoa Tips
The versatility of quinoa is evident in its ability to be combined with beans, nuts, seeds, or vegetables. It goes well with dried fruits or added to your favorite vegetable soups. Quinoa flour can be used to make cookies and muffins, and there is even a quinoa pasta that tastes great with your favorite Italian sauce.

SERVES 4

193 calories
2.5 g fat
37 g carbohydrates
5 g protein
1 g sugar
3 g fiber

INGREDIENTS
¼ cup hijiki
½ onion
½ cup quinoa
½ cup brown rice
½ teaspoon sea salt
5 cups water
¼ cup toasted pumpkin seeds

CHAPTER 6

Dark Chocolate Loves
Your Heart

Great news from the hallowed halls of scientific research: Chocolate contains beneficial nutrients that can improve your health. Your strong attraction to chocolate has confirmed what scientists are finding—chocolate can officially be considered a Superfood. In this chapter, you will find out what chocolate is the best to eat, how you can use it to improve your health, and a few secrets about chocolate you probably never knew.

What Makes It Super

How wonderful to find that something so delicious, decadent, and seemingly sinful can actually be good for you! Just one ingredient in chocolate is enough to classify it as a Superfood: polyphenol antioxidants, the same flavonoids found in green tea (see Chapter 14), and a natural protection against cancer. However, researchers from the Lombardi Comprehensive Cancer Center at Georgetown University have also discovered that pentameric procyanidin (pentamer), a natural compound found in cocoa, deactivates a number of proteins that likely work in concert to push a cancer cell to continually divide. What amazing news—chocolate may help to prevent cancer! Since chocolate contains over 300 chemicals, research scientists have been working overtime to learn more about this small cocoa nut. According to the Chocolate Manufacturers Association, dark chocolate contains almost eight times the polyphenol antioxidants found in strawberries; so, strawberries dipped in dark chocolate—a favorite treat of many—give you a double dip of anti-cancer protection.

Keep in mind that although chocolate contains beneficial ingredients, the forms it comes in can be pretty deadly to your health. Chocolate bars, cakes, cookies, and candies are often high in fat, sugar, and calories. Eat chocolate in moderation, and enjoy a piece of chocolate once in a while, preferably dark chocolate with its higher flavonoid content.

The University of Scranton conducted research showing how chocolate is relatively high in antioxidants compared to other foods. Cocoa powder ranked higher than dark chocolate and milk chocolate came in last. So, never fight that urge for a cup of hot chocolate before bedtime again.

The History of Chocolate

The cocoa tree, *Theobroma cacao*, is native to the rainforest areas of Central and South America. It was first harvested by the ancient Mayan people around 250 A.D.–900 A.D. They took the cocoa seeds and fermented, roasted, then ground them into a paste to be mixed with water, chili peppers, and cornmeal, plus a few other ingredients. This made a spicy, bitter drink, which played an important role in both their religious and social lives. Drinking this sacred brew was restricted to royalty, priests, and certain honored individuals. As part of religious services, the priests would make offerings of cocoa seeds to their gods and serve a chocolate drink during sacred ceremonies. (They obviously took their chocolate appreciation as seriously as many people do today.) At that time, sugar was not known to the people of Mesoamerica, so the pungent spices were probably used to balance the bitter taste of the chocolate.

There are three main beans in the chocolate world. The criollo bean is the superior-flavored bean reserved for only the finest, most-expensive chocolate. The more prolific forastero is the cocoa bean used for 90 percent of the world's chocolate production and for most commercial chocolate. Science went one step further and crossed the criollo with the forastero to create a high-quality hybrid cocoa bean called trinitario, known for its rich flavor.

The Aztecs Take Over

In the 1400s, the Aztecs, wielding considerable power amongst the Mesoamerican tribes, used the valuable seed from the cocoa tree for trading currency. The Aztec treasury was made up of large storehouses of cocoa beans. When Columbus returned to Spain in 1502, he took along the cocoa bean as a gift to the King of Spain, but there was no interest in the bitter-tasting seed. Then in 1519, Spanish Conquistador Hernando Cortés led an expedition into the depths of Mexico intent on relieving the Aztec people of their gold and silver treasures. Seen as "white gods, risen from the sea," Emperor Montezuma, along with his subjects, welcomed these strange-looking men in armor and served them a cold, bitter drink made from chocolate called *xocolatl*, which means "bitter water."

Chocolate Crosses the Ocean

In 1528, along with all the riches purloined from the Aztecs, chocolate sailed across the ocean to Europe, where it was introduced as a foamy, bitter drink named *chocolatl*. With a bit of innovation, the Spanish made the beverage more to their liking by adding sugar, cinnamon, and vanilla and eliminating the chilies. In its new form, cocoa spread from one royal court to the next, enjoyed for both its medicinal qualities and its delicious taste.

FACT

While visiting the court of Spain in 1679, Madame D'Aulnoy wrote of being served cocoa in a porcelain cup on a saucer of agate garnished with gold, with the sugar in a bowl of the same. She described an iced chocolate drink, a hot chocolate drink, and another with milk and eggs, which one took with a biscuit or dry, small bun.

Around 1850, the Cadbury and Fry chocolate companies thought to mix cocoa powder with milk, cocoa butter, and sugar to form a solid milk-chocolate bar. Since the moment of chocolate's introduction to Europe, the production and consumption of chocolate has grown to a global scale, with individuals proud to admit they are slaves to a chocolate addiction. According to Carol Off in her book *Bitter Chocolate: Investigating the Dark Side of the World's Most Seductive Sweet,* almost half of the world's production of cocoa comes from the Ivory Coast in West Africa, with Ghana, Indonesia, Nigeria, and Brazil rounding out the world's top-five cocoa producers.

Harvesting and preparing the beans is labor-intensive, and various economic and government forces have driven the price of the bean further and further down. Some cocoa farmers have resorted to using child labor to harvest the bean and satisfy the world's sweet tooth.

Despite its widespread popularity, chocolate is often dismissed as a form of junk food, and it is only recently that scientific studies have been done on the benefits of including chocolate in your diet.

Chocolate's Nutrient Content

The good news is that chocolate can provide adequate amounts of magnesium. On a sour note, chocolate is also high in oxalic acid and the caffeine-like substance theobromine, which when taken in excess can inhibit your body's ability to absorb minerals. This means calcium does not get absorbed properly, forcing your body to pull what it needs from your bones.

ALERT!

The caffeine-like substance in chocolate and cocoa, called theobromine, when taken in excess, can cause feelings of anxiety, nervousness, insomnia, heart disease, intestinal and stomach problems, and mood swings. Hyperactivity in children can also be attributed to a diet containing chocolate.

However, in a study done by Salk Institute researcher Henriette van Praag and colleagues, a compound found in cocoa—epicatechin—combined with exercise, was found to promote functional changes in a part of the brain involved in the formation of learning and memory. Epicatechin is one of a group of chemicals called flavonols, which have previously been shown to improve cardiovascular function and increase blood flow to the brain.

The nutritional content for 1 ounce of baking chocolate contains:

CALORIES	143	VITAMIN E	0.1mg
PROTEIN	4g	CALCIUM	28mg
CARBOHYDRATES	8.2g	MAGNESIUM	91.6mg
TOTAL FAT	15g	IRON	4.9mg
FIBER	5g	PHOSPHORUS	112mg
VITAMIN A	0 IU	POTASSIUM	235mg

Dr. van Praag's findings, published in the May 30, 2007 issue of *The Journal of Neuroscience,* suggest a diet rich in flavonols could help reduce the effects of neurodegenerative illnesses such as Alzheimer's disease and cognitive disorders related to aging.

Antioxidant Levels

According to study results published in the American Chemical Society's *Journal of Agriculture and Food Chemistry,* cocoa powder has nearly twice the antioxidants of red wine and up to three times what is found in green tea. Although scientists knew that cocoa contains significant antioxidants, they didn't know how rich in antioxidants it is until the ORAC test examined the antioxidant levels of various foods. The higher the ORAC score, the higher the level of antioxidants present in the food. Based on the U.S. Department of Agriculture/American Chemical Society's findings, dark chocolate tested the highest for antioxidants over other fruits and vegetables. Comparing the levels of antioxidants, dark chocolate came in with a score of 13,120; its closest competitor, milk chocolate, had levels of 6,740; and third was prunes, at 5,770.

Processing Chocolate

As a chocoholic, you may want to know everything about your favorite food, so let's begin with where it comes from. Cocoa is grown on plantations located twenty degrees from the equator in a rainforest atmosphere. This provides the right temperature for optimal growth and for the rainforest midge, insects that pollinate the cocoa tree's five-petal flowers. It isn't until the cocoa tree is four or five years old that it begins to produce fruit or pods, with an average tree producing only one or two pounds of dried beans a year. The cocoa seeds are located in the pod and are harvested twice a year. The cocoa pods are cut from the tree and the seeds are removed and laid out in trays to ferment for five days. At this stage, the seeds turn brown and lose some of their bitterness. The seeds are then dried and shipped to factories for processing.

At the factory, the beans are inspected for quality, then roasted in huge rotating cylinders for up to thirty hours. The outer cocoa-bean shell is removed and the cocoa nib is revealed inside. This cocoa nib is then ground into a liquid called cocoa liquor, which contains both the cocoa and cocoa butter. To separate the two, a giant press is used to squeeze out the cocoa butter, leaving behind the cocoa, which is then pulverized into cocoa powder. Ingredients such as cocoa powder, milk (for milk chocolate), sugar to balance the cocoa's bitterness, cocoa butter for richer flavor and smoother texture, soy lecithin to help warm chocolate pour into shape, and vanilla for flavoring are mixed together in large mixers.

Healing Properties of Chocolate

Let's face it, chocolate lovers of America, one of the best things about chocolate is that feel-good lift you get after eating a few pieces. It can be attributed to the caffeine present in small quantities or the theobromine, another weak stimulant present in slightly higher amounts. The combination of these two, in tandem with the other 298 chemicals present, may just provide the lift that makes your day a little better. As a matter of fact, chocolate also contains, phenylethylamine, a strong stimulant related to the amphetamine family, known to increase the activity of neurotransmitters in parts of the brain that control your ability to pay attention and stay alert.

The celebrated French physician Francis Joseph Victor Broussais (1772–1836) would prescribe a good-quality chocolate to help calm fever, nourish a patient, and restore the individual's health. Imagine your doctor writing a prescription for chocolate as a medicine to heal illness!

With findings like these, scientists continue to explore chocolate's effect on brain chemistry. Two researchers at the Neurosciences Institute in San Diego, California, Daniel Piomelli and Emmanuelle diTomaso, discovered in a 1996 study that chocolate contains pharmacologically active substances that have the same effect on the brain as marijuana, and that these chemicals may be responsible for certain drug-induced psychoses associated with chocolate craving. The chemical in question is a neurotransmitter known as anandamide, which is produced naturally in the brain, and is also a component of chocolate. This finding should not imply that eating chocolate will get you high; however, these particular compounds (and there may be more) provide that good feeling you get from eating quality chocolate.

Chocolate Lowers Cholesterol

Researchers from Pennsylvania State University studied twenty-three people in 2001, and found that those who included flavonoid-rich cocoa powder and dark chocolate in their diet had a slightly higher concentration of HDL—good cholesterol—when compared with the control group. Meanwhile, across the globe in Italy, researchers found that dark chocolate may help lower blood pressure in people with hypertension. The study also found that levels of LDL—bad cholesterol—in these individuals dropped by 10 percent. They noted in *Hypertension Journal* in August 2005 that this study used a very small test group of only twenty lucky subjects, but that darker chocolate with the most concentrated cocoa proved to have the most health benefits.

Chocolate and Your Heart

Including dark chocolate in your diet may benefit your heart, due to the phytochemicals mentioned earlier. The two positive effects these have on the body are the ability to block arterial damage caused by free radicals and inhibiting platelet aggregation, which could cause a heart attack or stroke. There have also been studies indicating that the flavonoids in cocoa relax the blood vessels, which inhibits an enzyme that causes inflammation.

ALERT!

Buy only the best chocolate and beware of inexpensive chocolates blended with wax, which contain very little real cocoa butter. Inexpensive brands are made with "partially hydrogenated palm oil," preservatives, and high amounts of sugar. Quality chocolate is made with real cocoa butter, the finest organic cocoa beans, minimal sugar, and an extensive refining process.

According to a recent study by Holland's National Institute of Public Health and Environment, chocolate contains up to four times the antioxidants found in tea. The study showed that chocolate, most importantly dark chocolate, contains 53.5 mg of powerful antioxidant catechins per 100 grams. By contrast, 100 ml of black tea contains a mere 13.9 mg of catechins. To your delirious taste buds, eating chocolate may appear to be the answer to all your health problems; after all, it has so many health benefits. In order to counter the sugar, saturated fats, and artificial flavorings in commercial candy bars, many people have turned to buying chocolate in its raw, organic form and making their own sweets.

Buying and Storage Tips

Chocolate needs to be stored at a cool temperature, in a dark place with good air circulation. Kept away from bright light, at 65°F and 50 percent humidity, unsweetened, dark chocolate can last up to ten years. In your own kitchen, dark chocolate can last up to one year (if you don't eat it before that!), or seven months for milk and white chocolate. Chocolate kept in the refrigerator should be wrapped in several layers of foil, then covered with plastic. Allow it to return to room temperature before unwrapping; this prevents "sugar bloom" from occurring, which is when moisture condenses on the surface of the chocolate, drawing the sugar to the surface to crystallize and form grey or white streaks. If you store your chocolate treats in the freezer, defrost them in the refrigerator, then remove and bring to room temperature before eating. True connoisseurs refuse to refrigerate their chocolates, insisting they be eaten within a month of purchase, since they contain no chemical preservatives.

Chocolate Peanut Butter Smoothie

SERVES 2

280 calories
13 g fat
32 g carbohydrates
14 g protein
22 g sugar
3 g fiber

INGREDIENTS

2 cups dairy or nondairy milk
1 large frozen banana
*2 heaping tablespoons peanut
 butter*
*1 heaping tablespoon
 unsweetened chocolate
 powder*
Sweetener of choice

This is the perfect recipe for when you want an instant chocolate fix.

1. Combine ingredients in a blender; purée until smooth.
2. Divide between two glasses; serve immediately.

Frozen Bananas

Frozen bananas are handy to have around for making milkshakes, smoothies, or spur-of-the-moment ice cream. Freeze ripe or overripe bananas ahead of time, by removing the peel and placing them in a freezer bag or freezer-safe container. They will keep in the freezer for several weeks.

Wheat-Free Brownies

SERVES 8, 2" × 4" BARS

320 calories
10 g fat
54 g carbohydrates
9 g protein
13 g sugar
6 g fiber

INGREDIENTS

1½ cups brown rice flour
*1 cup unsweetened cocoa
 powder*
¼ teaspoon sea salt
*1 (10-ounce) package soft silken
 tofu*
1 teaspoon orange extract
1 teaspoon vanilla extract
½ cup barley malt
½ cup maple syrup
1 cup low-fat soy or rice milk
⅔ cup walnuts, chopped

These are the perfect substitute brownie for individuals with gluten or egg allergies. The key to making these chewy is the brown rice flour. The silken tofu replaces the oil and keeps the fat grams way down, but to lower it even further, eliminate the walnuts and substitute juice-sweetened dried cranberries.

1. Preheat oven to 350°F.
2. In a medium-size bowl, combine flour, cocoa, and salt.
3. In a blender, purée tofu, orange extract, vanilla extract, barley malt, maple syrup, and milk.
4. Stir tofu mixture into flour mixture; add walnuts; mix well.
5. Pour into a lightly oiled 8" × 8" baking dish; bake for 30 minutes.

Dark Chocolate

When a recipe calls for chocolate, use dark chocolate (usually less sugar), or even better, cocoa powder. To substitute 1 ounce of unsweetened chocolate, use 3 tablespoons dry cocoa + 2 tablespoons sugar + 1 tablespoon mild-flavored vegetable oil.

CHAPTER 7

Mineral-Rich Sea Vegetables

As long as the oceans have covered the earth, there have been sea vegetables providing food for marine life, and later, for humans. In this chapter, you will find that the foods you eat for their vitamin and mineral content are far surpassed by what sea vegetables can provide you in one serving. The many varieties are also quick and easy to make, bringing the piquant taste of the sea to your dining table.

What Makes Them Super

Three billion years ago, from the depths of the oceans, single-celled organisms, most likely blue-green algae, became the singular meal for marine life. Today, there are close to 65,000 species of algae, 20,000 of which live in the ocean. Only about 100 of these species are edible for human consumption, eaten mostly in Asian countries, with Western cultures only now beginning to appreciate this complex Superfood.

More than the super-high amounts of nutrients sea vegetables provide, it is our connection to the sea itself that ties us to these foods. The human body is 70 percent water and begins its journey into life in the saline solution of the womb, a solution that has almost the same composition as seawater! The nutritional profile of sea vegetables is also complementary to your nutritional needs—containing ten to twenty times what land plants provide in the form of vitamins and minerals.

FACT

According to Shep Erhart, coauthor of *Sea Vegetable Celebration,* seeing the graceful way sea plants break with the waves calls to mind such words as *resilient*, *tenacious*, *supple*, *flexible*, and above all, *beautiful*. These energetic and aesthetic qualities are part of what your cells receive when you choose to eat sea vegetables.

A food that has sustained life for thousands of years, one that has been passed down from generation to generation, is finally getting the attention it deserves. Sea vegetables' beneficial composition and high nutrient content have been confirmed by modern scientific analysis. Studies of people who regularly incorporate edible seaweeds into their diets have been shown to have fewer problems from mineral depletion and live longer, healthier, more active lives.

The History of Sea Vegetables

Sea vegetables have a long history of being used as both food and medicine by cultures worldwide. The Japanese alone have been consuming sea vegetables for more than 10,000 years, as evidenced in their ancient burial mounds. In ancient China, sea vegetables were a noted delicacy served to honored guests and royalty. The Chinese also revered sea vegetables for their medicinal qualities. Ancient Chinese texts claim that, "there is no swelling that is not relieved by seaweed," and in many of today's alternative health programs, sea vegetables are used to treat swellings, lumps, edema, swollen lymph glands, and goiter.

Native Tribes

There are many types of sea vegetable, classified by their colors—reds, browns, greens, blue-greens, and yellow-greens—and each has a specific use for healing and detoxifying the body. In North America, archeological research reveals that Native American tribes in the Northwest harvested wild nori for food, known to them as *mei bil,* or "sea leaf." They would harvest the sea leaf in early spring and dry enough to see them through the year. Meanwhile, on the other side of the continent, other Native American tribes were harvesting kelp out of the Atlantic ocean. To these coastal peoples, seaweed was a prized possession both as a source of valuable nutrients, primarily minerals, and as a commodity of trade with the inland tribes.

Coastal Communities

In Europe, sea vegetables have been part of life in most ocean-bordered countries such as Ireland, Scotland, Iceland, and Norway for centuries. Evidence of sea vegetable consumption by coastal communities in New Zealand, Australia, and the Pacific Islands has also been found. Because of the high vitamin C content of sea vegetables, sea voyagers such as the Vikings and New England whalers would chew on seaweed to prevent scurvy.

Today, most sea vegetables are exported from Japan, but America has developed several successful manufacturers, including the Maine Coast Sea Vegetable Company on the East Coast and the Mendocino Sea Vegetable Company in northern California. Both companies provide clean, nutritious sea vegetables to natural-foods stores around the country, while other varieties, sold in Asian and natural-foods stores, are imported from Japan.

Sea Vegetables' Nutrient Content

Gram for gram, sea vegetables are higher in essential vitamins and minerals than any other known food group. These minerals are bio-available to the body in chelated, colloidal forms, which makes them more easily absorbed because they are able to retain their molecular identity while remaining in liquid suspension. The list of nutritional benefits attributed to sea vegetables can sound too good to be true; but consider that the Japanese people, who eat the highest amounts, also have the highest longevity rates of any group of people in the world.

FACT

Plants convert metallic minerals, which can be toxic to the body, into colloids, which have a natural, negative electric charge. These negatively charged minerals are easily absorbed by the body's cells and have been shown to increase the transport and bioavailability of other foods and supplements.

The following is a list of what sea vegetables can add to your daily diet:

- Sea vegetables can contain as much as 48 percent protein.
- Sea vegetables are a rich source of both soluble and insoluble dietary fiber.
- The brown sea vegetable varieties—kelp, wakame, and kombu—contain alginic acid, which has been shown to remove heavy metals and radioactive isotopes from the digestive tract, as well as strontium 90 from the bones.
- Sea vegetables contain significant amounts of vitamin A in the form of beta carotene, as well as vitamins B complex, C, and E.
- Sea vegetables are high in potassium, calcium, sodium, iron, and chloride.
- Sea vegetables provide the fifty-six minerals and trace minerals that your body requires to function properly.
- Sea vegetables contain fiber, iodine, omega-3 fatty acids, and very little fat, factors that can help with weight loss.

As you can see, the nutrient values are impressive, and so necessary in this time of refined, processed, and nutrient-depleted junk foods.

Types of Sea Vegetables

To get an idea of how sea vegetables compare in nutrient value to land-grown foods, it is necessary to consider each individual plant. Once you know a bit more about their super qualities, plan on buying one variety and cooking it in a few recipes before trying another. As you become more familiar with their delicious, unique flavors and their ease of preparation, begin to include a wider variety in your diet.

ALERT!

Vitamin B12, normally found only in animal products, is also found in sea vegetables. However, according to Paul Pitchford, author of *Healing with Whole Foods,* further testing shows this form of B12 to be an analogue, something that resembles B12 but cannot be utilized by the human body.

Arame

Arame is the perfect sea vegetable to introduce to your diet, due to its mild taste and ease of preparation. It grows near the Ise peninsula of Japan in bouquets of fronds, on rocks beneath the sea. When harvested, it is chopped into thin strips, boiled, and dried. Arame has a cooling nature, with a salty flavor. Medicinally, it is used to soften hardened areas in the body, and because of the high amounts of iodine, iron, and calcium, it is beneficial for the thyroid, lowering high blood pressure, and strengthening bones and teeth.

Here are a few tips for using arame in your kitchen:

- Before using, wash arame well to eliminate any sand or shells, and soak at least five minutes before cooking.
- Once soaked, arame can be used in stir-fry recipes, soups, and in salads.
- Be sure to store any leftover cooked arame in the refrigerator.

- Once the package of dried arame has been opened, you should store it in an airtight container in a dark, cool place, such as a kitchen cupboard, where it will keep indefinitely.

ALERT!

When preparing your recipe, remember that when soaked in water, sea vegetables double in volume, while some, like wakame, expand to seven times their dried state. Read the package directions carefully, or begin by soaking a small amount and increasing the amount as needed.

One-eighth cup (2 tablespoons) of arame contains:

CALORIES	4.5
PROTEIN	0.303 g
CARBOHYDRATE	0.914 g
TOTAL FAT	0.064 g
FIBER	0.050 g

Dulse

This red-and-blue colored north Atlantic sea vegetable grows as a flat, smooth frond from 6–12 inches long, and 6 inches wide, shaped like the palm of a hand. Dulse is:

- High in iodine
- Rich in manganese, which prevents scurvy
- A remedy for seasickness
- A palliative for the herpes virus
- A good substitute for salt

In addition to dried fronds, dulse is available in flake and powder forms. Dulse can be eaten out of the package, but should be examined first to eliminate any sand or small shells. Dulse can be soaked and eaten raw in salads, or cooked quickly and added to soups, vegetables, and cooked grains. Pan sauté it in olive oil for a topping to stemmed broccoli or as a snack by itself.

One-eighth cup (2 tablespoons) of dulse contains:

CALORIES	4.5
PROTEIN	0.303 g
CARBOHYDRATE	0.914 g
TOTAL FAT	0.064 g
FIBER	0.050 g

After opening, store dulse in an airtight container in a dry, dark place. Cooked dulse should be used soon after it is prepared or kept refrigerated.

Kelp

Kelp is a large, brown variety of algae, known to grow in shallow, nutrient-rich ocean forests. Kelp is a *Laminaria* species, which are the largest sea plants in the ocean. When taken for its high iodine content kelp is available as a supplement in powder, pill, or granular form. Kelp is also used for poor digestion, kidney and circulation problems, inflammation, immune stress, and to treat edema (water retention), goiter, arthritis, rheumatism, lymphatic swellings, and ovarian problems. Individuals can replace salt with kelp due to its slightly salty taste, and for the many vitamins, minerals, and especially trace minerals that it provides.

Kelp is delicious in soups and stews, stir-fried with vegetables, or cooked with beans or whole grains. When cooking beans, add kelp for its natural glutamic acid, a tenderizer that helps beans cook quickly and makes them more digestible. It also contains alginic acid, a substance used as a thickening and stabilizing agent in food production.

One-eighth cup (2 tablespoons) of raw kelp contains:

CALORIES	4.3
PROTEIN	0.17 g
CARBOHYDRATE	0.96 g
TOTAL FAT	0.005 g
FIBER	0.13 g

Kelp can be presoaked or added dry to foods with liquids. Remember that sea vegetables expand when soaked, and kelp absorbs up to five times its weight in liquid.

When storing dehydrated kelp, keep it in an airtight container in a dark, dry place, while cooked kelp should be kept refrigerated.

Kombu

Kombu is a wide-leafed sea vegetable harvested wild from the northern-most island of Japan. There are several varieties of kombu, with the most popular variety being Japanese ma-kombu (*Laminaria japonica*). In Japan, kombu is used to make over 300 products, including condiments and teas. Look for hand-harvested kombu consisting of the most tender central part of the leaf, which has the best flavor and texture.

Here are a few tips for using kombu in your kitchen:

- Add kombu to the cooking water of dried beans—it helps them cook faster and aids in digestion.
- Dehydrated kombu should be stored in an airtight container in a dark, dry place.
- Cooked kombu should be kept refrigerated.

Three and one-half ounces of kombu (100 grams) contains:

CALORIES	35	FIBER	0.3 g
PROTEIN	5.8 g	FOLATE	146 mcg
CARBOHYDRATE	5.1 g	CALCIUM	70 mg
TOTAL FAT	0.3 g	MAGNESIUM	2 mg

ESSENTIAL

Something to consider when reading about foods: "Excellent source" of a particular nutrient means they provide 20 percent or more of the Recommended Daily Value (RDV) for that nutrient. Foods that are a "good source" of a particular nutrient provide 10–20 percent of the RDV.

Kombu is well known for its flavor-enhancing characteristics and can be prepared in many methods: pickled, steamed, boiled, roasted, fried, broiled, ground, marinated, and toasted. Begin by adding a small piece of kombu to a soup-stock recipe, and watch how it enlivens the taste.

Laver/Nori

Wild laver leaf is harvested from the cold North Atlantic, and is the original form of nori before it is processed into thin, flat, roll-able sheets. Laver plants not in sheet form are best lightly roasted before use. Dry roasting brings out a nutty, salty flavor, delicious crumbled onto soups, salads, pasta, potatoes, or popcorn.

One-eighth cup (2 tablespoons) of laver contains:

CALORIES	3.5
PROTEIN	0.58 g
CARBOHYDRATE	0.51 g
TOTAL FAT	0.028 g
FIBER	0.03 g

Of the many sea vegetable varieties, laver is one of the highest in vitamins B1, B6, B12, C, and E, and contains significant amounts of vegetable protein, fiber, iron, and other minerals and trace elements.

Nori is the Japanese name for various edible seaweed species, including the wild laver plants that go into making the flat sheets used to prepare sushi rolls. The nori sheets are made by a shredding and rack-drying process that resembles papermaking. Nori is delicious dry roasted to bring out its nutty flavor, and can then be crumbled and used as a nutritious condiment over soups, salads, or grains. A few things to know about nori include:

- Nori is popular the world over for its use in sushi making. The glossy, purplish-black sheets are used to make sushi rolls called *maki*.
- Nori can be substituted for flour tortillas or pita bread, and when toasted and crumbled they are especially good with noodles or rice and hummus.

- Nori sheets are sold in boxes or sealed plastic envelopes; boxes usually contain about ten sheets.
- Nori should be kept free from moisture and stored in a dry place.

To toast a sheet of nori, hold it by the edge and pass it over the open flame of your gas burner or electric burner set to high. Do not linger over the heat, as it will toast quickly. Do one side and then turn it over and do the other side. Now you can use it to wrap rice and vegetables or crumble it as a condiment in your soup or salad.

Wakame

Wakame is closely related to *Alaria esculenta,* common in Atlantic waters. Black or dark green in color, alaria is similar to wakame in appearance, taste, and nutrition, but needs a longer cooking time than wakame.

A few things to know when cooking and storing wakame:

- Traditionally added to miso soup, wakame is also good with other vegetables, or in salads, stir-fry dishes, and rice dishes.
- Wakame and alaria are mostly found in natural-foods stores or specialty markets.
- Dehydrated wakame should be stored in an airtight container in a dark, dry place.
- Cooked wakame should be kept refrigerated.

Wakame is another sea vegetable that can expand to seven times its dried form. Begin by soaking 1–2 tablespoons at a time in warm water, then use both the soaking liquid and wakame to make your soup.

One-eighth cup (2 tablespoons) of wakame provides:

CALORIES	4.5
PROTEIN	0.303 g
CARBOHYDRATE	0.914 g
TOTAL FAT	0.064 g
FIBER	0.050 g

Some brands of wakame have a tough spine that needs to be sliced away after soaking, but most commercial wakame is processed to make preparation much easier.

Healing Properties of Sea Vegetables

Sea vegetables have traditionally been used in Asia to treat heart disease, hypertension, cancer, and thyroid problems. They have a cooling nature and a salty taste, and are effective for softening hardened areas and masses, such as tumors, in the body. They are effective detoxifiers, with diuretic properties and the ability to help cleanse the lymphatic system. They contain iodine, which is beneficial for the thyroid, and also alkalize the blood and relieve stagnancy in the liver. The latest nutritional research shows that sea vegetables have a thermogenic effect on the metabolism, which helps the body burn its own visceral fat. Taken all together, what you have is the ideal food for promoting weight loss where needed.

FACT

Scientific researchers are working to understand how sea vegetables can be used to successfully treat disease. One recent theory proposes that consumption of laminaria (kombu) explains the low breast-cancer rate in postmenopausal Japanese women. These studies hope to unveil the healing properties of these wondrous plants from the sea.

Buying and Storage Tips

In addition to the storage tips mentioned previously for each sea-vegetable type, there are a few generic tips you should know. For example, look for sea vegetables that are sold in tightly sealed packages, and avoid those that have evidence of excessive moisture. Some types of sea vegetables are sold in different forms; for example, nori can be found in sheets, flakes, or powder. Choose the form of sea vegetables that will best meet your culinary needs.

Store sea vegetables in tightly sealed containers at room temperature where they can stay fresh for at least several months.

SERVES 8

210 calories
12 g fat
23 g carbohydrates
4 g protein
1 g sugar
2 g fiber

INGREDIENTS

½ cup pine nuts, toasted
½ cup arame, cooked
3 cups cooked, long-grain brown rice (1½ cups uncooked)
1 cup cooked wild rice (½ cup uncooked)
2 green onions, chopped
½ cup parsley, minced
½ cup fresh mint, minced
1 teaspoon fresh thyme
2 tablespoons red wine vinegar
1 teaspoon ume plum vinegar
3 tablespoons extra-virgin olive oil

Wild Rice Mint Salad

This is the perfect way to introduce arame into your diet. The recipe is loaded with flavor, only complemented by arame's light salty taste. Serve with cold poached salmon topped with aioli mayonnaise and a fresh green salad.

1. Toast the pine nuts in a heavy, nonoiled skillet, shaking to evenly brown on all sides. Set aside in a bowl.

2. Soak arame in water 10 minutes. Drain; place in a small saucepan. Cover with water; bring to a boil and simmer 10 minutes. Drain and set aside to cool.

3. In a large bowl, combine brown rice, wild rice, onion, arame, parsley, mint, and thyme; mix well.

4. In a separate bowl, mix together red wine vinegar, ume vinegar, and oil.

5. Pour the dressing over the rice mixture; toss well. Add pine nuts and serve.

Wild Rice

A member of the grass family of plants, native to North America, and a staple in the diet of early Native Americans, wild rice is a large seed grown primarily in the Great Lakes region. A nutritional grain higher in protein than cultivated brown rice and low in fat, its mineral content is high in potassium and phosphorus.

Easy Miso Noodle Soup

This is a delicious soup made to relax and nourish the body after a long day. A white-colored miso will give a lighter taste than a dark red or brown miso. The darker the miso, the longer it has been fermented and the more live enzymes it will provide. Feel free to add other vegetables or a small fillet of fish to the soup.

1. Cut the onion in thin half-moon slices; julienne carrots into matchstick shapes; slice green onions on the diagonal into pieces.

2. Heat broth; and add onion, carrot, wakame, and tofu. Simmer until onion is just tender.

3. Ladle broth into individual bowls; dissolve 1 teaspoon of miso into each.

4. Add ½ cup of noodles to each bowl; ladle in soup with vegetables and tofu.

5. Top with pumpkin seeds and sliced green onions before serving.

Soba Noodles

Soba noodles are a traditional Japanese noodle made of buckwheat and wheat or spelt flour. They are a round, thin noodle that can be served either hot or cold with a variety of toppings. They go well in miso broth, with scallions, sesame oil, and bean sprouts or wrapped with other vegetables in a sheet of nori.

SERVES 4

180 calories
3.5 g fat
30 g carbohydrates
10 g protein
8 g sugar
5 g fiber

INGREDIENTS
½ onion
2 medium carrots
2 green onions
4–6 cups vegetable broth or water
1 tablespoon dried wakame
1 cube firm tofu
4 teaspoons mellow white miso
1 (8-ounce) package cooked soba noodles
4 tablespoons pumpkin seeds, toasted

CHAPTER 8

Garlic Is Nature's Antibiotic

In nature you can always find an antidote to what ails you. Take the simple garlic plant as an example: The power in each small clove can work as both an anti-inflammatory and an antibiotic dose of natural medicine. It also happens to taste fantastic and will enlighten your taste buds in a variety of cuisines. In this chapter, you will learn why this amazing plant is so popular and how it can help keep you healthy.

What Makes It Super

Almost every culture in the world uses garlic as a medicine in some form or other. According to data from the USDA's 1994–1996 Continuing Survey of Food Intakes by Individuals, 18 percent of Americans consume at least one food a day containing garlic. More garlic is eaten by Americans than French fries, ketchup, and fresh-market tomatoes. Garlic has made the Superfoods list because of its use as a flavor enhancer in recipes and as a powerful medicinal force in the botanical world. Garlic's Latin name is *Allium sativum,* but it is also known as rocambole, ajo, allium, stinking rose, rustic treacle, nectar of the gods, camphor of the poor, and poor man's treacle. The single ingredient that makes it a Superfood is allicin, a sulfur element known for its ability to cleanse and purify the body. Sulfur is found in the allium family, which includes garlic, onions, leeks, scallions, and chives.

FACT

Because foods from the allium family help you metabolize protein efficiently, they should be eaten with meals containing meat, poultry, fish, and other animal proteins. Slice the meat or fish and insert thin slices of raw garlic before cooking. Mince the raw garlic and sprinkle on top of the protein while cooking.

Garlic is by far the most pungent-tasting of the allium family, and possibly the most medicinal. Due to the extensive scientific research on garlic's health benefits, it is recommended in diets for individuals with cardiovascular disease. One German study published in *Toxicology Letters* indicates that consuming garlic can help reduce plaque formation, which can contribute to arteriosclerosis. Also, clinical studies conducted by Dr. V. Petkov at the Bulgurian Academy of Sciences found that consuming garlic on a daily basis helps to lower blood pressure. All of which means that eating garlic on a regular basis also decreases your risk for heart attack and stroke.

Each small clove of the garlic plant contains anti-inflammatory and antibiotic properties, assists with blood circulation, and is antifungal and antiparasitic. It is not only folklore that credits garlic with so many healing powers; studies done at the Mayo Clinic show garlic to be an effective blood thinner, and successful at reducing hypertension and fighting infections in patients. At the University of North Carolina, a study involving over 100,000 people found that eating only one clove of raw or cooked garlic daily may reduce the risk of both colon and stomach cancers. With these kinds of study results, major hospitals and universities continue to research garlic's allylic sulfides, the essential ingredient thought to be one of the most potent nutrients in the plant kingdom.

The History of Garlic

The first use of garlic was recorded some 6,000 years ago, when humans began writing down their history. More than likely, its beneficial properties helped the original tribes of hunters and gatherers survive the harsh living conditions of their time. Recorded history shows garlic moving from central Asia into Africa, where the Egyptians thought enough of it to bury their royalty with the precious bulbs. At the time, garlic was so valuable a commodity that it was given monetary value and used in barter.

ESSENTIAL

For centuries, garlic has been thought of as an aphrodisiac, because eating garlic can improve blood circulation to the groin. Proper blood flow to the groin promotes a strong physical arousal for the male. To ensure intimate success, make sure that both participants are eating garlic at the same meal.

When the pungent plant made its way to Europe, it picked up the name *garlic* from the ancient Anglo-Saxon word *garleac*, from *gar* ("spear") and *leac* ("plant"), in reference to the shape of its leaves. Old English herbal texts show garlic was grown in England before 1540, and was prized for its strengthening and purifying capabilities.

The ancient Greeks and Romans embraced garlic's powerful medicinal qualities, believing it would help strengthen athletes for the Olympic games. They also used it to heal infectious wounds, for pneumonia, digestive disorders, bronchitis, chronic cough, and snake bites. However, at the same time they condemned its odor. For instance, in ancient Greece, the public was not allowed to enter the temple of Cybele if they smelled of garlic, and the Brahmin priests of India were not allowed to eat it at all.

ALERT!

Eating garlic can cause intestinal flatulence in some people. A 1987 article in the *London Times* reported the plight of a French astronaut, who took some snacks containing garlic on a Soviet space flight. It seems the space shuttle's air conditioning was unable to handle the astronaut's digestive special effects.

Some cultures highly respect the medicinal properties of garlic and only use it for healing purposes. They advise against eating garlic in excess, as it is believed it can awaken desires and anxiety. According to an Indian yogic diet, garlic is considered to be rajasic, a food that causes overstimulation to the body. Rajasic foods arouse animal passions, hyperactivity, and a restless mind, while the point of yoga is to calm and stabilize both mind and body.

Garlic made its way to North America in the 1700s, and has edged its way into the palates of the American public decade by decade. As it became easier to travel to countries that use garlic as a culinary mainstay, and as more ethnic restaurants successfully implanted themselves into the heart of America, the garlic bulb has become a natural part of this country's cuisine. It may well be that the pungent garlic clove is responsible for expanding the once-narrow palate of the American public.

FACT

The giant garlic lookalike known as elephant garlic is only a distant cousin to the garlic family. Closer to a leek in flavor, it can be roasted until soft and used as a spread on breads or whisked into a sauce calling for a hint of garlic without the overpowering taste of real garlic.

Today, according to the food industry magazine *Agricultural Outlook*, China is the world's largest grower of garlic, accounting for 66 percent of the 13 billion pounds produced each year. On the other hand, garlic grown in the U.S. accounts for only 3 percent of the world's production, with 84 percent grown in California. Demand for garlic by the American public jumped 20 percent in 1999, to a record high of 660 million pounds! However, it is the home cook who purchases the highest amounts of raw garlic, some 56 percent, with the male population in America's western states dominating sales and consumption.

Garlic's Nutrient Content

Antiviral, antibacterial, antifungal, and antiparasitical are all properties of the simple garlic bulb. The flesh of each clove is contained within a papery skin, and only releases its smell when sliced or crushed. Once it has been exposed to the air, garlic quickly loses its medicinal properties, so eat it as soon as possible after cutting.

ALERT!

Consuming garlic can interfere with medication, so consult your doctor first. Eating excessive amounts of garlic can slow blood clotting, irritate the intestinal tract, and keep the thyroid gland from utilizing iodine properly when taken in concentrated doses.

One large head of garlic contains the following key nutrients:

CALORIES	98	IRON	0.48 mg
PROTEIN	8 g	SODIUM	4.82 mg
CARBOHYDRATE	16 g	MAGNESIUM	7.09 mg
POTASSIUM	113.68 mg	VITAMIN C	8.85 mg
ZINC	0.33 mg	MANGANESE	0.47 mg
CALCIUM	51.31 mg	B6	0.35 mg
SELENIUM	4.03 mcg		

The essential oil of garlic is the sulfur-rich allicin or allyl, which is found in the onion family and is the cause of garlic's pungent odor. Consequently, many people avoid taking garlic for fear of offending others in social gatherings. Instead, they buy garlic in capsule form, which contains small amounts of allicin. Consider that one clove of fresh garlic contains 18,300 mcg (micrograms) of allicin, while 600 mg of garlic extract only contains 3,600 mcg. This is a considerable difference, and one that can determine whether a healing treatment is successful or not. Many herbalists question the efficacy of these supplements without the presence of garlic's major ingredient, but allow for it helping in certain situations.

ALERT!

Read the labels on garlic supplements carefully, as some list the amount of alliin they contain, which is different from allicin. Allicin is formed enzymatically from alliin, but is only a precursor compound that on its own is of little or no value.

Garlic is also a good source of nutrients such as saponins, polyphenols, selenium, arginine, and vitamin C. You can obtain the many health benefits by using just one raw garlic clove in your cooking or salad dressings—that's all it takes to add great flavor and powerful nutrients to any meal.

Healing Properties of Garlic

It seems that every culture has found a use for garlic in their plant-based pharmacopeia. It has been used to treat everything from minor illness to major disease and inflammation, both internally and externally. If you could have one thing in your medicine cabinet, garlic would be the best choice. Its sulfur compounds are the key elements in preventing cardiovascular disease and for use as an antibiotic. In one study, garlic was tested on mice against an antibiotic-resistant strain of *staphylococci*. The results showed the garlic had protected the mice against the pathogen and significantly reduced any inflammation. The ailments that garlic is claimed to help includes:

- **Atherosclerosis:** helps to open the blood vessels in the body
- **Arthritis:** helps to reduce inflammation in the joints

- **Cancer:** helps reduce the risk of colorectal, gastric, and stomach cancers
- **Lymes:** used in concentrated form to kill lyme spirochetes disease
- **Candida albicans:** antifungal compounds destroys yeast overgrowth in the gut
- **Cardiovascular disease:** sulfur compounds reduce the formation of blood clots
- **Sore throat:** neutralizes bacterial infections in the throat
- **High cholesterol:** helps reduce levels of low-density lipoprotein (LDL) cholesterol
- **Food poisoning:** helps neutralize bacteria such as salmonella
- **High blood pressure:** using powdered garlic helps lower blood pressure
- **Eliminates heavy metals from the body**
- **Acts as an insect repellent**

Garlic has also been used topically to treat skin ailments such as warts, calluses, muscle pain, arthritis, and sciatica.

For centuries, military doctors have used garlic to treat battle-wounded soldiers. By applying the raw juice, diluted with water, to sterilized sphagnum moss and placing it over the open wound, the garlic prevents infection and allows for rapid healing. In your own home, you can use garlic to reduce swelling and draw infection out of a boil or abscess. Make a poultice by chopping garlic, mixing it with some olive oil, and placing it in a cheesecloth. Place the poultice over the abscess and give it time to draw out the impurities. This can also be used for carbuncles, skin ulcers, tumors, snake bites, and bee stings.

FACT

When included as a regular part of your diet, garlic can help reduce cholesterol levels in the blood and protect against stomach cancer. Its antibacterial properties help fight off the residual effects of colds and flu; its antifungal properties help prevent yeast infections; and at the same time, garlic can work to combat viral conditions. Now that's a Superfood!

Healing Garlic Oil

Garlic oil is simple to make at home and can be used for many common ailments.

1. Place 2 heads of pressed or minced garlic in a 16-ounce jar.
2. Add enough organic extra-virgin olive oil to cover the garlic.
3. Cap and store in a warm place for three days. A sunny windowsill is a good place, but put it in a warm place at night, then return it to the sill the next day.
4. After three days, strain the oil through cheesecloth and store in a cool place. It will keep indefinitely when capped tightly and stored in the refrigerator.

This oil can be used in the following ways:

- **For ear infections:** place drops (3 for children or 5 for adults) of the warmed oil into the infected ear, cover, and rest while the oil is absorbed.
- **For athlete's foot:** wash the feet well and mix 1 teaspoon of garlic oil with 5 drops of tea tree oil and rub into the feet, then cover with cotton socks. Apply morning and night until the infection is clear, then use one to two times a week for prevention purposes.
- **To strengthen the immune system:** as a salad dressing, add 2 teaspoons of garlic oil to ¼ cup extra-virgin olive oil, ¼ cup raw, unrefined apple cider vinegar, and 1 teaspoon of honey. Place ingredients in a small jar, shake well, and serve with love.

Prepare in small amounts and use within a month's time. Before finishing, have a fresh batch of garlic oil marinating in the wings.

Antibiotic Garlic Vinegar

Garlic vinegar is a simple recipe that is essential during cold and flu season. One teaspoon mixed with lemon juice and honey will provide antibiotic results without the harsh side effects of the pharmaceutical versions.

1. Peel and mince one head of garlic and place in an 8-ounce jar.
2. Add ¼ cup raw, unrefined apple cider vinegar and ¼ cup distilled water. Cover, swirl to mix, and set on the counter to marinate for 4–8 hours.
3. When done, strain through cheesecloth and return to the jar.
4. Add ¼ cup raw, unrefined honey; mix well. Cover and refrigerate.

When mixed with honey, the vinegar will keep for up to a week. You can use this concoction for:

- **Colds and flu:** 1–2 teaspoons in 8 ounces of juice or water. Sweeten for taste.
- **Sore throats:** 1 teaspoon garlic vinegar in 4 ounces of water. Use as a gargle.
- **Cuts, wounds, and skin disease:** Soak a clean cotton cloth with the garlic vinegar and place over the problem area. Wrap with another cloth and leave in place. Change the dressing 4 times a day.
- **Lyme disease:** 1 tablespoon in 8 ounces of water or lemon juice 2–3 times a day. (This is not a medical treatment, but can be used to help alleviate illness-related symptoms. The above recommendations are meant to be used in conjunction with your doctor's prescribed treatment protocol.)

ALERT!

When taking the garlic vinegar, be sure to mix it with four to eight ounces of water or juice. By diluting the concentration, you can better digest and absorb its healing properties. Do *not* take the mixture full strength; always dilute it first. You can also use it in a salad dressing along with olive oil and fresh herbs.

Both the garlic vinegar and the garlic oil provide a concentrated way to receive the beneficial properties of the garlic plant. You can dilute the garlic vinegar with extra vinegar and olive oil to use as a dressing for salads or vegetable recipes. The garlic oil can be drizzled over grilled meat, chicken, fish, or vegetables to add great taste, as well as healing properties, to a meal.

Buying and Storage Tips

Store your heads of garlic in a dry place, away from other vegetables. There are clay jars with holes in the sides that are used just to store garlic. The holes allow for the circulation of fresh air, which keeps the cloves from drying out and also inhibits the formation of mold. When purchasing, look for hard, unbruised heads of garlic without torn skins or sprouts. Once you have broken the skin of the garlic head, use it up over the course of the week. Once you have broken the skin of a clove, use it right away or you will lose any beneficial qualities.

Buying fresh from a local garlic grower is ideal, as many manufacturers store garlic for up to six months after it has been harvested and up to a year under controlled storage.

Roasted Garlic Aioli Mayonnaise

To save time or when you don't have a blender, you can use 1 cup of a good-quality store-bought mayonnaise in place of making it from scratch, although there's no comparison when made fresh. Add dried herbs of your choice for extra flavor. Serve aioli mayonnaise over vegetables, grilled meats, fish, or swirled into a thick purée of hot lentil soup.

1. Preheat oven to 375°F.
2. Wrap garlic in aluminum foil; bake for 20 minutes.
3. Allow to cool, remove foil, and slice across flat end of head.
4. Squeeze softened cloves out the end into a small bowl; set aside.
5. Pour ¼ cup of oil into a blender with egg, lemon juice, vinegar, and salt.
6. Turn on blender; pour remaining oil into mixture in a slow stream. The mayonnaise will thicken as you pour the oil.
7. Add roasted garlic to mayonnaise; pulse to combine.
8. Run blender additional 30 seconds after garlic has been added.
9. Keep mixture refrigerated in a glass container 5–7 days.

For Serious Garlic Lovers

The more garlic cloves you add to the mayonnaise the more pungent the flavor, resulting in an almost chili-pepper-like fire. If you prefer a heavier garlic flavor, try roasting two heads of garlic and mixing them both into the mayonnaise.

MAKES 1 CUP

1680 calories
173 g fat
22 g carbohydrates
10 g protein
1 g sugar
1 g fiber

INGREDIENTS
1 head garlic
¾ cup extra-virgin olive oil
1 organic egg
1 tablespoon fresh lemon juice
1 tablespoon raw apple cider vinegar
Pinch sea salt

270 calories
11 g fat
36 g carbohydrates
10 g protein
3 g sugars
3 g fiber

INGREDIENTS

6 cups chicken or vegetable
    stock
4 dried shiitake mushrooms
4 heads of garlic
1 teaspoon sea salt
14 ounces silken tofu
6 teaspoons extra-virgin olive oil
¼ cup parsley, minced
¼ cup pine nuts, toasted

Creamy Garlic Soup

The shiitake mushrooms add a distinctive flavor to the stock.
Once they have soaked, you can slice them and use them later
in a stir-fry or morning omelet.

1. Preheat oven to 375°F.

2. In a large saucepan, add stock and shiitake mushrooms; simmer gently while garlic is baking.

3. Wrap garlic in aluminum foil; bake 20 minutes, or until tender.

4. Remove garlic from oven, cool, remove aluminum foil, and slice off flat end of garlic head. Squeeze softened cloves into a bowl; set aside.

5. In a blender, purée roasted garlic, salt, silken tofu, and 2 cups stock until smooth.

6. Remove shiitake mushrooms from stock and set aside to use at another time. Add puréed tofu mixture to the stock; heat just until warmed through.

7. Ladle soup into individual bowls; drizzle a teaspoon of olive oil along surface. Top with minced parsley and toasted pine nuts.

Quick Garlic Bread

Slice a piece of sourdough bread and rub the top with a slice of garlic clove. Then brush the bread with olive oil and top with grated Romano cheese. Run under the broiler until golden brown and serve alongside the soup. Add a simple green salad to balance out the meal.

CHAPTER 9

Avocados Are Full of Good Fat

Avocados are a tropical delight with a tough outer skin and a buttery interior, that can be easily spread on a sandwich, diced into a salad, or mashed into the famous guacamole dip. In this chapter, you will discover that avocados are one of nature's most nutrient-rich foods, containing high amounts of fiber, folate, potassium, vitamin E, and magnesium. This very impressive list of health benefits qualifies the avocado as a Superfood.

What Makes Them Super

If recent research is any indication, avocados should be on everyone's list of the right food to eat. It is the monounsaturated fat in avocados that give it Superfood status. Only one other fruit comes close to having a comparable amount of monounsaturated fat, and that is the olive. The form of mono-unsaturated fat in both these foods is oleic acid, which has been shown to help lower cholesterol, prevent heart disease and arteriosclerosis, and lower your risk for cancer.

FACT

Oleic acid, also known as omega-9 fatty acid, is essential to the human body, which can manufacture only a limited quantity. However, the other essential fatty acids, omega-3 and omega-6, need to be present for the body to be able to produce oleic acid.

Fifty percent of the fat in avocados is oleic acid, which is also present in another Superfood, the cocoa butter used to make chocolate (Chapter 6). This beneficial fat and all of the nutrients it contains keeps your body well oiled, and can be used internally or externally as a skin conditioner and moisturizer.

Avocados' Versatility

There are many ways to prepare avocados, but most people prefer them raw and ripe. A quick and easy snack is to slice an avocado in half, sprinkle with some fresh lemon juice, and eat it right out of the shell. Then there's the basic guacamole recipe, probably one of the simplest yet tastiest ways to eat avocados. Just mash a ripe avocado with some lemon juice, minced onion, garlic, and salt. For a chunky salsa that also works as a side salad, chop tomatoes and avocado into cubes along with minced onion and garlic and toss with lemon juice. Any of these versions can be spread on bread, rolled up in a tortilla, or eaten with your favorite chips.

Quick Recipe Variations

It doesn't take much time to put together a tasty meal using avocado:

- Use chopped avocados as a garnish for black beans and rice.
- Add avocado to a tofu-based dressing recipe for extra richness and added color.
- Mix chopped avocados, onions, tomatoes, cilantro, lime juice, and seasonings for a quick guacamole.
- Mash ripe avocados, spread on whole-grain bread, and top with baked tofu and a slice of tomato.
- Combine sliced avocado with fennel, oranges, and fresh mint in a salad with a yogurt dressing.
- Top quartered avocado slices with corn relish and serve with a wedge of lime.
- Use as a garnish for vegetarian bean tacos or in burritos or wraps.
- Dice and add to a green leafy salad with tomato and sweet onion.

There's no reason to exclude avocados from your diet, even when you're counting calories, as the benefits justify the indulgence.

The History of Avocados

The first written reports of avocados come from the Spanish conquistador and cosmographer Martin Fernandez de Enciso, who recorded a description of the odd-looking fruit in his book *Suma De Geografia Que Trata De Todas Las Partidas Del Mundo* in 1518. The Spanish invaders reported finding avocados growing from northern Mexico through Central America and down into South America, where they had been cultivated since 8000 B.C. The Aztecs depended on the avocado as a staple in their diet, and gave it a name based on the fact that its shape is similar to the male anatomy—*ahuacatl*, or "testicles." The Spanish conquerors of the time found it a difficult word to pronounce, and instead called it *abogado*. The Aztecs used the avocado for its aphrodisiac qualities and believed it could improve sexual prowess when consumed. Due to this reputation, men and women avoided buying them lest they incite slanderous gossip.

Avocados were then introduced to Jamaica sometime in the mid-seventeenth century. When the English arrived in Jamaica, they called the avocado alligator pear, in reference to its shape and the leather-like appearance of its skin. Today, the Jamaican people simply call it a pear.

Avocados did not reach Florida and California until the twentieth century, where they are now mainly grown. Other major producers of avocados are Mexico, the Dominican Republic, Brazil, and Colombia.

FACT

While visiting Jamaica in 1672, W. Hughes, physician to King Charles II of England, wrote that the avocado was one of the rarest and most pleasant fruits he had tasted on the island. He learned from the natives that it nourished and strengthened the body, corroborating the spirits and acting as an aphrodisiac for the system.

The Avocado Fruit

Avocados are the fruit from the *Persea americana,* a tall evergreen tree that can grow up to sixty-five feet in height. There are many varieties, and being a year-round fruit they can vary in size and shape from season to season. The winter avocado is thin-skinned and pear-shaped, with a deep forest-green color, and weighs between six and sixteen ounces. The summer season produces more varieties, with skins that can be thick or thin, rough or smooth; with many pear-shaped and some round and plump. The skin color can vary from green to almost black, with a weight variation of ten to forty ounces.

You can easily grow an avocado tree by placing four strong, sharp-tipped toothpicks about 1 inch above the wide base of the seed. Place the wide end of the seed into a glass of water, balancing the toothpicks along the rim of the glass. Keep the water level constant until the seed sprouts roots and shoots, then plant it in soil.

Regardless of the seasonal variety, the inside meat of the avocado is always buttery smooth in texture, with a light yellow-green color. The large seed at the avocado's center should be discarded along with the skin; neither of these are edible.

Varieties of Avocado

There are two varieties of avocados available in the United States, and each differs in size, appearance, quality, and susceptibility to cold weather. The Hass variety is grown in California and has a tough, bumpy skin and buttery consistency. It is presently the most popular type. It was named for Rudolph Hass, a Wisconsin mailman who retired to Pasadena and obtained a patent for the Hass avocado tree in 1935. They are rich in healthy monounsaturated oil, with 18–30 percent oil in each avocado.

The other favorite is the West Indian avocado from Florida. The light-green Florida avocado is larger and juicier than the Hass variety, but it is less buttery and considerably lower in oil. The Florida avocado contains just 3–5 percent oil and roughly 25–50 percent less fat than the Hass variety.

Avocado's Nutrient Content

Avocados have nutritional values rare among the fruit kingdom. They contain no starch and very little sugar, yet they provide an excellent source of usable food energy. The temptation is to eat a whole, ripe avocado at a single sitting, but be aware that one whole California avocado has over 300 calories and 35 grams of fat, 8.5 grams being monounsaturated fat. Yet as a healthy snack, the avocado nutritionally beats out a handful of processed chips or high-fat cookies.

The nutrient content of 1 cup of puréed avocado provides:

CALORIES	235.06	BETA CAROTENE	477.13 mcg
TOTAL FAT	22.37 g	VITAMIN C	11.53 mg
CHOLESTEROL	0 mg	FOLATE	90.37 mcg
CARBOHYDRATES	10.79 g	VITAMIN K	29.20 mcg
DIETARY FIBER	7.30 g	CALCIUM	16.06 mg
SUGARS	1.31 g	MAGNESIUM	56.94 mg
PROTEIN	2.89 g	POTASSIUM	874.54 mg
VITAMIN A	893.52 IU	PHOSPHORUS	59.86 mg

The avocado is another whole food that is rich in the all-important mineral magnesium, along with potassium, which helps regulate blood pressure and prevent circulatory diseases, including high blood pressure, stroke, and heart disease. One cup of avocado contains 23 percent of the daily value for folate, which when combined with the monounsaturated fats and potassium, decreases your chances of cardiovascular disease and stroke.

FACT

Magnesium is an essential nutrient for healthy bone and cardiovascular systems (particularly in the regulation of blood pressure and cardiac rhythms), prevention of migraines, and prevention of type 2 diabetes. Ounce for ounce, avocados provide more magnesium than the twenty most commonly eaten fruits.

Avocados Strengthen the Immune System

In addition to their other heart-healthy qualities, avocados are rich in beta-sitosterol, a so-called phytosterol, which is the plant equivalent of cholesterol in animals. The avocado is one of the best sources of beta-sitosterol you can obtain from whole foods. Because beta-sitosterol is so similar to cholesterol, it competes for absorption with cholesterol and wins, thus lowering the amounts of cholesterol in your bloodstream. Based on both animal and laboratory studies, beta-sitosterol appears to inhibit excessive cell division, which may play a role in preventing cancer-cell growth.

Perhaps the most interesting research on avocados demonstrates that it is a powerful "nutrient booster," and can actually improve your body's ability to absorb nutrients. This was demonstrated in two separate studies.

In one study, adding about half an avocado to a mixed green and grated-carrot salad increased the absorption of the following nutrients in the subjects who ate the salad: alpha carotene by 8.3 times, beta carotene by 13.6 times, and lutein by 4.3 times, compared with the absorption rate of the same salad without avocado.

In a second study, adding a medium avocado (150 grams) to a serving of salsa increased the absorption of lycopene 4.4 times and the absorption of beta carotene 2.6 times compared with eating the salsa without the avocado.

Both studies showed that the healthy monounsaturated fat in the avocado caused a significant increase in the absorption of the fat-soluble carotenoid phytonutrients in the meal.

Healing Properties of Avocados

Although it may appear that avocados should be avoided in a weight-loss diet, if eaten in moderate amounts they can prove highly beneficial. At forty-eight calories per ounce, avocados are equivalent to skinless roast chicken breast, and they can actually help fight weight gain by making you feel satiated. It is this feeling of fullness that signals you to stop eating and helps to control your calorie intake.

On the cholesterol front, one study found that after seven days on a diet that included avocados, there were significant decreases in both total and LDL (bad) cholesterol, as well as an 11 percent increase in HDL (good) cholesterol.

Avocados Beat Cancer

Recent research indicates that the avocado is a potent warrior in the fight against prostate cancer. They contain the highest amount of carotenoid lutein of any commonly eaten fruit, as well as carotenoids including zeaxanthin, alpha carotene, and beta carotene, and significant amounts of vitamin E, all beneficial for maintaining a healthy prostate. One study showed that an extract of avocado containing these carotenoids and tocopherols inhibited the growth of prostate cancer cells. Interestingly, when researchers used lutein alone, the cancer cells were unaffected, thus demonstrating once again that it's the synergy of health-promoting nutrients in whole foods that makes the difference.

Buying and Storage Tips

Buy several avocados at a time; have one that is ripe and ready to eat, and a few at various stages of hardness. Here are a few things to consider when buying avocados:

- A ripe avocado is slightly soft, but should have no dark sunken spots or cracks.
- An avocado with a slight neck, rather than rounded on top, was probably tree-ripened and will have better flavor.
- A firmer, less-mature fruit can be ripened at home and will be less likely to have bruises.
- A firm avocado will ripen in a paper bag or fruit basket at room temperature within a few days.
- Avocados should not be refrigerated until they are ripe. Once ripe, they can be kept refrigerated for up to a week.
- A good test for ripeness is to stick a toothpick into the stem end; the fruit is ready to eat if the pick glides in easily.

ALERT!

Avocados contain substances called chitinases, that are associated with the latex-fruit allergy syndrome. If you have a latex allergy, you may very likely be allergic to avocados. Organic produce not treated with ethylene gas will have fewer allergy-causing compounds. In addition, cooking the food may deactivate the enzymes.

Avocados are a tropical fruit and are best eaten in late spring and summer, when they are in season. However, dry winter skin benefits greatly from the application of a mask of mashed avocado and fifteen to twenty minutes of feet-up relaxation.

Storing Avocados

Any leftover avocado can be placed in a container with the avocado seed and stored in the refrigerator. The seed will help slow down the browning of the flesh. You can also sprinkle the exposed surface of the avocado with lemon juice to prevent the browning that can occur when the flesh comes in contact with oxygen in the air. When shopping for avocados, select fruit that is unblemished, without cracks or dark sunken spots. Because it is difficult to find a ripe avocado in food markets, you can place unripe avocados in a paper bag and leave on the kitchen counter for a few days to ripen.

Preparing Avocados

Opening an avocado and removing the seed is the first step in using this super-delicious fruit. Begin by cutting around a ripe avocado lengthwise and twisting the two halves to separate. To remove the seed, take a knife and whack it sharply against the seed, then twist slightly. The seed will separate from the flesh and you will be able to easily remove it. Be careful taking the seed off the knife, as it can be a bit slippery. At this point, you can either peel the skin from the flesh and cut the flesh into long slices or cubes or, holding the avocado half in one hand, score the flesh with a knife, and using a spoon, gently scoop the flesh onto a plate or bowl.

To make rings or crescents, cut around the avocado crosswise before peeling, then peel the slices. Cut the rings in half to make crescent shapes. To make avocado balls, you can scoop the avocado meat from the unpeeled half shell with a melon-ball cutter or round spoon.

910 calories
87 g fat
38 g carbohydrates
9 g protein
4 g sugar
28 g fiber

INGREDIENTS

2 medium ripe avocados
2 tablespoons fresh lemon juice
2 tablespoons extra-virgin olive
  oil
⅛ teaspoon garlic powder
1 tablespoon chives
1 teaspoon sea salt
1 teaspoon ground cumin
Dash of hot sauce

Avocado Cumin Dip

The unique flavor of cumin complements the avocado without being overbearing. This dip is perfect with a south-of-the-border menu or spread on warm tortilla chips.

1. Peel and seed the avocados; in a medium-size bowl mash the meat until smooth.

2. Add remaining ingredients; mix to combine thoroughly.

3. Cover and keep in the refrigerator until ready to serve. Letting this dip sit for 15 minutes helps to blend the flavors.

Hot Sauce

Hot sauce with avocado helps to cut the slight blandness in a bare avocado and kick the taste up a notch. Instead of hot sauce, try using a pinch of cayenne pepper or red pepper flakes sprinkled into the dip—both will wake up your taste buds.

Avocado Reuben Sandwiches

Commercial Thousand Island dressing can be used, but for a taste treat make your own by combining 1 cup of mayonnaise with ½ cup of your favorite salsa. This recipe works well as a topping for turkey or veggie burgers as well.

1. Cut block of tempeh in half, then cut in half crosswise, making 4 thin slabs.

2. Lightly toast bread.

3. Heat oil in a heavy skillet; brown tempeh slabs on both sides.

4. Arrange 4 pieces of bread on separate plates; spread each with 1 table-spoon dressing. Top each slice with a slab of tempeh, spoonful of sauerkraut, a few slices of avocado, and a slice of cheese.

5. Place sandwich half under broiler to melt the cheese.

6. Spread another tablespoon of dressing on second piece of bread; lay it on top of cheese.

7. Slice each sandwich on the diagonal and serve immediately.

What Is Tempeh?

Tempeh is an Indonesian protein food made from cultured grains or soy. It is pressed into a block, packaged, and sold in natural-foods stores. Soy tempeh can be very low in carbohydrates, especially when you subtract the substantial amounts of fiber it provides. It is a very versatile food and a great vegetarian substitute for animal protein.

SERVES 4

660 calories
41 g fat
52 g carbohydrates
26 g protein
12 g sugars
14 g fiber

INGREDIENTS

1 (10-ounce) package soy tempeh
8 slices whole-grain bread
2 tablespoons olive oil
8 tablespoons Thousand Island dressing, divided
1½ cups sauerkraut
1 ripe avocado, sliced
4 slices Monterey Jack cheese

CHAPTER 10

Parsley: The Blood Cleanser

You may have noticed how many television cooking shows featuring Italian recipes call for the herb parsley. Parsley may be the most well known and utilized herb in the world today, not just as a garnish or to add color to a dish, but as an important ingredient in the recipe itself. In this chapter, you will discover what a tremendous nutrient boost you are getting from including parsley in your daily diet.

What Makes It Super

Just by adding some minced parsley to your salads, pasta recipe, grilled meats, or on top of your pizza, you are getting some of the essential vitamins and minerals your body needs. The problem is, that most people don't want to take the time to chop parsley, preferring to get a meal on the table fast. Once you learn that including this Superfood in your daily diet is like taking a vitamin tablet, you will probably get out your knife and start mincing.

Parsley comes from the *Umfelliferae* family of plants, and claims distant cousins celery and carrots as part of the family tree. The leaves and root of the parsley plant are the parts most commonly used in recipes for its aromatic flavor. The beneficial properties of parsley include:

- **Diuretic:** helps reduce water retention and swelling in your limbs and enlarged glands.
- **Carminative:** improves circulation and stimulation to body parts.
- **Expectorant:** helps excrete excess mucus from the lungs.
- **Nervine:** used to feed and tone the nerves.
- **Tonic:** used to strengthen blood and organs.

Parsley is loaded with the vital nutrients vitamins C, K, and A, along with compounds that purify your blood and expel toxins from your body. The body parts most affected by the properties in parsley are the kidneys, bladder, stomach, liver, and gall bladder. However, parsley needs to be taken in large quantities or consistently each day to be of any real benefit.

The History of Parsley

The name *parsley* comes from the Greek word for "rock celery," *petroselinon*. It is possible that parsley gets its Latin name from the distinctive characteristic of dissolving kidney and gall stones, since *petros* means rock. Another theory is that parsley was able to grow amongst the rocks in many ancient Greek gardens.

Long revered in Mediterranean countries, parsley has been cultivated for thousands of years, first as a medicine and later in daily meal recipes. Greek and Roman physicians used parsley in tonic recipes, antidotes for poisoning, for rheumatic stiffness, and to help dissolve stones. The ancient Greeks prized it so highly they would make victory laurels of parsley to drape around the necks of their victorious athletes.

Parsley Today

Sometime in the seventeenth century parsley was brought to the Americas, where it now grows in abundance. The most widely used culinary herb in the United States, it takes twelve pounds of fresh parsley to make one pound of dried. If you have a choice, use fresh parsley, which provides more flavor and health benefits than dried and requires little more than a quick mincing with a knife or snip of the scissors.

Use parsley with melted butter and garlic, toss in some cooked pasta and broccoli, then top with another Superfood, toasted walnuts. You can also juice parsley with carrots, celery, and cucumber for a healthy, refreshing vegetable juice or add it to a smoothie for added nutrition.

Parsley is a biennial plant, with the first year's leaves thought to be the best tasting. Both varieties—curly leaf and flat leaf—are biennials, but are usually treated as annuals, planted anew each spring.

There are two main varieties of parsley that you can find in your local food markets:

- **Flat leaf (*Petroselinum neapolitanum*):** Known as Italian parsley, it has a distinctive flat, saw-toothed leaf and a stronger, sweeter flavor than the curly variety. The flat-leaf variety is far more delicate and lacy, and gets very leggy. It grows to about eighteen inches in height and seeds in its second year. Unfortunately, in some countries it resembles the poisonous weed "fool's-parsley," causing people to avoid using it and grow the curly leaf instead. Its distinctive taste is at its best when sautéed with garlic and olive oil and served over roasted lamb and vegetables.

- **Curly leaf (*Petroselinum crispum*):** Milder tasting than the flat leaf, this variety lends itself to working as a team with other herbs. Its compact, dense, bright-green leaves tend to make it an attractive edging or container plant. Curly leaf can be used in just about any dish, bringing both color and just the right amount of flavor to the recipe. This variety grows as high as twelve inches tall and needs full sun and rich composted soil to grow.

FACT

To make healthy, great-tasting pesto, add a generous amount of parsley to the traditional basil, olive oil, garlic, pine nuts, and Parmesan cheese recipe. The flat-leaf variety of parsley can be a bit strong and tend to overpower the flavor of the basil, so use the curly leaf instead. The parsley helps neutralize your breath from the effects of eating raw garlic.

Growing Parsley

Starting a parsley plant from seed requires a long gestation period, which may have given rise to the saying that, "Parsley seeds must go to the devil and back nine times before sprouting." Begin by soaking the seeds overnight, then place in potting soil and keep in a warm place. It could take several weeks, so patience is called for here. Once they sprout, you can put them on a warm, sunny windowsill, water them regularly, and let them grow. You can replant once they are strong enough for the outdoors or pot them and keep them indoors or on the porch. They can grow to twelve inches in the sun, and surprise you with their full tufted leaves, delicious in everything from sauces to juices.

Parsley's Nutrient Content

Known mostly as the breath-freshening companion to raw garlic, parsley is a nutrient-dense herb high in vitamins C, A, and K; iodine; iron; and chlorophyll. Actually, parsley has a higher vitamin C content than citrus. Vitamin C is used to treat internal inflammation, making parsley an excellent ingredient in remedies to treat this problem. It is also used to protect against free radical damage. It contains certain volatile oils that have been shown to inhibit the formation of tumors, particularly in the lungs. The components of these volatile oils are the reason parsley can neutralize certain types of carcinogens, such as the ones that show up in cigarette and grill smoke. The components are myristicin, limonene, eugenol, and alpa-thujene. The curly leaf varieties are a richer source of myristicin.

A sampling of the nutrient content for 2 tablespoons of parsley include:

CALORIES	2.70	FOLATE	11.40 mcg
PROTEIN	0.22 g	VITAMIN K	123 mcg
CARBOHYDRATES	0.47 g	CALCIUM	10.35 mg
FIBER	0.25 g	IRON	0.46 mg
VITAMIN A	631.80 IU	MAGNESIUM	3.75 mg
VITAMIN C	9.97 mg	POTASSIUM	41.55 mg

ALERT!

Free radicals contribute to the development and progression of a wide variety of diseases, including atherosclerosis, colon cancer, diabetes, and asthma. Individuals who consume a diet high in vitamin-C foods have less of a risk for these kinds of disease.

Parsley is also rich in the flavonoids apiin, apigenin, crisoeriol, and luteolin. Flavonoids are known for their antioxidant activity and help prevent free radical damage to your body's cells; this results in protection against cancer and heart disease. Parsley's dark-green color provides needed oxygenating chlorophyll, increasing the antioxidant capacity of your blood.

Healing Properties of Parsley

As a healing herb, parsley excels in helping with urination difficulties, jaundice, kidney and bladder stones, and obstructions of the liver and spleen.

Parsley can be used in combination with other herbs, fruits, and vegetables to create healing remedies.

Parsley can be used for a wide assortment of health complaints:

- For kidney and bladder infections, combine parsley, echinacea, plantain, and marshmallow root.
- Two ounces of fresh parsley and apple juice works as a remedy for anemia and as a blood tonic.
- Parsley root can be used to treat jaundice.
- For female menstruation problems, parsley can be used in combination with buchu, cramp bark, and black haw.
- Two ounces of fresh parsley juice daily helps in cancer treatments.

Additionally, to treat edema or water retention, particularly caused by congestive heart failure, make a decoction (parsley tea) by placing one ounce of dried parsley leaves in sixteen fluid ounces of distilled water and simmer on low heat for fifteen minutes. Strain when done and consume six ounces three times a day. When the bladder and kidneys cannot let go of fluid, make a compress by soaking a cloth in the parsley tea and applying it to the swollen areas. The compress should be applied hot, but not burning, and changed as it cools during the thirty-minute treatment. At the end, apply a cold, wet towel to the area for only one minute. This helps to relax the kidney and bladder, open the pores, increase sweat, and reduce swelling.

FACT

In the macrobiotic diet, parsley is used as a daily condiment. Just a sprinkle of minced parsley on soup, grains, or veggies at each meal provides you with needed vitamins C and A and a variety of other nutrients. Rather than taking expensive supplements, get your nutrients from food, as nature intended.

Other health conditions that parsley can be used to treat are:

- Weak adrenal glands
- Optic and brain nerve weakness

- Ear problems such as: infections, earaches, and deafness
- Indigestion
- Gum and tooth problems
- Bad breath

The amounts of parsley taken for treatments can consist of one to two ounces of fresh parsley taken with meals or in capsule form. As a tea, drink two to three cups daily made from fresh or dried organic parsley.

Buying and Storage Tips

Fresh parsley should be covered and stored in the refrigerator when keeping a week or longer. If you will be using it over a few days, clip the tips of the stems and arrange in a glass of water. Set it on your counter where you can reach over and snip enough to garnish your food. Oftentimes, out of sight, out of mind can hold true for using fresh herbs in your cooking. If the parsley is there in front of you, more than likely you will find a way to use it.

QUESTION?

When making a white sauce, how can you get the taste of parsley without turning everything green?
Prepare the parsley by mincing the stems and then adding them to the sauce, instead of the parsley leaves. The leaves will leach color, turning the sauce a pale green shade, while the stems will provide the taste but not the color.

Preserving Fresh Parsley

The taste and aroma of parsley is stronger when eaten live and fresh, but it can also be frozen or dried. To freeze fresh parsley, wash off any sand or dirt and shake to dry. Place in freezer bags and into your freezer. Try to use frozen parsley within two months. To dry your own parsley, bundle fresh-cut stems and wrap the ends with twine. Hang the bunch of parsley upside down from a rafter or window frame. In this way, the volatile oils settle downward into the leaves, rather than into the stem. When completely dry and crisp, gently remove the parsley leaves, place in a glass jar, and seal tightly. Store in a cool, dry place out of the sunlight.

Making Pesto

With so many ways to use parsley in the kitchen, you can keep small pots on your windowsill or plant some in your herb garden so there is always plenty around to use at a moment's notice. There is no better combination than fresh parsley, basil, raw garlic, Parmesan cheese (optional), and a good-quality extra-virgin olive oil. This classic sauce, known as pesto, was born in the northern Italian city of Genoa. *Pesto* is the Genoese pronoun meaning "to pound" or "to crush," from the Latin root for *pestle*, as in *mortar and pestle*. Today, it can be made quickly in an electric food processor, but if you ever have the time, try working the ingredients by hand and see if you notice a difference in taste and quality.

Parsley Pesto Sauce

Simple, easy, and surprisingly quick to make using a mortar and pestle. Spread this pesto on salmon fillets and allow to marinate 30 minutes before grilling; nothing else is needed. Serve over cooked pasta, on bread, as a pizza topping, with cooked vegetables, or even mixed into cooked brown rice.

1. Add the walnuts to the grinding bowl or processor; grind to a pulp.

2. Add garlic to grinding bowl or processor; continue to grind.

3. Add parsley and basil in batches, along with a tablespoon of oil; continue to grind.

4. As ingredients break down, continue to add oil and salt to mixture until you have a thick paste.

5. Adjust consistency by adding more oil to make a sauce that is not too thick, yet not loose and runny.

What Parsley to Use

The Italian flat-leaf parsley will give a stronger, sweeter taste, while the curly leaf will complement the taste of the grilled salmon. Always look to complement the main entrée with your sauce, rather than overpowering it with an herb's aroma.

MAKES ¾ CUP

1350 calories
140 g fat
20 g carbohydrates
12 g protein
2 g sugars
10 g fiber

INGREDIENTS
⅓ cup fresh walnuts
3 cloves garlic
2 cups curly leaf parsley (no stems)
2 cups fresh basil leaf
½ cup extra-virgin olive oil
½ teaspoon sea salt

SERVES 6

210 calories
11 g fat
23 g carbohydrates
4 g protein
2 g sugars
2 g fiber

INGREDIENTS

1 cup quinoa
2 cups water or vegetable broth
½ teaspoon sea salt
1 cup fresh parsley
3 green onions
1 cup plum tomatoes
1 clove garlic
¼ cup extra-virgin olive oil
Juice of one fresh lemon
Sea salt to taste

Quinoa Parsley Tabbouleh

Make sure to seed the tomatoes for easier digestion, but also to prevent excess liquid from making your tabbouleh soggy.

1. In a heavy saucepan, combine quinoa, water, and sea salt; bring to a boil.

2. Reduce heat and simmer until all water is absorbed, about 15–20 minutes.

3. When quinoa is done, spoon into a large bowl and allow to cool.

4. While the grain is cooling, mince parsley and green onion; set aside.

5. Halve tomatoes lengthwise; scoop out seeds into a measuring cup or small bowl.

6. Chop tomatoes into small pieces; add to parsley and green onions.

7. Press and mince garlic; whisk it together in a small bowl with oil, lemon juice, and sea salt.

8. Strain and discard tomato seeds; add tomato liquid to lemon dressing.

9. Add parsley, green onion, and tomatoes to quinoa; toss well.

10. Add lemon dressing; mix well to combine all ingredients. Adjust seasonings with salt if needed.

High-Protein Meal

Using quinoa in this traditional Middle Eastern dish is especially beneficial for those individuals who cannot tolerate eating wheat couscous. This dish is high in protein and works well accompanied by vegetables and a bean dish to round out its protein content. It is also light enough to serve as a side salad to a fish or chicken entrée.

CHAPTER 11

Wild Salmon Keeps Your Skin Young

Watch the health shows on TV and read the health articles: The word is out that salmon is the number-one food for beautiful skin, a strong, healthy heart, and improved memory. In this chapter, you will learn about the world of the wild salmon and why the oil it provides is so important for your survival; but you will also learn about the dark side of the fish industry and how raising fish in tanks can cause you much more damage than good.

What Makes It Super

From the many news reports and scientific findings, you would think that salmon was the answer to all your health needs. Actually, it is the omega-3 fatty acids in salmon that puts this fish at the top of the Superfoods chart, but that's not all; it is also high in vitamin D, selenium, protein, and B vitamins. Omega-3 fatty acids can also be found in vegetable oils, and are not made by the body, so they must be imported through diet or supplements. After observing that the Eskimo population had a diet rich in fish oil and a low rate of heart disease, scientists began to take a serious interest in omega-3 fatty acids. Salmon is only one source for the two types of omega-3s: DHA (docosahexaenoic acid) and EPA (eicosapentaenoic acid).

The American Heart Association (AHA) recommends eating fish (particularly fatty fish) at least two times a week. The AHA considers salmon to be a good source of protein, without the high saturated fat that red meat products possess. Fatty fish like mackerel, lake trout, herring, sardines, and albacore tuna are other sources of omega-3 fatty acids. Scientific research has found that omega-3s taken as a supplement can significantly lower the risks associated with heart disease. Some studies have found that omega-3s can significantly decrease serum triglyceride levels, lower blood pressure, and reduce blood levels of homocysteine, high levels of which are associated with an increased risk of heart disease and stroke. Elevated homocysteine levels have also been linked to Alzheimer's disease, Parkinson's disease, and osteoporosis.

ALERT!

Omega-3 fatty acids are required for normal brain development of fetuses during pregnancy and for the first two years of life. If mother and infant are deficient in omega-3 fatty acids, the infant's immune and nervous systems may not develop correctly.

Omega-3s also help to thin the blood by discouraging platelets in the blood from clumping together, thus reducing the risk that the blood will clot and cause a heart attack. Preliminary research also suggests that omega-3 fatty acids from fish oil may help regulate the rhythm of the heart, as both EPA and DHA have been reported to help prevent cardiac arrhythmias. Potent anti-inflammatory agents, omega-3s help curb an overactive immune system, and thus are helpful in the treatment of autoimmune diseases such as rheumatoid arthritis, chronic inflammatory bowel disease, Crohn's disease, and psoriasis.

The History of Wild Salmon

Every year come early summer, salmon, having traveled thousands of miles during a two-to-five-year span, return home to spawn and die. They have been following this ritual in the cold waters of Alaska, the Pacific Northwest, eastern Canada, Norway, and Greenland for as long as history has been recorded, and probably well before that. Wild salmon thrive on zooplankton (tiny, single-celled organisms), which are a rich source of omega-3 fatty acids. When you eat the salmon, this heart-and-brain-healthy fat is delivered to your cells. That's the good news. The bad news is, that in the past fifty years our oceans have become overfished and polluted, resulting in the virtual extinction of U.S. Atlantic salmon. Instead, you will find that most Atlantic salmon sold in the United States is farm-raised, and all of it color enhanced with special feed also containing antibiotics. These fish are also genetically engineered to grow larger than their more natural cousins raised in the wild.

Wild Versus Farm-Raised

The year-round demand for salmon far exceeds its availability. In order to fulfill this demand, farms for raising salmon in captivity were created, and a new species of salmon was born. The farm-raised salmon contains less of the heart-healthy omega-3 fatty acids, with higher levels of chemical contaminants, and are most likely genetically engineered for size and color enhanced to make the flesh more appealing to a discerning public. This is what you will find in the supermarkets year-round and in restaurants featuring salmon on their menu.

Wild salmon, on the other hand, is high in omega-3 fatty acids, with a much lower level of chemical pollutants, and is not color enhanced or genetically modified for size. All in all, a much better addition to your diet.

ALERT!

Today, most salmon in the food markets are farmed, and there is a wide variation in price between inexpensive farmed salmon and expensive, fresh Alaskan salmon. Because farm-raised salmon are not always fed the marine diet that produces high amounts of omega-3 fatty acids, there is considerable controversy as to their omega-3 content.

Risks Associated with Pollutants

In the *Journal of Nutrition*, Barbara Knuth, Cornell professor of natural resources who specializes in risk management associated with chemical contaminants in fish, and Steven Schwager, Cornell associate professor of biological statistics and computational biology and an expert in sampling design and statistical analysis of comparative data, coauthored a benefit-risk analysis of eating farmed versus wild salmon. Schwager maintains that for a middle-aged man who has had a heart attack and doesn't want to have another one, the risks from pollutants are minor, and the omega-3 benefits him in a way that far outstrips the relatively minor risks from the pollutants. However, for the younger generation who are at risk of a lifetime accumulation of pollutants that are carcinogenic, and pregnant women, who are at risk for birth defects and IQ diminution and other kinds of damage to the fetus, those risks are great enough that they outweigh the benefits.

Knuth and Schwager's research found regional differences in contaminants in farmed salmon, with Chilean salmon showing the lowest levels and European (particularly Scottish) farmed salmon showing the highest levels. They maintain that careful consumers with a history of heart disease should choose farmed salmon from Chile for their high omega-3 content and relatively lower level of contaminants, and that farmed salmon from North America would be a better second choice than European farmed salmon.

The researchers' benefit-risk analysis showed that consumers should not eat farmed fish:

- From Scotland, Norway, and eastern Canada more than three times a year
- From Maine, western Canada, and Washington state more than three to six times a year
- From Chile more than about six times a year

Wild chum salmon can be consumed safely as often as once a week; pink salmon, sockeye, and coho about twice a month; and Chinook just once a month.

In a study appearing in *Environmental Health Perspectives* in May 2005, the research team reported that the levels of chlorinated pesticides, dioxins, PCBs, and other contaminants are up to ten times greater in farm-raised salmon than in wild Pacific salmon, and that salmon farmed in Europe are more contaminated than salmon from South and North American farms.

Salmon's Nutrient Content

Besides the potent omega-3 fatty acids, wild salmon contains a storehouse of nutrients to add to your diet. The nutrient content for 4 ounces of baked or broiled salmon contains:

CALORIES	261.95	FOLATE	39.69 mcg
PROTEIN	29.14 g	CALCIUM	31.75 mg
FAT	15.20 g	IRON	1.03 mg
CHOLESTEROL	96.39 mg	MAGNESIUM	138.35 mg
VITAMIN A	562.46 IU	PHOSPHORUS	420.71 mg
NIACIN, B3	11.34 mg	POTASSIUM	572.67 mg
VITAMIN B12	3.25 mcg	SELENIUM	53.07 mg
VITAMIN D	411 IU	OMEGA-3 FATTY ACIDS	2.09g

On days when you are having salmon, you can skip taking your omega-3 fish oil supplement, since you are getting all that you need from the real thing.

Healing Properties of Salmon

It's important to remember that your body does not make its own essential fatty acids, so you must import this nutrient in your food. People who eat diets with the optimum balance of essential fatty acids tend to avoid many common ailments. Cultures that have high omega-3 consumption from eating fish have far less mental depression than Americans whose diets are dominated by omega-6 fatty acids. In fact, in one epidemiological study, fish consumption was the most significant variable in comparing levels of depression and coronary heart disease.

FACT

The American Heart Association also recommends eating tofu and other forms of soybeans, canola, walnut, and flaxseed and their oils. These contain alpha-linolenic acid (LNA), which can become omega-3 fatty acid in the body. More studies are needed, however, to show a cause-and-effect relationship between alpha-linolenic acid and heart disease.

Cardiovascular Disease

In 1996, the American Heart Association released its Science Advisory, "Fish Consumption, Fish Oil, Lipids and Coronary Heart Disease." Since then, important new findings have been reported about the benefits of omega-3 fatty acids on cardiovascular disease. These include evidence from randomized, controlled clinical trials. New information has emerged about how omega-3 fatty acids affect heart function (including antiarrhythmic effects), hemodynamics (cardiac mechanics), and arterial endothelial function. These findings are outlined in their November, 2002 Scientific Statement, "Fish Consumption, Fish Oil, Omega-3 Fatty Acids and Cardiovascular Disease."

The ways that omega-3 fatty acids reduce CVD risk are still being studied. However, research has shown that they:

- Decrease risk of arrhythmias, which can lead to sudden cardiac death
- Decrease triglyceride levels

- Decrease growth rate of atherosclerotic plaque
- Lower blood pressure (slightly)

Meanwhile, epidemiologic and clinical trials have shown that omega-3 fatty acids reduce CVD incidence. Large-scale epidemiologic studies suggest that people at risk for coronary heart disease benefit from consuming omega-3 fatty acids from plants and marine sources. The ideal amount to take isn't clear, but evidence from prospective secondary prevention studies suggests that taking EPA+DHA ranging from 0.5 to 1.8 grams per day (either as fatty fish or supplements) significantly reduces deaths from heart disease and all other causes. For alpha-linolenic acid, a total intake of 1.5–3 grams per day seems beneficial.

Randomized clinical trials have shown that omega-3 fatty-acid supplements can reduce cardiovascular events (death, nonfatal heart attacks, nonfatal strokes). They can also slow the progression of atherosclerosis in coronary patients. However, more studies are needed to confirm and further define the health benefits of omega-3 fatty-acid supplements for preventing a first or subsequent cardiovascular event. For example, placebo-controlled, double-blind, randomized clinical trials are needed to document the safety and efficacy of omega-3 fatty-acid supplements in high-risk patients (those with type 2 diabetes, dyslipidemia, hypertension, and smokers) and coronary patients on drug therapy. Mechanistic studies on their apparent effects on sudden death are also needed.

Increasing omega-3 fatty acid intake through foods is preferable. However, coronary artery disease patients may not be able to get enough omega-3 by diet alone; these people may want to talk to their doctor about taking a supplement. Supplements could also help people with high triglycerides, who need even larger doses. The availability of high-quality omega-3 fatty-acid supplements, free of contaminants, is an important prerequisite to their use.

Health Benefits

Research is just beginning to show all of the benefits including omega-3 fatty acids in your diet can provide. By eating a piece of grilled salmon for dinner or taking a fish-oil supplement, you can effectively:

- Prevent both breast and colon cancers.
- Prevent age-related macular degeneration. In the Nurses' Health Study, those who ate fish four or more times a week had a lower risk of age-related macular degeneration than those who ate three or fewer fish meals per month.
- Mitigate autoimmune diseases such as lupus, rheumatoid arthritis, and Raynaud's disease. Multiple studies have substantiated that the anti-inflammatory abilities of omega-3 fatty acids are what help reduce the symptoms of autoimmune diseases, as well as prolong the survival of those who suffer from them.
- Relieve depression and a host of mental health problems. Because over 60 percent of your brain is fat, your mental health is severely affected by your intake of the essential fatty acids. Omega-3 fatty acids not only promote your brain's ability to regulate mood-related signals; they are a crucial constituent of brain-cell membranes and are needed for normal nervous system function, mood regulation, and attention and memory functions.

FACT

Some of the most interesting research on omega-3 fatty acids involves successfully treating mental depression, attention deficit disorder, dementia, hyperactivity, schizophrenia, bipolar disorder, and Alzheimer's disease.

When it comes to getting your omega-3 fatty acids, wild salmon is a simple, delicious answer. Not only is it delicious, is also high in protein, widely available in canned form, easy to prepare, and, more important, high in beneficial omega-3 fatty acids. If you eat wild salmon or other cold-water fish, like sardines or trout, two to four times a week along with a wide variety of whole grains, vegetables, fruits, and both vegetarian and animal protein, you can balance the ratio of fatty acids in your body and improve your cellular health. There's plenty of scientific evidence showing that including wild salmon in your diet will have a positive effect on your short- and long-term health.

Buying and Storage Tips

Naturally, the best wild salmon is freshly caught, but that is not always possible. Check with your local seafood markets to find out when U.S. Pacific wild Alaskan salmon is in season, and have it cut into steaks and fillets and wrapped for freezing. This way you can buy enough salmon, at a good price, to have for months to come. Frozen salmon can be an excellent alternative to fresh; just be sure to buy from whole-foods markets offering environmentally safe, high-EFA frozen fish.

The other thing you can do is buy canned wild Alaskan salmon or canned red sockeye salmon and store it in your cupboard for a quick meal. The canned fish can safely sit in your pantry for months before use. Canned sockeye salmon has 203 milligrams of calcium, which is 17 percent of your daily requirement. Don't let the presence of bones alarm you; the fish has been cooked and the bones are so soft they can be easily eaten, and are actually good for you.

Preparing Canned Salmon

You can prepare canned salmon at home or take along a few cans when traveling or camping out. The list of preparation ideas is as long as your imagination is wide. You can:

- Add salmon to a green salad for a delicious light meal
- Make salmon burgers by mashing with egg and breadcrumbs, then grilling
- Make it the way you do canned tuna, with mayonnaise, onion, and celery
- Add it to a hearty vegetable soup
- Replace the beef in meatloaf with it
- Add salmon to a traditional soufflé recipe
- Combine salmon with corn kernels, eggs, onion, and bread crumbs to make croquettes
- Prepare a delicious salmon pâté for special events
- Toss salmon with pasta, olive oil, garlic, fresh tomatoes, and basil
- Combine with corn meal and herbs to deep fry into salmon fritters

Since canned salmon is already cooked, it gives you a little more time to prepare the rest of your meal.

Preparing Fresh Salmon

Salmon steaks or fillets can be marinated, or just rinsed under water, then patted dry before cooking. Frozen salmon should be defrosted slowly in the refrigerator, to preserve the texture and flavor, then rinsed under water and patted dry. From this point, you can bake, broil, poach, grill, boil, sauté, fry, or steam it, because salmon is versatile and adaptable to any cooking method.

Salmon can be cooked with a honey-citrus glaze; with brown sugar and pecans; topped with minced garlic and olive oil; sprinkled with herbs de Provence and butter; poached in lemon juice or white wine; grilled with parsley butter; slathered with pesto; or baked with dill. There are many recipe ideas you can find, in cookbooks or online, simply by searching on Google for "salmon recipes," and your dinner plans are complete.

Salmon Cakes with Mango Salsa

If you cannot find almond or pecan meal, you can make your own by grinding a cup of raw almonds or pecans in a food processor until a flour consistency is achieved. Be careful not to run it so long it becomes an oily paste.

1. Preheat oven to 350°F.

2. In a medium bowl, combine salmon, chives, beaten egg, nut flour, and sea salt.

3. Mix well; form into 4 patties.

4. Place on a well-oiled baking sheet; bake 15–20 minutes, or cook in an oiled skillet, browning on both sides.

5. To make the salsa, peel and chop mango into small pieces; place in a medium-size bowl.

6. Mince red pepper and onion; add to bowl.

7. Peel and grate ginger, extracting juice by pressing the fiber against the side of a shallow dish; pour juice into bowl with mango mixture.

8. Juice the lemon; add to mango mixture; mix well.

9. Cover and refrigerate until ready to serve. For a hotter, spicier version, add a fresh, minced jalapeño pepper.

Grilled Salmon and Salsa

A beautiful fillet of grilled salmon would benefit from a few tablespoons of mango or tomato salsa. The juices will enrich the dry meat, and the sweet-sour taste will only complement the smoky flavor of the fish. Serve alongside some steamed broccoli tossed with garlic sautéed in olive oil and a salad of cooked kale and walnuts. A true Superfoods meal.

SERVES 4

260 calories
8 g fat
18 g carbohydrates
30 g protein
11 g sugars
4 g fiber

INGREDIENTS

1 (14-ounce) can wild Alaskan salmon
¼ cup minced chives
1 large egg, beaten
1 cup almond or pecan flour
Sea salt to taste
1 ripe mango
½ sweet Vidalia onion
½ red pepper
3-inch piece ginger root
Juice of one lemon

INGREDIENTS

1 (6-ounce) can wild Alaskan salmon
¼ cup minced sweet onion
¼ cup minced celery
2 tablespoons roasted peanuts
1 tablespoon mayonnaise
1 teaspoon Dijon mustard
Salt and pepper, to taste
2 tortilla wraps
2 large leaves of lettuce

Salmon Salad Wrap

Vary the amounts of mayonnaise and mustard to suit your taste, or substitute roasted pine nuts for the peanuts. Feel free to improvise to ensure you get just the flavors you love.

1. Open salmon and remove and discard any pieces of skin.

2. In a medium-size bowl, combine salmon, onion, celery, peanuts, mayonnaise, mustard, salt, and pepper; mix well.

3. Heat a skillet; warm 1 tortilla at a time. Remove to individual plates.

4. Divide salmon mixture; spread along one side of a tortilla.

5. Lay lettuce along length of mixture; roll up tortilla.

6. Slice wrap in half along the diagonal and serve.

Canned Salmon

Always keep a few cans of wild Alaskan or red sockeye salmon on hand for quick meals. In the off-season, when fresh wild salmon is not available, you can use the canned salmon to add to soups, stir-fries, pasta dishes, or as a pâté on crackers.

CHAPTER 12

Beans Lower Cholesterol

Beans are truly one of Nature's gifts to the human race. Not only are they an excellent protein source, they are good for your heart and lower your LDL cholesterol levels due to their high soluble fiber content. In this chapter, you may be surprised to learn how including beans in your diet can reduce your risk for heart attack and help prevent diabetes, both serious health issues for Americans today. You will also learn how to prepare your beans to eliminate digestive difficulties while preparing delicious, healthy, and body-strengthening recipes.

What Makes Them Super

The ideal vegetarian protein source, beans are low in fat and loaded with essential nutrients. There are over 1,000 species in the legume family, which includes beans, peas, lentils, and garbanzo beans, which means you won't soon become bored with rotating them around your weekly menu plan. They are the edible seed of certain leguminous plants such as split peas, peas, chickpeas, beans, and lentils. Not only do they provide a valuable source of protein to people, they contribute to the environment by fixing the atmospheric nitrogen in the soil in which they grow.

FACT

Dried legumes are classified into three groups: beans, peas, and lentils. They are eaten either whole or unhulled (outer husk intact) or split in half with or without their skins. Because they are a protein-starch combination, they can cause digestive gas, which can be neutralized by using ginger, kombu (sea vegetable), or bay leaf in the cooking process.

U.S. Dietary Guidelines

In January 2005, the sixth edition of the *Dietary Guidelines for Americans* was released. One of the major recommendations was for people to include three cups of beans on a weekly basis. The guidelines classify beans as a vegetable and as a nonmeat protein source because they contain nutrients found in both of the respective food groups.

Specifically, Americans are encouraged to eat nine servings (4½ cups) of fruits and vegetables daily, choosing a variety from the five veggie subgroups: dark green, orange, and starchy veggies; legumes (dry beans); and all other vegetables. Beans and legumes are spotlighted again in the *Dietary Guidelines for Americans* as a nutrient-rich carbohydrate source. Dietary fiber has numerous proven health benefits, such as reducing the risk of heart disease and some cancers, promoting regularity, and helping with weight maintenance.

Including Beans in Your Diet

According to the most recent U.S. Dietary Guidelines, servings of dry beans and peas can be counted either as vegetables (legumes subgroup) or in the meat and beans group. Generally, individuals who regularly eat meat, poultry, and fish would count their dry beans and peas servings in the vegetable group. Individuals or vegetarians who seldom or never eat meat, poultry, or fish would count most of their legume servings in the meat and beans group. Here are a few examples of what that might look like in your daily meal plan.

FACT

The *Dietary Guidelines for Americans,* published every five years since 1980 by the Department of Health and Human Services (HHS) and the Department of Agriculture (USDA), provides authoritative advice for people two years and older about good dietary habits to promote health and reduce risk for major chronic diseases.

For a diet of 1,800 calories per day, representing individuals who regularly eat meat, poultry and fish (not a complete list of daily foods eaten), you could eat:

- 3 ounces chicken or beef
- 2 ounces tuna fish
- ½ cup beans

The 3 ounces of chicken and 2 ounces of tuna fish equal 5-ounce equivalents in the meat and beans group, which meets the guideline's recommendation at this calorie level.

Therefore, the ½ cup beans counts as ½ cup of legumes to meet the .43 cup daily (3 cups per week) recommendation for legumes in the 1,800 calorie pattern.

Based on 1,800 calories per day, individuals or vegetarians who seldom or never eat meat, poultry, or fish, you could eat:

- 2 eggs
- 2 tablespoons peanut butter

- 1 cup tofu
- ½ cup chickpeas

The 2 eggs and 2 tablespoons peanut butter equal 3-ounce equivalents in the meat and beans group.

Two more ounces are needed to meet the 5-ounce recommendation. These 2-ounce equivalents are provided by the 1 cup of tofu. Since the meat and beans group recommendation has been met, the ½ cup of chickpeas then counts as ½ cup of legumes to meet the .43 cup daily (3 cups per week) recommendation for legumes in the 1,800 calorie pattern.

The guidelines make it easy to plan your weekly menu to ensure you receive the proper amounts of protein (from both vegetarian and animal sources), carbohydrates, and fats.

The History of Beans

Beans are one of the oldest recorded foods in history. Archeological digs have unearthed beans and lentils 5,000 years old in the Eastern Mediterranean, Mesopotamia, the Egyptian pyramids, Hungarian caves, the British Isles, the American continents, and up into India and the Middle East. Every culture has survived and flourished on the regular consumption of beans and lentils. Today, the legume family continues to nurture and sustain indigenous peoples the world over.

FACT

For most bean varieties, one pound of dried beans is equivalent to two cups dried or four to five cups cooked beans. The average cooking time is 1½–2 hours when simmered on the stovetop. Using a pressure cooker can reduce the cooking time by half. For optimal digestion, be sure to presoak the beans for six to eight hours before cooking.

A Few Types of Beans

There are many more beans awaiting your discovery than the more commonly used kidney, garbanzo, or lentil. Here is a sampling of what you can find in natural-foods markets:

- **Anasazi (a-na-SAH-zee) beans:** indigenous to the Native American Navajo tribes, *anasazi* means "ancient one." Cultivated since 1100 A.D., this heirloom bean has a sweet flavor, is fast cooking, and is reputed to cause less flatulence than other bean varieties. Can be used in place of pinto beans to make delicious refried beans.

- **Azuki beans:** also called aduki or black aduki beans. Usually a small red bean, with the less-common cousin being the black azuki. These beans have a sweet-sour flavor, are easy to digest, and cook faster than other beans. For healing purposes, they tonify the kidney and adrenal glands, detoxify the body, reduce swelling (either taken internally or as a poultice), and cleanse stagnant blood conditions.

- **Black turtle beans:** a member of the kidney-bean family, they are most often found in Latin American cuisine cooked with bay leaf, basil, onion, and green pepper. Helps support the kidneys and reproductive organs, acts as a diuretic (dispels fluids), and lessens the effects of urinary problems and menopausal hot flashes.

- **Cannellini, navy, and great northern beans:** smooth-textured, kidney-shaped white beans with a sweet, nutty flavor, they are mostly used in soups and salad recipes. They are thought to be beneficial to the lungs and help the elasticity and vibrancy of the skin.

- **Mung beans:** commonly used to make the Indian dish dahl, mung beans are a highly nutritious bean and easy to prepare. They are beneficial to the liver and gall bladder and act as a diuretic, helping to reduce swelling in the body. With 14 grams of protein, 55 grams of calcium, and 97 grams of magnesium in 1 cup of cooked mung beans, you cannot afford to live without this Superfood. Check the end of this chapter for a delicious mung-bean stew your family will love.

- **Lentils:** a good source of fiber, B vitamins, and protein without any fat. With 1 cup of cooked lentils you get 230 calories, 18 grams of protein, and 16 grams of fiber, all beneficial for your heart, circulation, adrenals, and kidneys.

According to nutrition researcher Paul Pitchford, soup broth made from mung beans can be used as an antidote for food poisoning, dysentery, diarrhea, painful urination, mumps, burns, lead and pesticide poisoning, boils, and edema.

Beans' Nutrient Content

The nutrient content of beans will vary with the many varieties; however, a basic overview for 1 cup of canned kidney beans would yield the following:

CALORIES	199.78	FOLATE	92 mcg
PROTEIN	13.36 g	POTASSIUM	607 mg
CARBOHYDRATE	37.12 g	CALCIUM	87 mg
FAT	0.36 g	IRON	3 mg
CHOLESTEROL	0 mg	ZINC	1.18 mg
DIETARY FIBER	13.6 g		

Notice the high fiber and protein levels that beans can add to a meal. Take another look at the calcium and potassium levels, and you can see why beans are part of the Superfoods list.

Healing Properties of Beans

A study published in the *Archives of Internal Medicine* confirms that eating high-fiber foods such as beans and lentils helps prevent cardiovascular disease. In this study, almost 10,000 American adults were followed for nineteen years. Those eating the most fiber—21 grams per day—had a 12 percent reduced risk for developing coronary heart disease (CHD) and 11 percent reduced risk for developing cardiovascular disease (CVD) compared to those eating the least fiber—5 grams—daily. Those eating the most water-soluble dietary fiber fared even better, with a 15 percent reduction in risk of CHD and a 10 percent risk reduction in CVD.

Beans and lentils are the perfect food for individuals with hypoglycemia and diabetes to have on a daily basis. The fiber content helps stabilize blood-sugar levels, while providing a steady, slow-burning source of energy. Along with the significant amounts of folate, iron, and magnesium they contain, your health is well taken care of.

Buying and Storage Tips

For the lowest cost, buy dried beans in bulk and cook in large batches, freezing some to be used later. If you are reluctant to cook your beans, you can buy canned organic beans and use those, but just make sure to look for low-salt brands and rinse them well before using.

ALERT!

Look for the Eden brand of organic beans in your natural-foods store. They cook the beans with the seaweed kombu, which helps reduce the gaseous qualities in the beans while replacing some of the mineral content destroyed in the heating process.

When buying in bulk, move the beans from plastic bags to glass mason jars and store in a cool, dry place. Try to use them as soon as possible because as dried beans get old, they toughen up and will not cook completely.

Cooking for Digestion

Because beans are a starch-protein combination, they are difficult to digest, one reason being that bacteria attacks the indigestible fiber that remains in the intestine, causing gas to form. However, there are a few things you can do to help make beans easier to digest:

- Presoak the beans for five to eight hours, then change the water before cooking. Presoaking also reduces the cooking time by a good half hour or more.
- Cover the beans with water, bring to a boil, cover, remove from heat, and allow to sit for one hour. Change the water and continue cooking.
- Change the soaking water several times.
- Add the salt and acidic ingredients such as tomatoes after cooking.
- Try pressure cooking the beans to reduce the gaseous qualities.
- Allow your digestive system to get used to beans by beginning with lentils and gradually adding beans to your diet.
- Begin with beans that are easier to digest such as navy, great northern, aduki, or black beans.
- Add a small piece of kombu seaweed, ginger, or bay leaf to the beans when cooking. These help reduce the gaseous qualities in the beans and the kombu replaces any minerals eliminated in the cooking process.
- Put a few drops of Beano in the first few bites of your meal. Beano is an enzyme product that works to digest the carbohydrates that would normally feed the intestinal bacteria.

So, you see, there is no need to be afraid of being able to digest beans now that you know how to prepare them properly.

Preparing Beans

The basic principle for cooking all beans is the same, no matter how you plan to use them in a recipe.

1. Before cooking, pick through the beans and remove any stones, broken beans, or other bits of debris.

2. Place the beans and enough water to cover in a large, heavy pot. Cover and allow to soak overnight or during the day. Drain the water and add fresh water before cooking.

3. To help reduce the flatulence properties, add a small piece of kombu seaweed or ginger to the water. Bring water to a hard boil, reduce the heat, and let the beans simmer until tender, usually about forty-five to fifty minutes. Skim any foam that rises to the surface. At this point, you can add vegetables and seasonings such as potatoes, carrots, peppers, basil, and bay leaf.

4. About fifteen minutes before the beans are done, add the salt and any acidic ingredients like tomatoes. The salt helps to bring out the full flavor of the beans; but adding salt and acidic foods too early inhibits the water's ability to penetrate the beans, leaving them hard and tough no matter how long you boil them.

5. When the beans are soft and tender, adjust the seasonings as needed.

In many cultures, the beans are seasoned in order to stimulate the digestive process and enhance the flavor, aroma, and appearance of the dish. In Spain, this is called adding a *sofrito*. To do so, add some oil to a skillet and sauté some chopped onions until slightly tender. Add ginger, garlic, tomatoes, and chopped parsley to the onions. Let it simmer for five minutes, or until the oil separates from the seasoning mixture. Add to the beans along with a small amount of water used to wash out the flavors left behind in the skillet.

INGREDIENTS

½ pound dried black beans
7 cups water
*3-inch piece kombu sea
    vegetable*
1 onion
1 green pepper
2 carrots
1 medium sweet potato
3 cloves garlic
*1 package organic chicken
    sausage (6 links)*
¼ cup extra-virgin olive oil
2 teaspoons cumin powder
1 teaspoon sea salt
2 tablespoons kuzu-root powder

Black Bean and Chicken Sausage Stew

You will want to make this stew to serve your guests and family, take along to a potluck dinner, or freeze in individual containers for future use. Otherwise, just halve the ingredients to serve six, and season with salt to taste.

1. In a large saucepan or pressure cooker, cover beans with water and soak overnight. In the morning drain, return to pot, and add 7 cups of water. Add kombu to beans; bring water to boil, reduce heat; and simmer until beans are tender, about 1 hour.

2. Meanwhile, chop onion, green pepper, and carrots; peel and chop sweet potato; and mince garlic. Slice sausage links and chop into bite-size pieces.

3. In a large Dutch oven, heat oil; sauté onion, pepper, carrots, and garlic until almost tender. Add cumin powder to onion mixture; stir well to combine. Add chopped sausage; allow to cook another 3 minutes. Add cooked black beans and liquid to sausage mixture; stir well.

4. Stir in sea salt; bring mixture to a boil, reduce heat, cover, and simmer until vegetables are cooked and tender, about 20 minutes, stirring occasionally.

5. In a small glass or measuring cup, dissolve kuzu-root powder with a small amount of water. Slowly add to black bean stew, stirring as you do so. It should begin to thicken immediately, so watch for level of thickness desired.

6. Cover and allow to simmer another minute or two. Remove from heat; adjust seasonings; and serve.

Methods of Cooking

You can speed up the process of cooking your beans by using a pressure cooker, which would cut the time in half. On the other hand, if you do not have the time, you can use canned black beans and prepare the vegetables with a quick sauté, then add all the ingredients to a slow cooker and cook on high for 3 hours or 5–6 hours on low.

Spicy Mung Beans in Coconut Milk

Mung beans are often sprouted and used in salads and to top off Asian-style stir-fries. Traditionally, they are cooked in India, similarly to this recipe, where the dish is called a moong dhal. There is no need to presoak these beans, as they cook quickly and are easy to digest.

1. Wash and sort through the mung beans, removing any stones or other debris. In a large saucepan or Dutch oven, bring the mung beans and water to a boil over medium high heat; cover, reduce, and allow to simmer until beans become tender, about 15 minutes.

2. Meanwhile, chop onion; mince garlic and pepper; and peel and mince ginger.

3. Heat oil and ghee in a skillet; sauté vegetables over medium-low heat, stirring from time to time, until onions are tender, about 4 minutes. Add curry powder and garam masala; stir well. Cook until spices release their aroma, about 1–2 minutes.

4. While onion-spice mixture is cooking, chop tomatoes; place in a blender or food processor and purée until smooth and liquid.

5. Pour tomatoes into mung beans along with onion-spice mixture. Add a small amount of water to skillet to "wash" out any remaining oil or spice adhering to the bottom of the pan; add to mung beans. Add coconut milk and salt to taste; stir well.

6. Reduce heat to simmer, cover, and cook another 30 minutes, or until beans have broken apart and flavors are well combined. (At this point, you could place the mung-bean mixture into a heated slow cooker and cook on low for a few hours until ready to serve.)

Clarified Butter

Clarified butter is regular butter that has had the milk solids and water removed, leaving behind a pure, golden-yellow butterfat. Also known as drawn butter, or ghee, it has a rich butter flavor with a shelf life of several months and a much higher smoke point than most oils. You can buy it ready-made in an Indian or natural-foods market.

SERVES 8

170 calories
8 g fat
20 g carbohydrates
7 g protein
3 g sugar
5 g fiber

INGREDIENTS

1 cup mung beans
4 cups water
1 onion
3 cloves garlic
1 hot pepper or 1 teaspoon red pepper flakes
2-inch piece fresh ginger
1 tablespoon coconut oil
1 tablespoon ghee (clarified butter)
1 teaspoon curry powder
1 teaspoon garam masala (Indian spices)
2 medium tomatoes
5½ ounces coconut milk
½ teaspoon sea salt

CHAPTER 13

Kale: A Powerhouse of Nutrients

Kale is one of those foods that is nutritionally good for you to eat, but is more often found as a garnish on a platter of lesser-quality foods. As a matter of fact, Pizza Hut is thought to be the largest consumer of kale in the United States, specifically using it to garnish their salad bars! In this chapter, you will find the leafy-green member of the Brassica family is given the respect it deserves. Loaded with cancer-fighting antioxidants, kale can move out of the shadows and finally claim center stage.

What Makes It Super

Kale is, literally, one of the healthiest foods in the vegetable kingdom, and it receives little or no respect for the benefits it can provide. The delicate curl of its deep green leaves and its earthy, bittersweet flavor can accompany any meal, and lift it to Superfood status. In Chapter 4, you were introduced to broccoli, another Superfood member of the *Brassica* family. Together with its cousin, you can receive strong protection against cancer and other disease by eating kale. What makes kale super is the availability of its organosulfur compounds, two of which are glucosinolates and methyl cysteine sulfoxides, that have been the subject of extensive research. With over 100 different glucosinolates found in plants, ten to fifteen are present in kale, and these precious few are what helps lessen the possibility of developing a wide range of cancers.

A Natural Detoxifier

Your body has its own natural detoxification process taking place throughout each day and night. Whenever your filtering organs become overloaded with toxins, chemicals, heavy metals, and other contaminants, they cannot effectively eliminate these dangerous poisons. Instead, these toxins end up being stored in your tissue and body cells. The foods that you include in your diet, such as kale and other *Brassica* vegetables, contain a potent glucosinolate phytonutrient, which actually boosts your body's detoxification enzymes, clearing potentially carcinogenic substances more quickly from your body.

Cancer-Prevention Studies

In a recent study, sulforaphane, found in kale and other members of the *Brassica* family, was tested to see if it could inhibit cancers arising from one's genetic makeup. Researchers at Rutgers University, Ernest Mario, Ah-Ng Tony Kong, and colleagues, tested laboratory animals bred with a genetic mutation that switches off the tumor-suppressor gene know as APC, the same gene that is inactivated in the majority of human colon cancers. They found that animals fed sulforaphane developed smaller tumors that grew more slowly, and had less risk of developing intestinal polyps the more sulforaphane they were given.

According to Dr. Kong, the study corroborates the notion that sulforaphane has chemopreventive activity. All of the research substantiated the connection between diet and cancer prevention, and it is now clear that the expression of cancer-related genes can be influenced by chemopreventive compounds in the foods that you eat.

FACT

More common members of the prestigious *Brassica* family of vegetables include: cabbage, broccoli, Brussels sprouts, cauliflower, kale, collards, mustard greens, rapini, bok choy, and broccoli rabe. With so many choices, take advantage of having a different variety each day of the week.

The History of Kale

Kale and other cabbage plants are thought to have originated in Asia Minor, and been brought to the eastern Mediterranean regions around 600 B.C. Having been shifted and traded between migrating tribes and prehistoric traders for so long, it is hard to identify where the species originated. The curly kale leaves were probably eaten by early hunters and gatherers; later, the plant was transferred to cultivated grounds and began to produce dense rosettes of leaves. The original *Brassica* we call a cabbage was a nonheading kind of plant with a prominent stalk or stem, and from this stock have sprung all forms of cabbages, cauliflower, Brussels sprouts, and kales. The kale and collard varieties of today are not far removed from this ancient ancestor, having been cultivated for at least the last 2,000 years.

Kale and collards were grown by the Greeks, and the Romans cultivated several varieties as well. These included plants with large leaves and stalks and a mild flavor, a crisp-leaved form and some with small stalks and small, sharp-tasting leaves. They also grew a broad-leaved form similar to today's collards, along with others with curled leaves and a fine flavor.

In the Middle Ages, European writers were describing a plant called cole popular with the peasant population. More than likely, the Romans carried these coles to Britain and France, during their military campaigns. Another theory claims that the Celts took them over in even earlier times. In the seventeenth century, colewort was brought to America and cultivated in Virginia.

Today, the two most common varieties are the dinosaur kale and the ornamental kale, also known as salad savoy. The dinosaur kale was first discovered in Italy at the end of the nineteenth century, while the ornamental kale was first cultivated in California in the 1980s.

Kale's Nutrient Content

Kale is an excellent source of calcium, iron, vitamins A and C, and the deep-green color is loaded with chlorophyll. It is a perfect low fat, nutritious food you can steam and serve with soft-cooked grains for breakfast, as a salad for lunch, or in a quick stir-fry for dinner. They are loaded with usable nutrients that your body will love. One cup of kale contains the following sampling of nutrients:

CALORIES	36.40	VITAMIN C	53.30 mg
PROTEIN	2.47 g	FOLATE	17.29 mcg
CARBOHYDRATE	7.32 g	VITAMIN K	547 mcg
FIBER	2.60 g	CALCIUM	93.60 mg
SUGAR	1.56 g	IRON	1.17 mg
FAT	0.52 g	MAGNESIUM	23.40 mg
VITAMIN A IU	9620 IU	PHOSPHORUS	36.40 mg
VITAMIN A RE	962 RE	POTASSIUM	296.40
BETA CAROTENE	5772 mcg	SELENIUM	1.17 mcg

Low in calories and high in beta carotene and potassium, you can't go wrong making kale a mainstay in your diet program.

Calcium and Kale

With all the buzz about getting enough calcium, many people are taking supplements with the promise that they can avoid losing bone density. What you should know is that eating calcium-rich foods is a much better way to strengthen your bones than getting your calcium in pill form. According to a study from Washington University in St. Louis, women who consumed an average of 830 mg (milligrams) of calcium per day in the foods they ate tested higher for bone mineral densities (BMDs) than women who took 1,033 mg of calcium in supplement form. If you feel, however, that you are unable to eat the required amounts of calcium-rich foods, the study also showed that women who received at least 70 percent of their calcium from food, plus took a calcium supplement, tested highest in BMDs, with an intake of 1,620 mg of calcium per day.

QUESTION?

How many weekly servings of cruciferous vegetables do you need to lower your risk of cancer?
Have three to five servings a week, or try to have one cup per day. Just like taking your daily multiple vitamin, eating foods that contain those vitamins should be done consistently over a week's time. One day have broccoli, the next kale, then Brussels sprouts, cauliflower, bok choy, mustard greens, and end the week with broccoli rabe.

Although you may think that dairy products are the best and only sources of ingesting calcium, there is a wide range of foods that actually allow you to digest and absorb your calcium better than pasteurized dairy products, and these include kale. Just by including kale and other calcium-rich vegetables in your weekly diet, you will be receiving the calcium your body requires for strong bones, proper estrogen metabolism, blood clotting, nerve conduction, muscle contraction, enzyme activity, and cell membrane function.

Healing Properties of Kale

Kale is thought to ease lung congestion and is beneficial to the stomach, liver, and immune system. Its lutein and zeaxanthin contents protect your eyes from macular degeneration, while indole-3-carbinol may protect you from developing colon cancer. Recent studies show that individuals who eat cruciferous vegetables on a weekly basis have a much lower risk of prostate, colorectal, and lung cancer. In a study conducted at the Fred Hutchinson Cancer Research Center in Seattle of over 1,200 men, those eating twenty-eight servings of vegetables a week lowered their risk of developing prostate cancer by 35 percent; while those including just three or more servings of cruciferous vegetables a week lowered their risk by a whopping 44 percent.

FACT

A Netherlands Cohort Study on Diet and Cancer showed that over the course of six years, 100,000 people benefited with a 25 percent lower risk of colorectal cancers from eating vegetables, while those eating the most cruciferous vegetables did almost twice as well, dropping their cancer risk by 49 percent.

Kale and Smoking

A study of Chinese women in Singapore, a city in which high air-pollution levels put stress on the detoxification capacity of residents' lungs, found that in nonsmokers, eating cruciferous vegetables lowered risk of lung cancer by 30 percent. In smokers, regular cruciferous vegetable consumption reduced lung cancer risk an amazing 69 percent!

Kale Protects Your Eyes

Scientific research tells us that age, color of eyes, smoking, and exposure to sunlight can increase your risk for developing age-related macular degeneration (ARMD) and cataracts, which contributes to nearly half the blindness in the world. The Eye Disease Case-Control Study found that those with the highest blood levels of lutein and zeaxanthin, two antioxidants found in kale, were 70 percent less likely to develop ARMD than those with the lowest levels. Individuals who consumed leafy green vegetables such as kale, spinach, and collard greens for five or more servings per week had a 43 percent less risk of ARMD than those who consumed the greens once a month or less.

ALERT!

Rather than looking to supplements for your protection, research suggests that food sources are your best bet for eye-protective antioxidants. Lutein and zeaxanthin are found in the eye's macula in a ratio similar to that found in foods. Lutein is most effective when accompanied by other antioxidants, such as fruits and vegetables.

The Nurse's Health Study showed that, while kale can protect your eyes from macular degeneration, it also guards them against forming cataracts. In the study, the nurses who ate cooked greens more than twice a week had one-third fewer cataracts requiring surgery than those who ate them less than once a month.

Buying and Storage Tips

Kale is considered a cold-weather crop, but it is available all year round. However, once it has been nipped by a good frost, it is at its most flavorful and tender. To get the most benefit from your kale, be sure to choose organically grown varieties, as their phytonutrient levels are higher than conventionally grown kale. Otherwise, when ready to use, wash the leaves well with a vegetable wash made for removing petroleum-based pesticides and herbicides. Rinse well and shake to dry.

Store fresh kale in the refrigerator and use within the week of purchase. When kale sits too long the leaves will turn yellow, signaling that the time to be cooked has long passed.

Cooking Kale

To retain nutrients when cooking kale, you can use the water-sauté or light-steam methods.

- **Water-sauté method:** Wash and drain the kale, then run a sharp knife along the stem to remove the leaves. Pour half-inch of water into a large skillet and add the kale leaves. Cover, bring to a simmer, and cook until tender, about six to seven minutes. Remove kale to a colander and rinse with cool water to stop the cooking process. Gently squeeze out any water and chop the kale.
- **Steam method:** Place a half-inch of water in a large saucepan and arrange a steamer basket on the inside of the pan. Add the kale, cover, and bring to a boil. Reduce heat and allow to steam until kale is tender, about six to seven minutes. Remove kale to a colander and rinse with cool water to stop the cooking process. Gently squeeze out any water and chop the kale.

Preparing your greens using one of these two methods has been shown to retain the most phytonutrients and maximize their availability to your body. You can prepare the kale at any time during the day and store it in the refrigerator until needed. Try to use it up within three days to retain nutrients and freshness.

Easy Uses for Kale

Those big, curly leaves can be considerably reduced in size in the cooking process, so cook up a big bunch of kale at one time and keep it on hand to use in any of the following ways:

- Toss the kale with garlic sautéed in olive oil.
- Add kale to soups just before serving.
- Add kale to mixed salad greens and toss with a lemon vinaigrette.
- Serve kale as a side vegetable with a dab of butter, salt, and pepper to taste.
- Add kale to a vegetable stir-fry.

- Mash kale into hot potatoes with butter and the potato cooking liquid.
- Roll up kale in a bean and rice burrito.
- Make a wrap with kale, sliced chicken, avocado, and mayonnaise.
- Top a pizza crust with kale and add sautéed garlic, pine nuts, and feta cheese.
- Serve kale with pasta and red sauce or a white clam sauce.
- Leave the cooked leaves long and use to roll up rice and ground turkey, then smother in a spicy red sauce.

You are only limited by your imagination with this versatile and nutritious Superfood. If you have difficulty getting the kids to eat it, try puréeing the cooked kale in their favorite tomato sauce and serving it over pasta. Just don't tell them what you did, and they'll never know.

INGREDIENTS

1 bunch fresh kale
1 bulb fresh fennel
1 teaspoon anchovy paste (or 3
    anchovy fillets)
1 shallot
¼ cup extra-virgin olive oil
2 tablespoons balsamic vinegar
½ teaspoon garlic powder
1 teaspoon agave syrup
2 tablespoons mayonnaise
¼ cup toasted pumpkin seeds

Kale Fennel Salad

Use a high-quality mayonnaise such as the Vegenaise brand found in natural-foods stores. Commercial brands are loaded with flavorings, colorings, and preservatives, plus refined sugar, which you want to avoid.

1. Wash and drain the kale. Run a sharp knife down the length of the stem to remove the leaf and set aside.

2. Cover the bottom of a large skillet with ½" of water; set kale into the pan. Cover, bring to a boil, reduce heat, and simmer until kale is tender but still bright green.

3. While kale is cooking, slice the fennel into narrow strips and set aside.

4. In a blender or using a mortar and pestle, combine anchovy, shallot, oil, vinegar, garlic, agave, and mayonnaise; mix to a dressing consistency.

5. Rinse cooked kale under cool water, drain, and press out water. Chop kale well; place in a medium-size salad bowl along with the fennel.

6. Spoon dressing over salad; toss well, or serve dressing on the side and serve salad on individual plates.

7. Top with toasted pumpkin seeds before eating.

A Low-Glycemic Sweetener

Agave syrup is made from the same cactus plant that tequila is made from. It is a low-glycemic sweetener that won't spike your blood sugar. Use it in place of honey or maple syrup when sugar is called for in your recipes.

Roasted Kale

This is a simple recipe requiring four ingredients, and yields a crisp, chewy kale even your kids will enjoy snacking on. You can also slice up some collard greens or Swiss chard as a substitute for kale, or mix them all together for a tasty medley.

1. Preheat oven to 375°F.

2. Wash and trim kale by pulling leaves off the tough stems or running a sharp knife down the length of the stem.

3. Place leaves in a medium-size bowl; toss with extra-virgin olive oil and garlic powder.

4. Roast for 5 minutes; turn kale over and roast another 7–10 minutes, until kale turns brown and becomes paper thin and brittle.

5. Remove from oven and sprinkle with sea salt. Serve immediately.

Quality Sea Salt

Commercial salt is highly refined—99.5 percent is made up of sodium chloride, with additives of anticaking chemicals, potassium iodide, and sugar (dextrose) to stabilize the iodine. Instead, look for a high-quality sea salt, which is loaded with minerals, and in moderation, can actually give you energy.

SERVES 2

170 calories
8 g fat
21 g carbohydrates
7 g protein
0 g sugar
4 g fiber

INGREDIENTS
6 cups kale
1 tablespoon extra-virgin olive oil
1 teaspoon garlic powder
1 teaspoon sea salt

CHAPTER 14

Green Tea: Sip Your Antioxidants

Green tea is the second most-consumed beverage in the world, water being the first. Used medicinally for centuries in India and China, green tea has finally gone global and found a place in the Western world. In this chapter, you will read about the most recent studies that add to the large body of knowledge regarding tea's potential ability to reduce risk for several chronic diseases, including heart disease and certain cancers. Regardless of how you like to drink your tea, you will come to appreciate the power that is unleashed when tea leaves meet the perfect temperature of water.

What Makes It Super

Slightly bitter in taste and traditionally taken without milk or sugar, green tea is a simple yet complex beverage. The Japanese dedicate intricate ceremonies and rituals to its preparation, while in America it is combined with herbs, flowers, and berries to give variety to its taste. The super-active constituents in green tea are a form of antioxidants called polyphenols (catechins) and flavonols. You have been introduced to both of these antioxidants in several other Superfoods, such as blueberries (Chapter 3), chocolate (Chapter 6), and parsley (Chapter 10). It is the high antioxidant activity of green tea that makes it beneficial to your health. These antioxidants protect your body from the oxidative damage caused by free radicals, so that your risk for diseases such as cancer, heart disease, suppressed immune function, and accelerated aging are lowered. The many scientific studies on green tea provide a significant list of health benefits:

- Green tea's antioxidants protect against DNA damage and slow the initiation and progression of cancerous tumor growth.
- Green tea significantly protects the immune system, as in the case of cancer patients undergoing radiation or chemotherapy. White blood cell count was maintained more effectively in cancer patients consuming green tea during treatment.
- Green tea has been shown to prevent obesity in studies of mice receiving green tea in their diets. They showed a significant suppression of food intake, body weight gain, fat tissue accumulation, lower levels of cholesterol and triglycerides, and leptin levels in serum showed a decrease.
- Green tea has been found to help lower blood pressure, prevent cancer and osteoporosis, lower your risk for stroke, and promote heart health.
- Green tea may help to prevent sunlight damage, such as wrinkles and skin cancer.

There are so many health benefits from drinking tea that on September 18, 2007, scientists from around the world convened for the Fourth International Scientific Symposium on Tea & Human Health to review the latest findings on the potential health benefits of tea, including studies on how it may help maintain a healthy body weight, control blood sugar, and even help us think more clearly.

FACT

Most studies are conducted on green and black teas, which are both from the *Camellia sinensis* plant, and have yielded similar results. In 2006, Americans consumed well over 50 billion servings of tea, or over 2.25 billion gallons. About 83 percent of all tea consumed was black tea, 16 percent was green tea, and a small remaining amount was oolong tea.

Decaffeinated Versus Caffeinated Tea

Decaffeinated green tea is simply a more processed form of green tea, removing a certain amount of caffeine from the leaves. Due to this form of processing, green tea will have some of its nutrient content decreased. All green teas undergo some processing, in the form of applied heat used to stop the natural oxidation process that occurs with freshly picked tea leaves. However, since this heat processing is minimal, the vast majority of nutrients are left intact.

The three basic ways caffeine gets removed from tea leaves are:

- **The Effervescence Method:** To draw the caffeine out from the tea leaves, compressed carbon dioxide (CO_2) is combined with water. The tea leaves are soaked in this solution, then removed, and the solution is passed through an activated carbon filter to get rid of the caffeine. The tea leaves are then returned to the solution to restore any lost flavoring components.
- **Chemical Method:** The tea leaves are soaked in water to allow for the release of caffeine (and other substances) from the leaves. The tea leaves are removed and a chemical solvent, ethyl acetate, is added to the caffeinated water to extract the caffeine. Once the caffeine has been extracted, the tea leaves are reimmersed in the water to allow the natural flavors to be restored.

- **Hot Water Method:** Tea leaves are boiled in water for approximately three minutes to sufficiently reduce the caffeine content of the leaves—about 80–85 percent.

One recent research study showed that only 5 percent of the key phytonutrients (catechins) were lost in the hot-water method using fresh green tea leaves. Far more catechins were lost when decaffeinating dried or dried/rolled tea leaves. Your best and healthiest buy is the water-decaffeinated green tea or effervescence-decaffeinated green tea. According to one green tea study, flavanol content varied from 21.2 to 103.2 milligrams/grams for regular teas and from 4.6 to 39.0 mg/grams for decaffeinated teas. The antioxidant values varied from 728 to 1686 trolox equivalents/grams tea for regular teas and from 507 to 845 trolox equivalents/grams for decaffeinated teas. (Trolox equivalents/grams is a form of measurement used when measuring each antioxidant component separately and their interactions with other antioxidants.)

ALERT!

The chemical method of decaffeination can leave residues of ethyl acetate in the water to be reabsorbed by the tea leaves. Ethyl acetate occurs naturally in several common fruits in trace amounts, but in high doses it is considered toxic to the body, known to disrupt activity in the liver, respiratory system, and central nervous system.

Despite the nutrient loss that occurs in the decaffeination process, this degree of loss should not prevent you from receiving many of the benefits of decaffeinated green tea.

The History of Green Tea

The origin of green tea is so old that it is difficult to trace its beginnings, but using written documents, we can trace its use back over 4,000 years ago in China. Legends about green tea are considered more myth than reality, such as the story of the Chinese Emperor and medical expert, Sheng Nong, who is said to have discovered tea as a medicinal herb in 2737 B.C. One day while boiling water under a tea tree, the leaves fell into Sheng's pot, and after drinking some of this tea water, he fell in love with the taste. Following this discovery, tea was used as a spiritual offering and then, as its healing powers were revealed, as a medicinal herb.

Trading in Tea

Over time, the Buddhist monks began to grow it around their monasteries and later, during the Ming dynasty, the tea trade took an upper share in the state economy. As the Buddhist monks traveled between China and Japan, they brought the tea leaves with them. During the sixth century, a Japanese Buddhist priest, Myoan Eisai, brought green tea to Japan. He was also known for introducing the Rinzai school of Zen Buddhism. Hundreds of years later, during the sixteenth century, a Portuguese missionary carried the tea leaves back with him and introduced tea to the European palate. With a step by step progression, the simple yet powerful leaf became a major commodity for trade between China and the Western world; and as more European cultures assimilated tea into their daily diets, the import of tea rose from 100 pounds a year to over 5 million pounds per year.

Presently, there are more than 3,000 varieties of tea available around the world, and it's a beverage that, because of its complexity and variety, attracts both connoisseurs and ceremony. From the British institution of teatime to formal Japanese tea ceremonies, no other beverage, save perhaps wine, inspires such ritual and debate.

Japanese Green Tea

Drinking tea in Japan is a very serious business, to the extent that they honor the serving of tea with a simple, yet complex ceremony. The quality and grade of the tea is an important aspect, with the best Japanese green tea said to come from the Uji region of Kyoto. Japanese green teas are sold in specialty and natural-foods stores with different names for different varieties, flavors, and purposes, including:

- **Bancha:** a common leaf tea from the sencha plant, harvested as a second-flush between the summer and autumn months. With larger leaves than the first-flush sencha, but with a weaker flavor.

- **Genmaicha:** a light, delicious tea made up of a combination of maisha leaves and roasted brown rice.
- **Gyokuro:** from a grade of green tea known as tencha. Gyokuro, or Jade Dew, refers to the pale green of the infusion. The flavor of the tea is influenced by the leaves being grown in the shade.
- **Hojicha:** a roasted green tea, hojicha means "pan fried."
- **Kukicha:** the roasted twigs of the tea tree, produced by harvesting one bud and three leaves.
- **Kabusecha:** another form of the sencha tea leaves, it means "covered tea," having been grown in the shade. It produces a lighter, more delicate flavor than regular sencha.
- **Matcha:** this is the tea used in the Japanese tea ceremony. A high-quality powdered tea, it is also used to make green-tea ice cream and other forms of sweets.
- **Sencha:** probably one of the most common green teas brewed in Japan, made from leaves exposed directly to the sunlight, which may be why *sencha* means "broiled tea."

Have several varieties on hand to try at different times of the day; this way you won't get tired of any one taste too quickly.

Green Tea's Nutrient Content

Tannins in tea are large polyphenol molecules and form the bulk of the active compounds in green tea, while catechins make up nearly 90 percent of the tannins.

Although there are no vitamin and mineral components to green tea, there are significant quantities of catechins present:

- Epicatechin (EC)
- Epigallocatechin (EGC)
- Epicatechin gallate (ECG)
- Epigallocatechin gallate (EGCG)

The most powerful of the catechins appears to be the EGCG, which accounts for 10–50 percent of the total catechin content; its antioxidant activity is about 25–100 times more potent than vitamins C and E. One cup of green tea may provide 10–40 mg of polyphenols, and has antioxidant activity greater than a serving of broccoli, spinach, carrots, or strawberries. Research shows that green tea may also reduce cholesterol and triglycerides, enhance immune function, enhance weight loss, and lower your risk for developing cancer. Now that's a Superfood!

ALERT!

The stimulant in green tea, called theine, was first discovered in 1827. Once it was shown to be identical to the caffeine in coffee, the word theine was replaced with the word caffeine. Green tea contains a quarter the amount of caffeine as coffee; or, 5 ounces of coffee has 80 milligrams of caffeine, while green tea contains 20 milligrams.

Healing Properties of Green Tea

John Foxe, Ph.D., Professor of Neuroscience, Biology, and Psychology at City College of the City University of New York, presented the results of several ongoing human trials at the 2007 Fourth International Scientific Symposium on Tea and Human Health. He found that theanine from tea actively alters the attention networks of the brain. Theanine is an amino acid present almost exclusively in the tea plant. After drinking tea, theanine, which is present in green, black, and oolong varieties, is known to be absorbed by the small intestine and to cross the blood-brain barrier, where it affects the brain's neurotransmitters and increases alpha brainwave activity. This alpha brain rhythm is known to induce a calmer, yet more alert, state of mind.

The subjects were asked to complete a variety of attention-related computerized tasks after drinking 250 mg of either theanine or placebo. Dr. Foxe and his team monitored brain activity using electrophysiological measures and found that after having theanine, individuals showed significant improvements in tests for attention and that activity in cortical regions responsible for attention functions was enhanced. What's more, just twenty minutes after consuming theanine, the blood concentrations of theanine increased and the brain's alpha waves were impacted. It lasted about three to four hours, which, they found, may be why people tend to drink a cup of tea every three to four hours during the day.

QUESTION?

What do the ancient Chinese books of medicine say about the health benefits of green tea?
It is noted that drinking green tea aids in quenching thirst and in digesting food, reduces phlegm, wards off sleepiness, stimulates renal activity, improves eyesight and mental prowess, dispels boredom, and helps to digest greasy food.

Tea and Your Brain

Both human and animal epidemiological studies suggest that drinking catechin-rich tea is inversely correlated with the incidence of dementia, Alzheimer's disease, and Parkinson's disease. This may help to explain why there are significantly lower rates of age-related neurological disorders among Asians than in Europeans or Americans.

Research suggests that the effects of theanine, in combination with caffeine, help to induce a more calming, relaxed state, but one that allows the mind to focus and concentrate better at tasks. A cup of tea contains an average of 20–25 mg of theanine.

Dr. Silvia Mandel, of the Eve Topf Center for Neurodegenerative Diseases in Israel, has been studying the effects of tea on brain functions in laboratory and animal models for over a decade. Her most recent studies looked at animal models of neurological diseases such as Parkinson's and Alzheimer's. Her group provided an amount of purified EGCG equal to about two to four cups of green tea per day to animals with induced Parkinsonism as part of their diet to evaluate how their symptoms improved or progressed. They found that when the animals are fed green-tea EGCG, the polyphenol appeared to prevent brain cells from dying, and showed improvements in reducing compounds that led to lesions in the brains of animals with Alzheimer's disease.

Dr. Mandel found that not only may the EGCG help prevent brain cells from dying, it appears that the polyphenol may even rescue the neurons once they have been damaged, and help them to repair. In the past, it was thought that once brain cells were damaged, there was no way to repair them. The major question science is asking, is whether these promising results are reproducible in humans.

FACT

Jeffrey Blumberg, Ph.D., professor, Friedman School of Nutrition Science and Policy, and director, Antioxidants Research Laboratory, at Tufts University, Boston, found that the list of health benefits associated with tea consumption is ongoing and growing. Unlike medications, there are no known medical reasons not to enjoy tea as part of a healthy diet and lifestyle.

Green Tea and Health

Research scientists from top medical institutions in Asia, the Middle East, Europe, and North America presented their findings concerning the benefits of tea at the Fourth International Scientific Symposium on Tea and Human Health:

- Tea flavonoids may improve cardiovascular health by reducing inflammation and improving blood vessel function.
- Tea drinking may play a role in gene expression that is involved in cancer cells.

- Tea may play a role in shifting metabolism to favor weight loss and better manage blood sugar levels.
- Tea is a major contributor of flavonoids in the U.S. diet.

Lenore Arab, Ph.D., Professor of Internal Medicine at the University of California, Los Angeles, believes that the scientific community around the world is making tremendous advancements in better understanding the mechanisms by which tea may reduce risk for heart disease, certain cancers, type 2 diabetes, and maintain neurological function.

Buying and Storage Tips

Purchase your green tea from a store with a high inventory turnover to ensure quality and fresh taste. With green tea, it is best to buy loose rather than in tea bags, as the leaves are uncrushed and usually of a higher quality. Cheap tea bags are often a combination of inferior-quality leaves, powdered tea, dust, and bits of branches.

At home, place your teas in a container with a tight-fitting lid, as the tea leaves tend to absorb other aromas. Store in a dark, cool place and use within six months for optimal flavor.

Preparing Green Tea

Green tea brewing time and temperature varies with individual teas. The hottest brewing temperatures for water are 180°F–190°F, and the longest steeping times two to three minutes. The coolest brewing temperatures are 140°F–150°F, and the shortest times about thirty seconds. For a medium-strength cup of Chinese green tea, simply pour boiling water over ½–1 teaspoon of tea and allow to steep for three to five minutes. You can use the same leaves to make a second and third infusion, which some people prefer to the first steeping. It is taken without adding any sweetener or cream. Lower-quality green teas are steeped hotter and longer, while higher-quality teas are steeped cooler and shorter.

Green Tea Cucumber Apple Cooler

This is a light, refreshing drink with multiple benefits from the cucumber, apple, and green tea. Sweeten to taste with the stevia powder or sweetener of choice.

1. Wash cucumber, apple, and parsley well.
2. Cut and section as appropriate to fit a juicer slot.
3. Juice all ingredients; add green tea and sweeten to taste.
4. Serve immediately, while juice is still fresh and nutrient dense.

Overbrewing Tea

If the tea is left to steep too long in the hot water it will develop a strong, bitter taste. Loose tea needs a shorter steeping time than a tea bag, but if you steep for under five minutes, you can't go wrong with the flavor.

SERVES 4

40 calories
0 g fat
9 g carbohydrates
1 g protein
7 g sugar
2 g fiber

INGREDIENTS
1 large cucumber
1 sweet apple
Handful of fresh parsley
1 cup chilled green tea
Pinch of stevia powder

MAKES 2 GALLONS

150 calories
1 g fat
45 g carbohydrates
1 g protein
6 g sugar
2 g fiber

INGREDIENTS
2 gallons water
12 lemon decaf green tea bags
8 dried lime tea bags
16 ounces organic lime juice
1–2 teaspoon stevia powder

Lime Green Tea Punch

The ginger and lime give this punch a sharp, refreshing taste that the stevia complements well. Begin with one teaspoon and add until you have the desired sweetness. Feel free to substitute your favorite sweetener of choice.

1. Remove the tea bags from their wrappings along with the string attached to the bag.

2. In a large pasta-cooking pot, bring water to a boil.

3. Turn off heat; add tea bags. Cover; allow to steep until water has cooled.

4. When cool, remove tea bags; add lime-juice concentrate and stevia powder. Stir well to dissolve sweetener.

5. Ladle into a punch bowl; add chopped fruit if desired. Serve over ice in a glass.

Desert Lime Tea

The addition of dried lime from the Arabian Desert provides an additional dose of vitamin C along with a neat citrus flavor. Traditionally harvested and dried in the hot desert sun, it combines beautifully with the crisp ginger flavor of the green tea.

CHAPTER 15

Pumpkin Seeds Help the Prostate

Most people think of pumpkin seeds only as the stuff attached to the slimy insides of the Halloween pumpkin they carve each year. Not only is the flesh of the pumpkin one of nature's most nutritious fruits, but those white seeds are also brimming with a combination of protein, carbohydrates, and fats that your body can utilize for optimal health. Once you have read about the amazing qualities of pumpkin seeds in this chapter, you will never throw them out again once the pumpkin has been carved.

What Makes Them Super

Pumpkin seeds, also known as pepitas, nestle in the core of the pumpkin, encased in a white-yellow husk. The pumpkin is really a fruit, even though they are used in many recipes as a vegetable. A member of the *Cucurbitaceae* or gourd family, what makes pumpkins super is their low fat and sodium content, plus their orange coloring contains massive amounts of lutein and vitamin A in the form of beta carotene. These antioxidants are powerful agents in preventing certain cancers. Pumpkin flesh is rich in potassium; fiber; vitamins C, E, and K; and many minerals. The dark-green seed of the pumpkin has its own superpowers and has been used for centuries to treat a number of ailments; two of the more unusual being freckles and snake bites. Today, the superpowers of pumpkin seeds have been found to help prevent prostate cancer in men, protect against heart disease, and also have anti-inflammatory benefits.

The History of Pumpkin Seeds

Pumpkins are considered to have been the first food to travel from the New World to be cultivated in Europe. The English name pumpkin dates back to sometime before the 1600s, but the fruit has its true roots in American soil. Pumpkins were a staple in the Native American diet and a part of their healing medicines long before the pilgrims showed up and claimed it for their Thanksgiving day meal. Outside the United States, pumpkin seeds show up in the traditional cuisine of Mexico and other parts of the Americas. Today, pumpkin seeds are produced commercially by the United States, China, India, and Mexico.

Pumpkin Seed's Nutrient Content

This super seed contains a number of minerals, such as zinc, magnesium, manganese, iron, copper, and phosphorus, along with proteins, monounsaturated fat, and the omega fatty acids 3 and 6. They can be eaten raw; roasted; or blended in water, strained, and the water then taken as a form of tea. One ounce of roasted, unsalted pumpkin seeds contains:

CALORIES	148	POTASSIUM	229 mg
FIBER	1.1 g	ZINC	2.11 mg
FAT	6 g	IRON	4.24 mg
CARBOHYDRATES	3.81 g	MANGANESE	855 mg
PROTEIN	9.35 g	MAGNESIUM	151 mg
VITAMIN A	108 IU	PHOSPHORUS	332 mg
FOLATE	16 mcg	CALCIUM	12 mg
VITAMIN K	13.4 mcg	BETA CAROTENE	65 mcg

Although high in fat and calories, one teaspoon of toasted pumpkin seeds is the perfect topping for soups, grains, or vegetables.

Pumpkin-pie filling can be made from a pie pumpkin, averaging about eight inches in diameter. Remove the pulp and seeds. Preheat the oven to 375°F, place the pumpkin halves flesh-side down on a baking sheet, and bake until flesh is tender, about forty minutes. Allow to cool, scrape out the flesh, and set aside to use in your pie recipe.

Healing Properties of Pumpkin Seeds

Pumpkin seeds have a sweet-sour-bitter taste and contain diuretic properties, meaning they are good for reducing any swelling in the body. According to nutrition research author Paul Pitchford, pumpkin seeds are effective in ridding the body of worms, such as round and tape worms, and they help relieve feelings of nausea and motion sickness. For these particular conditions, chew one to two ounces of raw pumpkin seeds on a daily basis until the condition is resolved. The dark, nutrient-rich pumpkin-seed oil is effective for helping control cholesterol levels, while providing enough zinc to help keep aging bones strong.

Other health benefits from consuming pumpkin seeds include reducing inflammatory symptoms of the skin such as eczema and psoriasis, as well as for arthritis conditions. Due to their high phytosterol content, they help lower the LDL cholesterol in the blood, enhance immune response, and decrease your risk of certain cancers.

Pumpkin seeds contain 30–40 percent oil, which is nutrient-rich and contain both saturated and unsaturated fatty acids. Scientific research studies have discovered pumpkin-seed oil is beneficial for bladder and urethra function, healing wounds and burns, as a diuretic, and provides needed L-tryptophan for the brain to ease mild depression.

Prostate Health

Touted as a "man's health food," pumpkin seeds are effective in helping combat prostatic hypertrophy (BPH), an enlargement of the prostate gland that commonly affects men over fifty years and older. BPH is caused by the hormone testosterone, and its conversion product, dihydrotestosterone (DHT), overstimulating the prostate cells. Pumpkin-seed oil happens to contain certain ingredients found to interrupt the multiplication by testosterone and DHT of prostate cells. The omega-3 fatty acids found in pumpkin seeds not only support the prostate, but also help with memory and brain function.

FACT

Zinc is an essential element commonly deficient in individuals eating a low-animal-protein, high-cereal diet. The phytic acid in cereal and flour products binds to zinc, inhibiting its absorption in the intestines. Dermatitis, retarded growth and sexual development, poor wound healing, and loss of taste, smell, and appetite are a few indications of zinc deficiency.

Bone Protection

Pumpkin seeds are a good source of zinc, a trace element essential for the proper metabolism of nutrients. Although osteoporosis is usually associated with older women, it is commonly found in men who are deficient in zinc. A study of 400 men, ranging in age from forty-five to ninety-two, published in the *American Journal of Clinical Nutrition,* found a clear correlation between not getting enough dietary zinc, low blood levels of the trace mineral, and osteoporosis in the hip and spine. Since zinc is also essential for prostate health, men should take in at least 15mg a day. A handful of pumpkin seeds, approximately ¼ cup, provides about 4mg of zinc.

Buying and Storage Tips

Pumpkin seeds are available in packaged containers or from bulk bins found in many natural-foods stores. When purchasing from the bulk-bin section, make sure the pumpkin seeds are kept covered and the seeds are fresh. Look to see that there is no evidence of moisture or insect damage and that the seeds look firm and not shriveled. Take a good smell, and if the seeds smell the least bit rancid or musty, avoid buying them. The high oil content can begin to turn the seed rancid if exposed to air for too long. This is why you should store your pumpkin seeds in an airtight container in the refrigerator or freezer at home, to keep them fresh and edible for up to two months.

FACT

Pumpkin-seed oil, which is known as "green gold," has a pleasant and mildly rich flavor and should be used unheated in salad dressings, smoothies, or drizzled over steamed vegetables and greens. You can purchase it online or at your local natural-foods market.

When purchasing pumpkin-seed oil, read the label to ensure the manufacturer has not diluted it with sunflower-seed oil. Extracting the oil from pumpkin seeds is a complicated and expensive process, reflected in the cost to you. Make sure the oil has been kept refrigerated both in the store and once you take it home.

Growing from Saved Seed

What a great lesson for both you and your children to learn about how food grows in nature from a small seed. First, you will need to gather seeds from your Halloween pumpkin for planting once the spring frosts have ended. Actually, you will need to take the seeds from a variety of different pumpkins to ensure good germination. You can tell by the size and shape of the pumpkin you choose just how your pumpkins will look when they are ripe for harvest.

Here are ten steps that will guide you through growing your own pumpkins:

1. Extract the seeds and rinse them well using a mild detergent and warm water. Be careful that the water is not too hot, and do not let them soak in the water.
2. Place the seeds in a strainer to drain.
3. Set up a screen in a cool, dry area and spread the seeds out on the screen.
4. For the first few days, move the seeds around, turning them over as you stir them.
5. Let the seeds dry on the screen for up to three weeks or longer, until completely dry.
6. Store the dry seeds in a glass jar, but not airtight. If the seeds are even slightly damp, mold will grow and they will rot. An envelope will also work well for storage purposes.
7. Write the name of the seeds and the date on the container and store in a cool, dry place until ready for use.
8. Sow seeds in the garden from May 15th to June 15th, or you can start the seeds indoors two weeks before planting outdoors.
9. Choose a sunny spot—the sunnier the better; you want to get at least six hours of direct sunlight. The time to plant is once the spring rains have receded and the temperature has reached the low 70s.
10. Soak the seeds you will be planting the night before to soften the outer shell, making sprouting occur faster.

Most pumpkins need 110–140 frost-free days to grow to maturity. So make sure you allow enough time before the autumn chill sets in.

Using Pumpkin Seeds

Pumpkins can grow to over a foot in diameter, and once they have been split open, they reveal a hollow center filled with white seeds and loose fiber. Having a handful of roasted seeds as a snack or tossing them into a trail mix are great ways to make use of their nutrients; but there are many other ways to use these versatile and tasty little seeds. Here are ten suggestions:

1. Toast and eat the seeds as a snack, with or without the shell.
2. Shelled seeds can be ground to make a Mexican mole sauce for chicken or fish.
3. Shelled, toasted seeds can be sprinkled over sautéed vegetables.
4. Sprinkle shelled and toasted seeds on soups and salads.
5. Grind raw, shelled seeds with fresh garlic, herbs, olive oil, and lemon juice for a salad dressing.
6. Replace nuts in your favorite cookie or granola recipe with shelled pumpkin seeds.
7. Raw or toasted shelled seeds can be added to hot or cold cereals.
8. Finely grind and add to rice and vegetables to make veggie burgers.
9. Replace nuts and use seeds to make toffee and brittle.
10. Ground or whole seeds can be added to yeast and quick breads.

As you come to appreciate all the elements of this versatile plant, especially the taste of pumpkin seeds, you will find more and more uses for them in your weekly menus.

Toasting Pumpkin Seeds

There are several ways to toast seeds in their shelled or unshelled form. Let's begin with the unshelled seeds you have extracted from the pumpkin:

1. Give them a quick rinse with water, then wipe off any excess pulp with a clean dishcloth. Spread the seeds out on a paper bag and leave overnight to dry out.
2. The next day, preheat your oven to 300°F. Lay out the seeds on a cookie sheet and season with a spray of olive oil, garlic powder, and sea salt.

Place in the oven and bake for thirty minutes, shaking from time to time, until golden brown.

Toasting the small, green-shelled pumpkin seeds can be done very easily using a heavy skillet.

1. Heat a small, heavy skillet over medium-low heat and add a cup of raw, shelled pumpkin seeds.
2. Keep moving the seeds around the pan or shake the pan from time to time to evenly distribute the heat.
3. Within a few minutes, the seeds will begin to make a popping sound as they brown.
4. Reduce the heat to low and continue to toast until all the seeds have browned, then pour the seeds into a small bowl.
5. At this point, you can add a dash of soy sauce while the seeds are still hot and stir well. Be moderate; the heat from the seeds will dry the liquid, giving it a subtle flavor and salty taste.

Store the toasted pumpkin seeds in a glass container and keep on hand to sprinkle over grains, vegetables, soups, or as a quick snack in the afternoon.

Pumpkin Seeds and Raisins

A simple yet delicious snack you can make in just a few minutes. The heat from the toasted pumpkin seeds softens the raisins, creating a contrast in texture and a sweet-salty flavor.

1. Measure the raisins into a bowl large enough for the seeds as well. Set aside. Have the tamari ready at hand.

2. Heat a small, heavy skillet over medium-low heat; add pumpkin seeds.

3. Move seeds around pan to ensure each seed is toasted. As they brown they will make a sound like knuckles cracking.

4. Once seeds are brown and toasted, remove to a small bowl; add tamari. Mix well to coat seeds. The heat will dry the soy sauce. (Be moderate—too much tamari will make the seeds soggy.)

5. While seeds are still warm, add to raisin bowl; mix well. Set aside and allow to cool naturally. Store covered in a glass bowl in refrigerator.

The Five Tastes

Getting the five basic flavors in the course of a meal, or even a day, will help alleviate food cravings. The five tastes include: sweet, salty, bitter, pungent, and sour. This Pumpkin Seeds and Raisins recipe provides you with sweet from the raisins, salty from the tamari, and a slightly bitter taste from the pumpkin seeds; three out of five flavors for your taste buds.

MAKES 1½ CUPS

530 calories
13 g fat
100 g carbohydrates
15 g protein
49 g sugars
6 g fiber

INGREDIENTS
½ cup raisins
1 cup toasted pumpkin seeds
3 drops tamari soy sauce

INGREDIENTS

1½ cups yellow cornmeal
½ cup whole-wheat flour
1 tablespoon baking powder
1 teaspoon sea salt
3 eggs
1¼ cup low-fat or nondairy milk
1 tablespoon honey
¼ cup melted butter

Pumpkin Seed Cornbread Stuffing
The Cornbread

This cornbread recipe can be used to make stuffing or served on the side warm with a pat of butter and a drizzle of honey.

1. Preheat oven to 350°F.

2. In a large bowl, sift together cornmeal, flour, baking powder, and sea salt.

3. In a separate bowl, whisk together eggs, milk, and honey.

4. Add liquid mixture to dry ingredients; stir until just combined.

5. Meanwhile, melt butter; gently stir into cornbread mixture.

6. Pour batter into a greased 8" × 12" baking dish and bake 35–40 minutes, or until center is firm and golden brown.

7. When done, remove from oven, set aside, and allow to cool before handling.

Pumpkin Seed Cornbread Stuffing
The Stuffing

Complete each step of the preparation before putting the stuffing together. You can then bake it separately in the oven or stuff your turkey before baking. You can also make the stuffing a day ahead and refrigerate before baking it the next day.

1. Preheat oven to 350°F.

2. Crumble cornbread into a large bowl; set aside.

3. In a heavy skillet over medium heat, heat olive oil; sauté peppers, onion, and garlic until tender.

4. Meanwhile, in a food processor, purée pumpkin seeds, broth, tamari, and cayenne until smooth.

5. Add pumpkin seed purée and sautéed vegetables to crumbled cornbread; mix well to combine flavors.

6. Spoon into an oiled baking dish; bake 20 minutes.

Stuffing

The traditional holiday stuffing is most often made from bread crumbs, celery, pan drippings, herbs, and spices. Why not try something different with the addition of heart-healthy pumpkin seeds and cornmeal? Give it a preholiday tryout and serve with small Cornish hens with a cherry yogurt sauce and a side of autumn-ripe Brussels sprouts.

310 calories
15 g fat
38 g carbohydrates
10 g protein
6 g sugars
4 g fiber

INGREDIENTS
1 pan Pumpkin Seed Cornbread (see page 176)
2 tablespoons olive oil
2 red peppers
1 medium onion
2 cloves garlic
1½ cups toasted pumpkin seeds
⅔ cup vegetable broth
1 teaspoon tamari soy sauce
½ teaspoon cayenne pepper

CHAPTER 16

Nutrient-Rich Microplants

There are a few plants in nature that are extremely
concentrated with vitamins and minerals, surpass-
ing even kale and broccoli. Although microplants are
related to dark leafy vegetables, they provide a higher
level of nutrients than other foods. These microplants
consist of blue-green algae, chlorella, spirulina, wheat
grass, and barley grass. In this chapter, you will learn
the importance of including microplants in your diet.
They were the beginning source of life for this planet,
and they continue to nourish humans today.

What Makes Them Super

Microplants come in many forms and colors, harvested both from the sea and dry land, and nutritionally each one is an excellent source of two important phytochemicals: chlorophyll and lycopene. These super-powerful nutrients support your body's ability to detoxify heavy metals, pesticides, and other toxins, plus they are loaded with nutrients to boost your immunity to disease. Microplants, commercially known as green foods, contain a concentrated combination of phytochemicals, vitamins, minerals, bioflavanoids, proteins, amino acids, essential fatty acids, enzymes, coenzymes, and fiber. This means a whole lot of nutrition in small amounts of food. Dr. Richard Schulze, author of *Get Well,* refers to microplants as nature's blood transfusion.

It may be a bit confusing to discern which microplant is right for you to take, but don't worry, there are products on the market that combine these Superfoods into one formula, making it easy to stir into fresh juice and drink your nutrients.

Individually, the most common microplants sold in natural-foods stores include:

- **Blue-green algae (cyanophyta):** one of the first life forms, scientists have found 3.5 billion years of earth's existence encoded in the RNA/DNA (nucleic acids) of these primitive organisms. Presently available in loose powder or capsule form, blue-green algae contains beta carotene and more nucleic acids than any plant or animal food. Actually, blue-green algae are composed of hundreds of types of algae, spirulina, aphanizomenon, and microcystis being a few.
- **Chlorella (chlorophyta):** is a single-cell, freshwater green microalgae that is the Superfood of choice for over 10 million people worldwide. The first known form of plant life with a true nucleus, it has survived for 2.5 billion years because of its extremely tough outer cell wall and its ability to quadruple in quantity every twenty hours, making it the fastest-growing plant on earth! NASA believes it to be the ideal food for long-term space travel and colonization. It is useful for removing heavy metals, pesticides, and other toxic carcinogens from the body. It contains less protein and beta carotene than

spirulina, with twice the nucleic acid and chlorophyll. Its cleansing and rejuvenating properties are considered to fight aging, Alzheimer's disease, sciatica, palsy, seizures, multiple sclerosis, and general nervous system issues.

- **Spirulina:** a microscopic, spiral-shaped, blue-green algae native to shallow, brackish lakes; also known as a cyanobacteria. It has been esteemed as a Superfood for centuries by people inhabiting the regions surrounding Mexico's Lake Texcoco and Africa's Lake Chad, Lake Nakura, and Lake Rudolf. It is one of the most heavily researched, nutritious, well-rounded foods on Earth, being one of the single-celled plants of the blue-green algae family. Spirulina provides more than 100 vitamins and minerals and is 60 percent digestible vegetable protein, with high concentrates of beta carotene, antioxidants, B vitamins, iron, and chlorophyll. It's also a rare food source of GLA (gamma-linolenic acid), an essential fatty acid.

- **Wheat grass:** a variety of grass similar to barley, oats, and rye, it is grown in fields across America, but the wheat grass referred to here is grown indoors in trays for approximately ten days and then pressed into fresh juice. The tray-grown grass is used primarily for therapeutic purposes. The sixty-day-old field-grown grasses, available in dehydrated powder or tablets, are used primarily as nutritional supplements. Wheat-grass juice is made from sprouting wheat berries, and is very high in chlorophyll. The chlorophyll helps cleanse the body, neutralize toxins, slow the aging process, and prevent cancer. Wheat-grass juice is also effective when applied as an external poultice for burns, poison-oak rash, and wounds.

- **Barley grass:** Barley grass is another green grass that is high in chlorophyll. The young green leaves of barley absorb crucial nutrients from the soil. When barley leaves are twelve to fourteen inches high, they contain vitamins, minerals, and proteins necessary for the human diet, plus chlorophyll. These necessities are easily assimilated throughout the digestive tract, giving your body instant access to vital nutrients. Green barley leaves contain a multitude of enzymes, which supply the spark that starts the essential chemical reactions our bodies need to live.

These microplants (blue-green algae, spirulina, chlorella, wheat and barley grass) are well known by scientists as nutritious and safe to eat. With over thirty years of international scientific research and thousands of published peer-reviewed papers documenting their safety and nutritional and therapeutic health benefits, microplants should be a part of everyone's daily diet. Scientific research continues to investigate each one of these amazing foods, so new discoveries are always forthcoming.

For your present needs, there are quality "green" powder drinks that are a combination of all the listed microplants, plus fruits, vegetables, sprouted grains, and probiotics. Makers of the leading green drinks claim that one to two tablespoons of this concentrated powder mixed in water will provide you with the equivalent of five to six servings of vegetables. Check the label for ingredients and nutritional breakdown.

The Benefits of Chlorophyll

The word *chlorophyll* derives from the ancient Greek *chloros* and *phyllon*, meaning "green leaf." This is the green pigment that colors most plants, algae, and cyanobacteria. Actually, chlorophyll is a molecule specifically designed to absorb sunlight and use this energy to synthesize carbohydrates from CO_2 and water. This process is called photosynthesis, and is the basis for sustaining the life processes of all plants. Since animals and humans obtain their food by eating plants, photosynthesis can be said to be the source of our life as well.

Chlorophyll helps oxygenate the blood; deodorizes breath and body odor; strengthens body tissue; contributes to cell and tissue strength by aiding the blood in carrying oxygen; promotes intestinal microflora; and stops bacterial growth in wounds. It's molecular structure is so similar to the structure of our red blood cells, it is often referred to as "the blood of plant life." Chlorophyll can be purchased in liquid form and taken as a supplement in a concentrated form.

Microplants and Chlorophyll

Since microplants contain high amounts of chlorophyll, they nourish, purify, and suppress inflammation in the body. The best way to ingest chlorophyll is by eating the microplants: barley and wheat grass, chlorella, spirulina, and blue-green algae, plus other Superfoods such as kale, collards, spinach, broccoli, and chard. But it is the microplants chlorella, spirulina, and blue-green algae that contain more chlorophyll than any other foods, often double the amounts, depending on how and where they are grown.

The History of Microplants

Four billion years ago, in our planet's evolution of life and growth, cyanobacteria, the blue-green algae people consume today, was thriving in an oxygen-depleted atmosphere, breathing carbon dioxide and making oxygen as a waste product; all done through photosynthesis. It was the beginning of life on this planet. Small amounts of microalgae such as chlorella and spirulina provide a tremendous wealth of nutrients that are essential to health, yet are increasingly absent in today's toxic diet of heavily processed foods.

Today, spirulina and chlorella are easily cultivated and grown in scientifically designed algae farms that do not form scum on the surface of the water. Blue-green algae is harvested from natural lake conditions, as well as from cultivated algae farms. Although the microalgae spirulina, chlorella, and blue-green algae, and the cereal grasses wheat and barley unite under the term *microplants*, they have a distinctly different history from each other.

Cereal Grass

Agronomists have determined that barley grass was first cultivated as early as 7000 B.C., probably in the dry lands of southwestern Asia. It is a very hardy plant and can be grown under a greater variety of climatic conditions than any other grain. There is written mention of the grain as long ago as 2800 B.C. in Babylon, and the athletes of ancient Greece drank a barley mush in preparation for athletic events. Astounding amounts of vitamins and minerals are found in the green barley leaves and slender stalk of the wheat grass. These include potassium, calcium, magnesium, iron, copper, phosphorus, manganese, zinc, beta carotene, B1, B2, B6, C, folate, and pantothenic acid. Green barley leaves also contain significant amounts of chlorophyll.

FACT

African flamingos get their pink color from eating a super-rich diet that includes the pink-tinted microalgae known as spirulina. In the same way, if you were to drink excessive amounts of fresh carrot juice, your skin would take on an orange tint.

The Chinese honored the healing properties of wheat grass as far back as 2800 B.C. The Romans and Egyptians had similar ceremonies for worshiping cereal grasses and grains. Early research about immature pasture grass was done in England in the 1800s. Modern research into the nutritional content of cereal grasses, such as wheat, barley, and oats, began in 1935 when chemists at the University of Wisconsin described the growth-stimulating factor of grass as distinct from all the known vitamins. This work was inspired by the agricultural chemist Dr. Charles F. Schnabel, who started a movement to make cereal grass available for both livestock and human consumption. Around the same time, Dr. Ann Wigmore popularized the use of indoor-grown, fresh-squeezed wheat-grass juice for the therapeutic treatment of cancer patients who had been pronounced incurable.

Microplants Nutrient Content

The nutritional content for each microplant varies according to amounts and growing conditions. The nutritional content for two tablespoons of a combination of spirulina, blue-green algae, chlorella, barley, and wheat grass, plus a few green vegetables includes:

CALORIES	50	VITAMIN B6	6 mg
FAT	0.5 g	VITAMIN B9	269 mg
CARBOHYDRATES	6 g	VITAMIN B12	11.2 mcg
FIBER	3.6 g	VITAMIN C	60 mg
PROTEIN	6.4 g	VITAMIN E	21 mg
VITAMIN A	7000 IU	SELENIUM	29.2 mcg
VITAMIN B1	6 mg	IODINE	38.4 mcg
VITAMIN B2	7.2 mg	IRON	2.22 mg
VITAMIN B3	40 mg	ZINC	1.9 mg
VITAMIN B5	10 mg		

The Recommended Daily Allowance (RDA) for most of the nutrients listed are over 100 percent, with the B vitamins exceeding 300, 400, and 500 percent. This in just two tablespoons of powdered microplants! The extraordinary vitamin and mineral content of these Superfoods is in their natural forms and are more healthful, more absorbable, and more effective than any bulk vitamin supplements.

Healing Properties of Microplants

Microplants are considered to be complete foods and an easily assimilated source of nutrients. Scientific research has been extensive and remarkable in revealing a superior source of vitamins and minerals compared to regular dietary supplements. Of all the Superfoods you can buy, microplants should be number one on your next shopping list.

Microalgae

In 1979, Russian scientists published initial research on the immune-stimulating effects on rabbits from lipopolysaccharides in spirulina. These discoveries are significant for human health as well. Overused antibiotics have created highly resistant bacteria; most antibiotics are no longer effective. Now scientists want to identify probiotics that strengthen the immune system to prevent disease and cancer. Based on this animal research, as little as 3 grams per day of spirulina may be effective for humans. It seems to turbocharge the immune system to seek out and destroy disease-causing microorganisms and cancer cells.

Immunologist and Professor M. A. Qureshi, Ph.D., released a study sponsored by Earthrise Company of California entitled *Immunomodulary Effects of Spirulina Supplementation in Chickens*. The study showed that less than 1 percent of spirulina added daily to a chicken's diet greatly improved T-cell and thymus function. Dr. Qureshi found that spirulina boosted cells called *macrophages*, the first line of your body's defense. The importance of these macrophage cells is their ability to communicate with T-cells to coordinate the fight against infections. Spirulina caused the cells to increase in number, become more active, and display more effective microbial killing.

ALERT!

Due to the abundance of ineffective antibiotics used on farm factories to protect animals from disease, scientists are actively testing spirulina as a broad-spectrum vaccine against bacteria. They are hoping that it may also protect against other disease-causing microbes and cancer.

Scientists in China and Japan have independently studied the nutritional benefits of microalgae for decades. They have found that these ancient plants have healing capabilities when used properly and in the right doses. In their research with spirulina, they found that when it was fed to mice, it increased macrophage function, antibody production, and infection-fighting T-cells. Another study found spirulina extracts inhibited cancer by boosting the immune system. The active phytonutrients are a polysaccharide (a complex sugar molecule) named calcium spirulan (Ca-SP), unique to spirulina; and phycocyanin (the blue pigment found only in blue-green algae).

Spirulina and HIV-1

In April 1996, scientists from the Laboratory of Viral Pathogenesis, Dana-Farber Cancer Institute, and Harvard Medical School, Boston, Massachusetts, and Earthrise Farms, Calipatria, California, announced ongoing research concerning a water extract of *Spirulina platensis* that inhibits HIV-1 replication in human-derived T-cell lines and in human peripheral blood mononuclear cells. The research found that a concentration of 5–10 μg/ml was found to reduce viral production.

Another group of medical scientists has published new studies regarding calcium spirulan. It inhibits replication of HIV-1, herpes simplex, human cytomegalovirus, influenza A virus, mumps virus, and measles virus in-vitro, yet is very safe for human cells. It also protects human and monkey cells from viral infection in cell culture. According to peer-reviewed scientific journal reports, this extract holds great promise for the treatment of HIV-1, HSV-1, and HCM infections, which is particularly advantageous for AIDS patients who are prone to these life-threatening infections.

QUESTION?

What is calcium spirulan?
Calcium spirulan is a polymerized sugar molecule unique to spirulina, containing both sulfur and calcium. Hamsters treated with this water-soluble extract had better recovery rates when infected with an otherwise-lethal herpes virus 9.

Barley Grass and Your Heart

People who regularly consume powdered organic barley-grass juice supplements could be providing a boost to their cardiovascular system, according to research recently published in the peer-reviewed scientific journal *Diabetes and Metabolism* (2002). Ya-Mei Yu and Chingmin E. Tsai, from Fu Jen University in Taipei, together with fellow Taiwanese researchers from China Medical College in Taichung, found in a clinical study that supplementation with barley grass reduced the levels of cholesterol and oxygen-free radicals in the blood of type 2 diabetics. In the study, thirty-six randomly selected type 2 diabetics were randomly assigned to receive daily supplements of barley grass, a combination of vitamins C and E, or a combination of barley grass and vitamins C and E for four weeks. Past research has indicated that antioxidant vitamins C and E taken together can significantly reduce the risk of cardiovascular disease.

As in everything, Mother Nature does it better. So in summation of what microplants can do for your health, they:

- Strengthen your immune system
- Help with the removal of heavy metals and pesticides
- Improve your digestion
- Improve bowel elimination
- Improve mental focus
- Increase and sustain your energy level
- Alkalinize your blood pH

If you were stranded on a desert island without any food, you would survive quite nicely on a diet of microalgae, sea vegetables, and fish, all Superfoods of the highest quality (with the sea salt easily provided.)

Dr. Richard M. Gold, Ph.D., L.Ac., author and professor at Pacific College of Oriental Medicine, advises individuals concerned about their cardiovascular health to focus on a diet consisting of a lot of green foods, particularly organic barley grass.

Buying and Storage Tips

Green foods can be purchased from your local health-foods store or online. They are available in both capsule or powder form. Look for a reputable manufacturer offering a blend that is certified organic. There are also blends providing four to six servings of concentrated fruits, vegetables, and sprouted whole grains along with the microalgae and cereal grass. Although this may not seem very appetizing, you can improve the taste with the two recipes located at the end of this chapter.

Pure, 100 percent spirulina or chlorella powder are dark green or blue-green in color and have no other colored particles. Your body feels energy within minutes of taking them because the powder is naturally digestible. It provides quick energy and nourishment between meals or in place of a meal. Doses are two or more tablespoons per day. You can add it to your favorite fruit or vegetable juice in a blender. Start with one teaspoon (5 grams) and add flavors or spices to suit your taste. Later on, you can increase the amount. Many regular users take one heaping tablespoon (10 grams) per drink. Use pure spirulina or chlorella in place of the suggested microplant powder in the provided recipes. Store all your microplants in a cool, dry place or well sealed in the refrigerator. Once opened, they will keep for up to a month.

242 calories
13 g fat
27 g carbohydrates
16 g protein
15 g sugars
11 g fiber

INGREDIENTS

1 cup vanilla-flavored hemp-
    seed milk
½ cup frozen blueberries
1 tablespoon microplant powder
    of choice
1 tablespoon flax-seed meal
1 tablespoon hemp-seed protein
    powder
Sweetener of choice, preferably
    stevia powder

Morning Power Green Smoothie

Feel free to vary the fruit using frozen strawberries, blueberries, or banana. Add water to find the right consistency for your palate and adjust the sweetness to suit your taste.

1. Combine all ingredients in a blender and purée until smooth.

2. Serve immediately, while chilled and fresh, chewing well to better release the enzymes needed to digest the proteins, carbohydrates, and fats.

The Hemp Seed

The hemp seed is an achene (uh-keen), similar to sunflower seeds, and has been used as a food source for centuries. A nutritional breakdown of hemp oil shows it to contain a perfect 3:1 ratio of both the required essential fatty acids (EFAs) for long-term human consumption. Hemp seeds also contain nine essential amino acids, vitamins, minerals, and the antioxidants your body requires for life-sustaining fuel.

Spicy Blended Green Salad

You can make this with all the ingredients you usually love to put in a salad. Avocado will thicken and add richness to the final blend, but only add the avocado to a blender; do not attempt to juice.

1. Wash the vegetables well and chop into pieces big enough to fit into either a juicer or blender.

2. If juicing, do all the vegetables first, then stir the remaining ingredients into the juice, mixing well. If blending the vegetables, add all the ingredients to the blender and purée until smooth.

3. Serve immediately with a celery stalk in the glass.

Blending Fruits

The fiber in fruits and vegetables is designed to slow down the rush of sugar to the bloodstream that can happen after eating fruit or sugar-rich carrots and beets. Blending all the vegetables with water, on the other hand, allows the nutrients and fiber to remain intact and gives you the benefits of fiber, sugar, and nutrients.

SERVES 2

100 calories
0.5 g fat
22 g carbohydrates
5 g protein
6 g sugars
6 g fiber

INGREDIENTS
4 carrots
4 celery stalks
2 kale leaves with stem
Handful fresh parsley with stems
2 tablespoons microplant
   powder
1 teaspoon tamari soy sauce
Dash of hot sauce
1 teaspoon apple cider vinegar
   or lemon juice

CHAPTER 17

Oats: The Wonder Grain

Despite having been a staple for many years in the diets of people worldwide, oats really earned cult status in America in 1997, when the FDA announced that including oats in your daily diet could substantially reduce your chances for coronary heart disease. This proclamation included the oatmeal you eat for breakfast, any baked goods made from oat bran or oat flour, and the whole-oat grain itself. In this chapter, you will learn why eating your breakfast of oats can keep you and your family's hearts healthy and immune systems strong.

What Makes Them Super

With the FDA announcement, the American public took eating their oats more seriously. The question everyone wanted answered when the FDA made oats a Superfood was, what did it contain that was so effective in fighting heart disease? The answer turned out to be the soluble fiber in oats known as beta glucan, and oats contain more soluble fiber than any other grain. Soluble fiber is the kind that dissolves in water, so the body turns it into a thick, viscous gel, which then moves very slowly through your body.

FACT

Beta glucans are polysaccharides which occur in the outer layer, or bran, of cereal grains. Pertaining to human nutrition, they act as soluble-fiber supplements and texturing agents found most abundantly in oats and barley and less in wheat and rye grains.

The health benefits from adding soluble fiber to your diet include:

- Your stomach stays fuller longer, providing satiety
- It slows the absorption of glucose into the body, helping you avoid sugar highs and lows
- It inhibits the reabsorption of bile into the system, forcing your liver to import cholesterol from your blood, which serves to lower your blood-serum cholesterol levels

This combination of soluble fiber and nutrients in oats is what makes them a superior Superfood. They are also an affordable grain that you can buy in any food store, they take little time to prepare, and children, teenagers, and adults already know and love them. Regardless of why you began eating oats, continuing to do so can only improve your health.

What Makes an Oat?

Oats are part of the cereal family known as grains, which includes barley, wheat, spelt, rye, quinoa, and rice to name but a few. These cereal grains are really just the edible seeds of certain grasses that are easily grown in large quantities, and in many countries constitute the main ingredient in that populace's diet. In 1931, there were twenty-five species of oats cultivated; today there are only three. Since oats are an annual grass whose life cycle is completed once they have grown their seeds, they are left to dry in the fields before harvesting. In America, the oat grass is machine harvested, which first cuts the grass, then beats the plant in order to separate the grain from the straw. Finally, it winnows the grain in order to separate the grains from the lighter plant chaff.

ALERT!

When the media grabbed hold of the FDA's approval of oats, they pushed the story that all you had to do was eat oat bran to lower your cholesterol. This proved not to be the case, unless other aspects of one's diet were taken into consideration and appropriate changes made. Lowering saturated fat and dietary cholesterol in the diet also helped lower cholesterol levels in the blood.

What is left is the whole grain, consisting of three parts:

- **Oat bran:** the soluble fiber-rich outer layer that contains B vitamins, minerals, protein, and other phytochemicals
- **Endosperm:** the middle layer that contains carbohydrates, proteins, and a small amount of B vitamins
- **Germ:** the nutrient-packed inner layer that contains B vitamins, vitamin E, and other phytochemicals

The synergy of these three components is what makes oats (and all other grains) so nourishing and health supportive. This is the whole grain in its glory, before it has been stripped of its bran, endosperm, and germ and all their powerful nutrients, antioxidants, and phytonutrients, to become a refined carbohydrate.

Sowing Your Wild Oats

It is not a coincidence that the clichés "sowing your wild oats" and "feeling your oats" refer to notions of sexual activity and a youthful vitality. Both eating the oat seed and drinking a beverage made from oatstraw have long been known to enhance the libido by restoring sexual vigor. This is due to the nourishing yet soothing properties of the plant, which help tonify the nervous system, ease internal inflammation, act as a diuretic, and provide needed nutrients to the endocrine system. All in all, a most effective love tonic for those in need.

The History of Oats

The botanical name *Avena sativa* translates to "cultivated oat." A strong member of the grain family, the English referred to them as oats, groats, wild oats, naked oats, tartarian oats, and bristle-pointed oats. They were the last of the major cereal grains to be domesticated, around 3,000 years ago in Europe, and apparently originated as a weed that grew within cultivated fields of various other crops. Because of the many species and subspecies, it is difficult to accurately track its history, but many researchers point to Asia Minor as the place of origin.

Somehow, oat seeds made their way to Europe, where according to John K. Williams in *A Brief History of Oats—And How You Should Eat Them,* the Greeks and Romans looked down their noses at them, considering them nothing more than a diseased version of wheat. The Romans grew oats to be used as horse feed, and made fun of the Germanic tribes or "oat-eating barbarians," who evidently took offense and brought down the Western Roman Empire.

FACT

In Samuel Johnson's dictionary, oats were defined as "eaten by people in Scotland, but fit only for horses in England." A Scotsman's retort to this: "That's why England has such good horses, and Scotland has such fine men!"

The oat grass was first brought to North America in 1602, where it was planted on the Elizabeth Islands off the coast of Massachusetts. It is known that George Washington sowed 580 acres of the grain, no doubt to feed his herd of horses. Today, the major production of oats are grown in the middle and upper Mississippi Valley, with more oats being grown for animal feed and less than 5 percent of oats grown for human consumption.

Oats' Nutrient Content

New discoveries, combined with what's already known about oats, have shown that their health-promoting powers are truly impressive. Oats are low in calories and high in fiber and protein. They're a rich source of magnesium, potassium, phosphorus, zinc, copper, manganese, selenium, thiamine, and pantothenic acid. They also contain phytonutrients such as polyphenols, phytoestrogens, and lignins, and they are an excellent source of multiple tocopherols, which are important members of the vitamin E family. The high-fiber content of oats also makes them an excellent cleansing grain for both your intestines and your blood.

It takes ten minutes to cook regular rolled oats, while the thinner, quick-rolled oats cook in two to three minutes. Instant rolled oats, which are the least nutritious, have already been cooked and dehydrated, and just need boiling water to reconstitute them. For the highest nutritional value, use the regular rolled oats and save the instant kind for camping trips.

One cup of oatmeal cooked in water contains the following nutrient content:

CALORIES	166	CALCIUM	20 mg
PROTEIN	6 g	IRON	2.1 mg
CARBOHYDRATES	32 g	MAGNESIUM	63.2 mg
FIBER	4 g	MANGANESE	1.37 mg
TOTAL FAT	4 g	PHOSPHORUS	178 mg
VITAMIN A	0 IU	POTASSIUM	164 mg
FOLATE	14 mcg	ZINC	2.3 mg

Actually, one cup of cooked oatmeal can be a large serving, when half a cup will do fine, without making one feel over full. The daily recommended allowance for whole grains is 5–7 servings, but those servings should be about half a cup of cooked grains or pasta and only one slice of bread at a time. Also, the fats in oats are a healthy form, with a lipid breakdown of 21 percent saturated, 37 percent monounsaturated, and 43 percent polyunsaturated.

In addition to the benefits of soluble oat fiber, the germ and bran of oats contain a concentrated amount of phytonutrients, including caffeic acid, a naturally occurring compound shown to be a carcinogenic inhibitor; and ferulic acid, a potent antioxidant that is able to scavenge free radicals and protect against oxidative damage. It also seems to be able to inhibit the formation of certain cancer-promoting compounds.

FACT

Oat protein is nearly equivalent in quality to soy protein, which has been shown by the World Health Organization to be the equal to meat, milk, and egg protein. The protein content of the hull-less oat kernel (groat) ranges from 12–24 percent, the highest among cereals.

Types of Oats

There are a number of different ways that oats are processed for your cooking pleasure. It can get confusing, unless you know what they are and how to prepare them. The following is a description of the types of oats available in food markets, listed from the least to the most processed:

- **Whole-oat groats:** minimally processed the outer hull has been removed. Very nutritious and delicious, but need to be presoaked for four to eight hours and cooked for a few hours. An alternative is to cook them overnight in a slow cooker.
- **Oat bran:** the outer casing has been removed from the groat. The bran is particularly high in soluble fiber. Oat bran can be used as an addition to baking recipes, or even raw in smoothies.

- **Steel-cut oats:** also known as Irish oats, they have been chopped into small pieces, have a firmer texture than rolled oats, and are often preferred for hot oatmeal cereals.
- **Rolled oats:** oat groats that have been steamed and flattened with huge rollers so that they cook quicker, in about five to fifteen minutes.
- **Quick oats:** groats that have been cut into several pieces before being steamed and rolled into thinner flakes, thus reducing the cooking time to three to five minutes. While they cook quicker, they lack the hearty texture and nutty flavor of the less-processed varieties.
- **Instant oats:** groats have been chopped into small pieces, pre-cooked, dried, and flattened with a big roller. They cook instantly with the addition of boiling water. This form of processing removes all traces of the original texture and rich flavor of the groats, plus many of the nutrients.
- **Oat flour:** whole-oat groats have been ground into a powder, which may contain some gluten, but not enough to make it rise like wheat flour. To make oat flour at home, place rolled oats in a blender or food processor and purée until desired consistency.

A tough, old cowboy once counseled his grandson that if he wanted to live a long life, he should sprinkle a pinch of gunpowder on his oatmeal every morning. The grandson did this religiously and lived to the age of 110. He left four children, twenty grandchildren, thirty great-grandchildren, ten great-great-grandchildren, and a fifty-foot hole where the crematorium used to be. —Anonymous Joker

Healing Properties of Oats

According to Paul Pitchford, author of *Healing With Whole Foods*, oats have a warming thermal nature, a sweet and slightly bitter flavor, are soothing, restore nervous and reproductive systems, strengthen the spleen and pancreas, build and regulate qi energy, remove cholesterol from the digestive tract and arteries, and strengthen cardiac muscles.

One of the richest silicon foods, oats help renew the bones and all connective tissues. Oats also contain phosphorus, required for brain and nerve formulation during youth.

Its cholesterol-lowering soluble fiber, beta glucan, has been shown to lower total cholesterol by 8–23 percent in individuals with high cholesterol (above 220 mg/dl) when they consumed just 3 grams of soluble oat fiber per day—roughly the amount in a bowl of oatmeal. Given that each 1 percent drop in serum cholesterol translates to a 2 percent decrease in the risk of developing heart disease, this is a significant effect.

Oats for Your Skin

Due to their anti-inflammatory properties, oats can be used for a skin-softening facial mask or wrapped in cheesecloth and placed in a hot tub of water to help ease dry and itchy skin.

To make an oatmeal honey mask: Take ½ cup of oatmeal and blend it to almost flour consistency. Place in a small bowl and add 1 tablespoon of honey and one beaten egg white. Mix well to form a paste and spread over clean face; relax for fifteen to twenty minutes. Remove the mask when done and rinse face well. This will leave skin smooth and soft.

Try adding oat milk to your bath water. Begin by tying a handful of oatmeal into a piece of cheesecloth. While the water is running, hold the oatmeal under the faucet or let it hang while the water soaks through the cloth. With the tub full, place the oat bag in the water with you, squeezing it from time to time to release its milky properties. Use it to scrub your body and face so the juices can soften and cleanse your skin.

Because they have the best amino-acid balance of all the cereal grains, oats can be used as water-binding agents in skin-care products. You will find that oat grains and oat straw appear in some shampoos, dusting powders, moisturizers, and skin-cleansing bars.

Oatstraw

Oatstraw is made up of the green stalk of the plant, the leaves, and the grain. It has a higher vitamin A and vitamin C count than just the grain alone. It is soothing to the nervous system, nourishes the endocrine system, and removes inflammation from the body. This allows any internal swelling to subside and release extra fluid.

Buying and Storage Tips

At home, store whole grains in airtight containers in a cool place, preferably the refrigerator or freezer; otherwise, buy only the amount you will consume within the month. Oats, for example, have more natural oil than many people realize, and can become rancid if they're stored in a warm environment.

Cooking Ideas

Many of you have only experienced oats in the form of oatmeal, and instant oatmeal at that. There are few grains as delicious as whole oats cooked overnight in a slow cooker and served with a drizzle of maple syrup and fresh butter. Here are a few things to remember when cooking with oats:

- Presoaking whole oats can reduce the cooking time.
- Once whole oats or oatmeal are cooked, they will keep in the fridge for two to three days.
- Oats freeze well if you want to make extra and freeze in portion sizes.
- Rolled oats can be added to soups to thicken a purée and add a cream-like texture.
- Soak a few tablespoons of rolled oats in hot water for five minutes and add to your morning smoothie.
- Replace bread crumbs with puréed oatmeal in meatloaf or burgers for added fiber.

It's time to change your perspective and look at oats in a whole new way. Experiment with some of the ideas listed and you will find that oats will fit very nicely into your weekly menu plans.

220 calories
14 g fat
21 g carbohydrates
7 g protein
10 g sugars
3 g fiber

INGREDIENTS

¾ cup rice syrup
1½ cups toasted almond or peanut butter
1 teaspoon vanilla extract
½ cup flax-seed meal
⅓ cup unsweetened coconut
½ cup rolled oats
⅓ cup raisins
⅓ cup chopped walnuts

Energy Oat Bars

Rice syrup is a thick, mild sweetener that helps bind the bars together. It has a low glycemic index, meaning it won't spike your blood sugar. If you want a sweeter bar, substitute ½ cup of agave or maple syrup or honey.

1. In a large, heavy saucepan, heat rice syrup on low until thin and runny, about 2 minutes.

2. Add almond butter and vanilla; stir well.

3. Remove from heat; stir in remaining ingredients; mix well.

4. Spoon into an 8" × 8" casserole pan; spread; slice into 20 pieces.

5. Cover and chill in the refrigerator or freezer.

Protein Energy Bars

Most energy bars on the market today are loaded with sugar and a lot of worthless ingredients at a steep price. Here you can make your own, freeze them, and have a quick bite before a workout or as a treat between meals.

Whole Oats and Raisins

A very simple recipe you will make over and over again. Children love oats made this way and so will you. You can cook them on the stove all day or use a 1.5-quart slow cooker and make your life a whole lot easier.

1. Before going to bed, combine oats, salt, raisins, water, and cinnamon in a 1.5 quart slow cooker. Turn on low; let cook overnight.

2. In the morning, chop walnuts; stir oats and spoon ½ cup into individual bowls.

3. Top with walnuts, a drizzle of maple syrup, and a splash of milk.

Warm Winter Food

Whole oats cooked slow over a long period of time will warm your body and keep your energy levels balanced throughout the morning hours. For a more savory recipe, eliminate the raisins and cinnamon and serve with sautéed greens and toasted pumpkin seeds. Delicious either way!

SERVES 4

330 calories
13 g fat
46 g carbohydrates
9 g protein
9 g sugars
7 g fiber

INGREDIENTS

1 cup whole-oat groats
Pinch of sea salt
⅓ cup raisins
5 cups water
½ teaspoon cinnamon powder
½ cup toasted walnuts
Maple syrup, to taste
Splash of milk

CHAPTER 18

Sweet Potatoes: Rich in Vitamin A

There are not many foods you can reach for in spring, summer, autumn, and winter that have the versatility of the sweet potato. In this chapter, you will discover what you are missing by leaving this incredible vegetable out of your diet. Once you learn how easy they are to prepare and how good they are for your health, you and your family will include them for dinner more often than just Thanksgiving.

What Makes Them Super

What makes a sweet potato a Superfood is its high amounts of beta carotene—equal to that of carrots—and the fact that for 90 calories per sweet potato, you get a huge amount of health-building nutrients. Beta carotene is a major fighter against cancer, heart disease, asthma, and rheumatoid arthritis. The bright-orange flesh of the sweet potato contains carotenoids that help stabilize your blood sugar and lower insulin resistance, making cells more responsive to insulin, and aiding your metabolism.

Sweet potatoes can be prepared as a cold salad, a rich stew, French fries, baked potato, or as a spread on focaccia bread. You can bake, sauté, steam, boil, fry, or roast sweet potatoes, and they always taste great. Sweet potatoes are a highly nutritious food, easy to prepare, delicious to eat, and very beneficial for your health. Yet, many Americans only eat them during the winter holidays, and usually smother them in brown sugar and marshmallows.

The American Yam

People are often confused about the difference between sweet potatoes and yams. The moist-fleshed, orange-colored root vegetable sold in American food stores and labeled a yam is actually a variety of sweet potato. The name comes from the African word *nyami,* referring to the root of the true yam plant. This white-fleshed variety of sweet potato was first introduced to the American palate in the mid-twentieth century, and while there are attempts to distinguish between the two, in reality, the traditional Dioscoreae family of yam is not generally available. These true yams are nothing like the sweet potato, but are a tuber native to Africa, very starchy, not very sweet, and can grow as large as 100 pounds.

The American Sweet Potato

There are about 400 varieties of sweet potato, varying in size, shape, and color. They are grouped in two separate categories based on their baked texture, which can be firm, dry, and rather mealy or soft and moist. In both these types, the taste is sweet and starchy, with different varieties having their own unique flavor.

The flesh of the sweet potato can be white, yellow, or orange, with a thin outer skin in shades of white, yellow, orange, red, or purple. The shapes can vary from short and blocky with rounded ends to long and wide with tapered ends.

Sweet potatoes belong to the Convolvulaceae plant family, and are known to be relatively low in calories, with no fat. They are rich in beta carotene, one sweet potato having five times the recommended daily allowance of vitamin A, as well as being loaded with potassium. The potassium helps maintain fluid and electrolyte balance in the body's cells, as well as normal heart function and blood pressure.

FACT

According to Dr. Earl Mindell, wild Mexican yams, which are related to the sweet potato, seem to have anti-weight-gain, anti-cancer, and anti-aging properties. No doubt this is due to the high beta carotene and potassium content that not only helps prevent disease, but keeps you young and healthy as well.

The History of Sweet Potatoes

The botanical name for sweet potatoes, *Ipomoea batata*, was derived from the Native American tribes of Louisiana who were growing them in native gardens as early as 1540. They referred to sweet potatoes as "batatas." However, they originated farther south, in Mexico, Central and South America, and the West Indies. Sweet potatoes are considered one of the oldest vegetables known to man and have been consumed since prehistoric times. This was evidenced by sweet-potato relics dating back 10,000 years discovered in Peruvian caves.

New World Potatoes

When Columbus returned home to Spain following his first voyage to the New World, he brought the sweet potato with him. What a delightful surprise for the Spanish, who immediately began cultivating them and were soon exporting them to England, where they were enjoyed by King Henry VIII in spice pies. From there, the French took them into the gardens of Louis XV, and later, having loved them as a child in Martinique, Empress Josephine helped make them popular. By the sixteenth century, they were brought to the Philippines by Spanish explorers and to Africa, India, Indonesia, and southern Asia by the Portuguese. To this day, in Africa, they remain an important staple of the native diet.

Southern Soil

Around the sixteenth century, the sweet potato landed in America's southern soil, namely North Carolina, Georgia, and Louisiana. It was the Southerners who adopted the name *yam* to distinguish the darker-skinned orange sweet potato from the other varieties. It became such an important part of southern cuisine that during the American Revolution and Civil War, they were said to have sustained the fighting soldiers. Today, sweet potatoes are a featured food in many Asian and Latin American cultures, with the main commercial producers of sweet potatoes being China, Indonesia, Vietnam, Japan, India, and Uganda.

Sweet Potatoes' Nutrient Content

In 1992, the Center for Science in the Public Interest did a study comparing the nutritional value of vegetables. It was used to show how eating vegetables provided more nutrients than the most popular artery-clogging fast foods. The study was based on the following criteria:

- Fiber content
- Complex carbohydrates
- Protein levels
- Vitamins A and C
- Iron
- Calcium

According to this criteria, the vegetable that ranked the highest in nutritional value was the sweet potato with a score of 267, a full 184 points over its nearest competitor, the white potato, at 83 points. In addition, the Nutrition Action Health Letter did a study rating fifty-eight vegetables for their USRDA for six important nutrients, similar to the ones listed above, but including folate, iron, and calcium. Once again, sweet potatoes topped the list with a score of 582 points, with its nearest competitor, the carrot, coming in at 434 points.

Nutritional Data

Having a baked sweet potato with a dab of butter and a drizzle of maple syrup can be a meal or a dessert. Coupled with a mixed green salad and a tart vinaigrette dressing, you will feel full for hours to come. However, it is important to know just what you are getting with that big tuber, so here is the nutritional value for one sweet potato:

CALORIES	90	VITAMIN C	20 mg
FAT	0 g	VITAMIN E	1 mg
CARBOHYDRATES	21 g	CALCIUM	38 mg
PROTEIN	2 g	CAROTENOIDS	11,552 mcg
DIETARY FIBER	3 g	POTASSIUM	475 mg
VITAMIN A	19,218 IU	MAGNESIUM	27 mg
FOLATE	6 mcg		

This is the perfect diet food, one that not only provides plenty of nutrients and fiber, but one that will also satisfy your taste for something soft and sweet.

What You Should Know

The North Carolina sweet potato industry has compiled a list of information they feel is important for you to know about these deliciously sweet spuds. The data is pretty amazing, and supports the scientific findings concerning sweet potatoes' Superfood status.

- It would take twenty cups of broccoli to provide the 38,000 IUs of beta carotene (vitamin A) available in one cup of cooked sweet potatoes.

- Sweet potatoes have four times the USRDA for beta carotene when eaten with the skin on.
- Sweet potatoes are a source of vitamin E, plus they're fat free.
- Sweet potatoes provide many essential nutrients, including vitamin B6, potassium, and iron.
- Cup for cup, sweet potatoes have been found to provide as much fiber as oatmeal.
- Sweet potatoes are fat-free, cholesterol-free, and low in sodium and calories.

ALERT!

Due to the possibility of pesticide residue on your sweet-potato skin, make sure to buy organic when possible, or grow your own crop during the summer and autumn months. Otherwise, use a vegetable wash designed to remove any surface chemicals in a way the water cannot.

Although overlooked and underrated, the sweet potato's taste appeals to all ages, and can support your health by reducing your risk for stroke, heart disease, and many forms of cancer.

Healing Properties of Sweet Potatoes

Look no further than the American Cancer Society, the American Heart Association, and the North Carolina Stroke Association for positive endorsements of the sweet potato's healing abilities. Not only does it lower your risk for diverticulosis, colon and rectal cancers, diabetes, and obesity due to its high fiber content, it also has a unique configuration of proteins containing potent antioxidants. Recent studies have found unique root-storage proteins in sweet potatoes that have been observed to have significant antioxidant capacities. In one study, these proteins had about one-third the antioxidant activity of glutathione—one of your body's internally produced antioxidants. Although future studies are needed in this area, count on these root proteins to help explain sweet potatoes' healing properties. Another study by Columbia University showed that consuming high levels of vitamin E delayed the progression of Alzheimer's disease by about seven months. Although present in a number of Superfoods, only sweet potatoes provide vitamin E without the fat and calories.

Sweet Potatoes and Diabetes

With that sweet, delicious taste you might think otherwise, but sweet potatoes are considered a key food in preventing diabetes. It earned this designation in recent animal studies in which the sweet potato helped stabilize blood-sugar levels and lowered insulin resistance in test subjects.

FACT

Insulin resistance is a condition caused when the body's cells won't respond to the hormone insulin. Under normal conditions, insulin acts as the key to unlock your cells in order for sugar to pass from the blood into each cell.

What we do know from scientific research is that different foods have different effects on blood-glucose levels. Some of its blood-sugar regulatory properties may come from the fact that sweet potatoes contain high concentrations of carotenoids. Research has suggested that physiological levels, as well as dietary intake, of carotenoids may be inversely associated with insulin resistance and high blood-sugar levels. So, the next time you have the urge for something sweet, how about a baked sweet potato? It's one vegetable guaranteed to satisfy your sweet tooth while nurturing the rest of your body.

Rich in Antioxidants

The healing properties of sweet potatoes come from their high amounts of vitamin A (in the form of beta carotene) and vitamin C. These two free-radical fighters are very powerful antioxidants that work in your body to help eliminate chemicals that damage cells and cell membranes, and are associated with the development of conditions like atherosclerosis, diabetic heart disease, and colon cancer. By eating foods containing these nutrients, you can lower your risk of developing these conditions. Both vitamins A and C have anti-inflammatory properties, which can be helpful in reducing inflammation in conditions such as asthma, osteoarthritis, and rheumatoid arthritis.

Sweet potatoes are a good source of vitamin B6, which is needed to convert homocysteine, an interim product created during an important chemical process in cells, called methylation, into other benign molecules. High homocysteine levels are associated with an increased risk of heart attack and stroke, but eating sweet potatoes can help in their prevention.

For those who smoke, or are frequently exposed to secondhand smoke, sweet potatoes, loaded with vitamin A, just may save your life. A study by Richard Baybutt, associate professor of nutrition at Kansas State, discovered a common carcinogen in cigarette smoke, benzopyrene, induces vitamin-A deficiency, leading to emphysema. He recommends that a diet rich in vitamin A can help counter this effect. Baybutt speculates that there are a lot of people who live to be ninety years old who are smokers, which is probably due to their diet. The implications being that those who start smoking at an early age are more likely to become vitamin-A deficient and develop complications associated with cancer and emphysema, which is compounded if they also have a poor diet.

Buying and Storage Tips

Sweet potatoes are available year-round in supermarkets and natural-foods stores. When buying, choose organic potatoes that are firm to the touch without any cracks, bruises, or soft areas.

At home, store in a cool, dark, and well-ventilated place, where they will keep fresh for up to ten days. Store them loose rather than in plastic or paper bags. Also keep them away from exposure to sunlight or temperatures above 60°F, since this will cause them to sprout or ferment.

Preparing Sweet Potatoes

With a little imagination, the sweet potato can be the center attraction for a meal or a complement to the main course. When planning your next meal, consider a few of these sweet possibilities:

- Cut two large sweet potatoes into French-fry slices, toss with olive oil, dried basil, and garlic powder, and roast in a 375°F oven for twenty to thirty minutes.
- Peel and chop a medium sweet potato and add to your favorite bean-stew recipe.
- Chop a small sweet potato, a few beets and carrots, toss with oil, and roast in a 400°F oven for twenty-three to thirty minutes.
- Bake or boil a medium sweet potato, then mash the flesh with some tahini (sesame butter), lemon juice, and maple syrup.
- Peel and chop a small sweet potato and cook it overnight in a slow cooker with one cup of millet, four cups of water, and a pinch of sea salt.
- Serve baked sweet potatoes warm with a dollop of butter and a dab of unrefined honey and cinnamon.
- Peel and chop two sweet potatoes and place in a baking dish with a cup of orange juice, a handful of dried plums, sprinkle of cinnamon, and a drizzle of maple syrup. Bake covered at 350°F for forty minutes.
- Mash baked or boiled sweet potatoes with butter and rice milk and serve in place of white potatoes.

ALERT!

Avoid buying sweet potatoes displayed in the refrigerated section of the produce department, since cold temperature negatively alters their taste. The same applies to home storage, so do not store in the refrigerator, or they will become dry and mealy when cooked.

Serve with greens, in a stir-fry, as a topping for shepherd's pie, or as a base for filet mignon; the possibilities are endless, and the process can be simple and easy or as complicated as a sweet-potato Bundt cake. Whatever you decide to make, you will be doing your health, as well as your taste buds, a great service.

Sweet Potato Corn Cakes with Wasabi Cream

Silken tofu makes an excellent dairy-cream substitute for both sweet and savory recipes. The lemon juice and sweetener are used to mimic the sweet-sour taste of real cream. A finely grained salt can be substituted for the ume plum vinegar.

1. Preheat oven to 375°F. Pierce sweet-potato skin with a fork; bake until tender. Cool, then peel potato.

2. Dice green onions.

3. In a large mixing bowl, combine corn meal, baked sweet potato, corn kernels, and green onions.

4. In a small bowl, whisk egg; add to cornmeal mixture.

5. Use your hands to form mixture into patties; set on a plate.

6. Heat a small amount of oil; fry patties until brown, turning to do both sides.

7. Place on a platter and keep warm in a low-heat oven while making wasabi cream.

8. Combine tofu, wasabi powder, vinegar, lemon, and sweetener in a blender or food processor; purée until smooth.

9. Divide corn cakes on individual plates; top each cake with a dollop of wasabi cream.

Japanese Horseradish

Wasabi is a member of the cabbage family and is cultivated in Japan. Known as Japanese horseradish, the root has a hot, strong flavor that can get your nose irritated and running if too much is eaten. Wasabi is traditionally served with sushi (raw fish), and was once used medicinally as an antidote for food poisoning.

SERVES 6

170 calories
2.5 g fat
30 g carbohydrates
8 g protein
3 g sugars
4 g fiber

INGREDIENTS
1 large sweet potato
4 green onions
1 cup corn meal
⅔ cup corn kernels
1 egg
Light vegetable oil for frying
1 (10-ounce) package silken tofu
1 tablespoon plus 1 teaspoon
    wasabi powder
1 tablespoon ume plum vinegar
Juice of ½ lemon
Pinch of sweetener such as
    stevia or sugar

INGREDIENTS

3 large sweet potatoes
1 cup vegetable broth
4 cups water
1 cup red lentils
½ teaspoon cinnamon powder
*2 teaspoons garam masala
    (Indian spices)*
1 teaspoon cumin powder
½ can coconut milk
Sea salt to taste

Sweet Potato Coconut Soup

Despite the sweet ingredients, this is a hearty and delicious soup. Increase the coconut milk to a full can if you want a richer coconut flavor. If you want to take the time, you can toast the cinnamon, garam masala, and cumin in a dry skillet over medium-high heat. Once they release their aroma, remove from the heat and add to the soup mixture.

1. Peel and chop potatoes; rinse and drain lentils.
2. Combine all ingredients except coconut milk and salt in a large sauce-pan; bring to a boil.
3. Reduce heat; simmer until potatoes are tender.
4. Skim off any foam that forms on the surface while cooking.
5. When done, add coconut milk and sea salt.
6. Using a hand wand or a blender, purée until smooth.
7. Serve topped with toasted pine nuts and a dollop of plain yogurt.

Garam Masala

This combination of Indian spices is a traditional mix of cinnamon, roasted cumin, green or black cardamom, nutmeg, cloves, and mace. Garam masala helps warm the body and adds depth to a recipe. Make your own by buying the ingredients separately and grinding them in an electric coffee grinder or with a mortar and pestle.

CHAPTER 19

Walnuts Provide Essential Fatty Acids

As a Superfood, walnuts are the preferred choice here, but it should be clear that all nuts and seeds are small powerhouses in themselves. So powerful, in fact, that just by having a serving of nuts five times a week you can significantly reduce your risk for heart disease. In this chapter, you will learn about the walnut's tremendous nutritional benefits and how it can be used to raise the culinary standards of your menu plans.

What Makes Them Super

If for no other reason, the walnut is a Superfood because it's the only nut that provides significant amounts of alpha-linolenic acid, one of the three omega-3 fatty acids. Because your body cannot produce this acid, you need to provide it daily from other sources. All it takes is seven walnuts to supply your daily need for these essential fatty acids. Omega-3s are your brain food (see Chapter 11 for more on omega-3 fatty acids), and the high amounts of unsaturated fat helps lower the LDL, or bad cholesterol, in your blood and increase HDL, or good cholesterol. By eating a handful of walnuts a day, you can reduce your risk for heart disease.

FACT

Walnuts were the first whole food to receive a heart-health claim from the U.S. Food and Drug Administration. Have them as a snack or combine half a cup of fresh blueberries, half a cup of plain yogurt, five walnut halves, and a splash of vanilla extract; a delicious way to get your nutrients.

That is because the plant-derived omega-3s in walnuts are thought to lower blood triglyceride levels. Triglycerides are the fatty compounds that circulate in your blood, sticking to artery walls and eventually blocking the flow of blood to your heart. By eating walnuts, the omega-3 fatty acids are absorbed by the LDL particles, which in turn triggers the liver cells to remove this bad cholesterol from the blood. For every two walnut halves that you consume, the liver will lower the LDL particles by 1 percent. The many studies done on walnuts' ability to lower cholesterol levels have shown that for every 1 percent drop in LDL, there is a 2 percent decrease in coronary heart-disease risk. Just remember that more is not necessarily better, and eating too many walnuts can lead to considerable weight gain.

To determine if walnuts help lower LDL cholesterol, scientists at the University of California–Davis, their Agricultural Research Service, and the University of Padua, Italy, spent six and a half months feeding walnuts to 100 hamsters. The study was used to see if walnuts had any effect on the build up of endothelin, the compound known to cause inflammation in arteries and the sticky plaque that develops on blood-vessel walls. Using the common store-bought English walnut, they found that endothelin was successfully suppressed in the arteries of the test hamsters.

The History of Walnuts

It is hard to say with certainty which food-bearing tree is the oldest, but archeological digs have given that honor to the walnut tree, dating it back to 7000 B.C. It is thought to have originally grown wild in prehistoric Central Asia until invading Persians brought it home to what is now Iran. Over the centuries, both the meat of the walnut and its oil sustained invading armies, who spread it from one continent to another. At some point, the Romans gave it the name *Juglans regia*, Latin for "walnut tree." In those ancient times, the dark reddish-brown juice of the nut was used to dye wool for clothes and blankets.

In Greek mythology, the walnut tree shows up in the story of Dionysus, the god who fell in love with the mortal Carya. Upon her death, Dionysus bestowed immortality upon her by transforming her into a walnut tree. Upon hearing the news, Carya's father had a temple built in her honor, with the temple columns sculpted into the shapes of young women called caryatids, translated as "nymphs of the walnut tree."

ALERT!

Nuts were meant to be eaten fresh from the shell, and since it takes some time and effort to do so, you end up eating fewer walnuts than if they were already shelled for you. The work it takes to shell a few walnuts will be rewarded with a clean taste and oil-fresh nut.

Archaeological excavations reveal that eight thousand years ago, Neolithic tribes in the Perigord region of Southwest France were roasting walnuts over an open fire, no doubt using a stone to mash them with a few herbs and berries. This combination may have been ideal spread over the roasted shank of some exotic creature of the time.

Harvesting Walnuts

From first planting to first harvest, walnut trees can take twelve years to produce fruit. They are grown in orchards, and when mature the nuts fall to the ground or are removed by machines that shake the walnuts from the trees and then gather them up. From there, they are taken to the processing plant, washed, sun-dried, and stored for further drying.

To make walnut oil, the walnut kernels are ground and roasted in cast-iron kettles, resulting in a warm paste. This is then placed in a hydraulic press to separate out the oil, which is then filtered and bottled. The walnut fiber that remains is later sold to bakeries or used for cattle feed.

The Walnut's Nutrient Content

The walnut kernel is a highly concentrated food that contains all the protein, calories, and nutrients that the plant will need to grow into a tree thirty feet tall. Protected by a tough outer shell, it is a health-filled powerhouse that requires eating only a small amount of to get all of its benefits.

Although high in fatty acids, walnuts contain an abundance of vitamins and minerals. The nutrient content in one cup (100 grams) of walnuts includes:

CALORIES	654	POTASSIUM	441 mg
PROTEIN	15.23 g	ZINC	3.09 mg
FAT	65 g	COPPER	1.586 mg
CARBOHYDRATE	15.8 g	VITAMIN B6	0.537 mg
FIBER	6.7 g	VITAMIN C	1.3 mg
CALCIUM	98 mg	VITAMIN A	29.2 mcg
IRON	2.91 mg	VITAMIN E	2.916 mcg
MAGNESIUM	158 mg	VITAMIN A	41 IU
PHOSPHORUS	346 mg	FOLATE	98 mcg

If you are only eating ten walnut halves, the total fat content would be 18.5 grams, with 11.4 grams of omega-6 fatty acids. Those ten walnut halves would total 196.2 calories, 4.1 grams of carbohydrates, and 4.57 grams of protein. To work off those calories you would need to take a brisk thirty-minute walk around the neighborhood, which also helps ward off heart disease.

Walnut Oil

In the history of food oils, the majestic olive tree has transformed the landscape of countries in exchange for the commerce it generated. Walnut oil was just as significant, although more beneficial health-wise, than olive oil because of the high amounts of omega-3 fatty acids. As a folk medicine, walnut oil was used for everything from skin conditions and hair loss to sexual dysfunction and tuberculosis. As one of the richest sources of polyunsaturated fat found in nature, walnut oil contains 60 percent linoleic acid and 12 percent alpha-linolenic acid. One tablespoon a day used in your salad dressing or drizzled over cooked vegetables provides you with the government-recommended daily dose of these heart-healthy fatty acids.

A walnut looks like a little brain, with a left and right hemisphere, upper cerebrums, and lower cerebellums. Even the wrinkles or folds on the nut are just like the neocortex. Research shows that walnuts help develop over three dozen neurotransmitters for brain function.

Healing Properties of Walnuts

Every part of the walnut, with all its nutrients, has been used to benefit the human body in some way. The high B6 content helps alleviate premenstrual syndrome (PMS) in women. The vitamin E and zinc contents help keep skin smooth and supple, while the polyphenolic compounds help prevent allergic skin conditions such as eczema, especially in children.

If you take a close look, you will see that the nut itself is composed of three elements:

- First is the edible part, called the kernel, which is formed by two ivory-colored lobes or hemispheres covered by a dark-brown skin. This is the part that looks like the human brain.
- Second is the protective outer shell, or endocarp, which has been used over the centuries in a number of ways, including for the treatment of diarrhea, anemia, and hair loss.
- Third is the soft, fleshy husk, called the pericard. Versatile and beneficial, it has been used to make a stain for wood, as a hair dye, and as a fine liqueur. When boiled with the walnut leaves, it can be used medicinally as a remedy for anemia, rickets, and as a gargle for sore throats.

In China, walnuts have been used to treat impotency and to enrich the quality of sperm. Because they help strengthen kidney energy and moisten the lungs and intestines, walnuts are used as a remedy for inflammation, coughing, wheezing, and asthma difficulties.

ALERT!

Raw walnuts can harbor parasites, so it is better to soak them in a bath of one pint water to fifteen drops of grapefruit-seed extract or roast them before eating. The grapefruit-seed extract destroys parasites and bacteria, and the heat from roasting will help kill off the organisms as well.

Buying and Storage Tips

Walnuts sold in the shell should be fresh. Before buying, give them a shake, and if they rattle around inside the shell, they have become old and dry. Make sure the shells are undamaged and have no scars or wormholes. Look for newly harvested walnuts abundant in the fall and early winter.

Once they have been shelled, walnuts can go rancid quickly. When buying walnuts in bulk, keep them in tightly closed bags or jars and store in the refrigerator or freezer.

Stored in this way, walnuts will keep for six months and sometimes up to a year.

Cooking with Walnuts

Walnuts are extremely versatile for cooking purposes and can be used raw, roasted, or toasted to enhance the taste of a recipe, while providing needed nutrients. Some of the ways you can use walnuts are:

- Served roasted as an appetizer
- Coated with melted butter and honey to make a sweet, crunchy treat
- Added raw to salads
- Baked in muffins, cakes, and cookies
- Added to a bread or grain stuffing
- Chopped and stuffed into an apple, wrapped with puff pastry, and baked
- Combined with raisins, dried cranberries, pumpkin seeds, and peanuts for snacking
- Chopped and added to bread dough just before baking
- Puréed with water, maple syrup, and vanilla to make a rich cream sauce

ALERT!

Storing your walnuts in the freezer not only preserves their freshness, it keeps them out of reach for snacking purposes. Remove only the amount you will need for a day's use—about fourteen walnut halves. This way, you can eat your nuts without putting on extra weight.

When cooking with walnuts, be creative and let your imagination guide your taste buds. Although walnuts are high in fat, they are a good source of protein, which makes them a perfect food for individuals with weak appetites, the elderly, and those underweight due to illness. In these cases, and for those who cannot chew their food well, walnuts can be puréed in the blender with water, fruit, yogurt, and sweetener to make a delicious, healthy meal shake.

SERVES 8

180 calories
8 g fat
20 g carbohydrates
7 g protein
1 g sugars
6 g fiber

INGREDIENTS
½ cup walnuts
2 green onions
1½ cups cooked lentils
¾ cup cooked brown rice
3 tablespoons tamari soy sauce
¾ cup rolled oats
2 tablespoons almond butter

Lentil Walnut Pâté

1. Preheat oven to 375°F.

2. Chop walnuts and green onions in food processor.

3. Combine remaining ingredients in food processor; process until smooth.

4. Spoon into a lightly oiled 8" × 8" baking pan; bake for 30 minutes.

5. Cool and serve with crackers, rice cakes, or as a sandwich spread.

What to Do with Walnuts

Walnuts can be served roasted as an appetizer or coated with melted butter and honey to make a sweet, crunchy treat. Leave them raw and add them to salads, bake them in muffins and cookies, or toast them and serve over cooked grains or pasta. They can be added to stuffing (especially good with stuffed zucchinis or tomatoes), or you can chop them and add them to a baked apple or pear.

Roasted Walnut Tapenade

This is a versatile sauce that can be served over grilled chicken, meat, or lamb dishes. It will also serve well as a dip with vegetable crudités or thin slices of toasted bread.

1. Preheat oven to 350°F; roast walnuts until lightly browned, about 8 minutes. Remove from oven and allow to cool.

2. Chop walnuts in a food processor using the pulsing action.

3. Add olive paste and garlic; continue to pulse for a chunky texture.

4. With the chute open, add olive oil in a slow stream while you pulse ingredients.

5. Add water, vinegar, and sea salt; continue to pulse until you have a smooth paste-like consistency.

Roasting Walnuts

To roast walnuts, preheat the oven to 350°F. Spread the walnuts out on a baking sheet and place them in the oven for about 8–10 minutes. Make sure to set an oven timer to remind you when they are done. To toast them, place them in a skillet with a little bit of oil and cook over medium-low heat, stirring often.

MAKES 2 CUPS

1700 calories
176 g fat
20 g carbohydrates
16 g protein
6 g sugars
7 g fiber

INGREDIENTS
1 cup walnut halves
4 teaspoons olive paste
2 cloves garlic
½ cup extra-virgin olive oil
½ cup water
2 teaspoons balsamic vinegar
½ teaspoon sea salt

CHAPTER 20

Yogurt Replants Your Intestines

What a gift this food is to your overtaxed digestive system. Live, probiotic yogurt is a Superfood that has been around for over 4,000 years. Most beneficial of all is the abundance of live cultures found in yogurt that provide beneficial microflora where it is most needed, in your large intestine. In this chapter, you will learn how beneficial yogurt can be for your body, how it has sustained many cultures through the ages, and how you can make rich, delicious yogurt easily in your home.

What Makes It Super

Yogurt is high in ten important nutrients, including calcium. Yogurt is a health food that the whole family can enjoy for both its taste and its nutritional value. Eaten extensively in India, as well as many other countries, yogurt is considered a medicinal part of the Ayurvedic diet, especially freshly made probiotic-rich yogurt, which is abundant in good bacteria that aids digestion while destroying harmful organisms.

QUESTION?

What is an Ayurvedic diet?
This way of eating was first recorded in India some five thousand years ago. Living according to the Ayurvedic principles is part of an overall health plan, which includes a specific diet for each individual, supportive herbs for the body, meditation for the mind, yoga practice for strength and flexibility, and several different massage techniques to treat particular health issues.

Yogurt's super-beneficial organisms, plus its high nutrient content, are not the only benefits you receive from eating it on a weekly basis. Yogurt is a high-protein food that can also be used medicinally to help with intestinal bloating, stomach disorders, and to relieve both constipation and diarrhea.

The American Journal of Clinical Nutrition published an article by Simin Nikbin Meydani, Ph.D., in 2000, showing how yogurt may help make the immune system more resilient, help protect the intestinal tract, and help increase your resistance to immune-related diseases such as cancer and infection, particularly gastrointestinal infection. Again, this is due in part to the live and active cultures, called *Lactobacillus casei* (LAC), found in yogurt.

The History of Yogurt

Legend claims that an angel taught Abraham how to make yogurt. Yogurt is made by adding friendly bacterial cultures, called probiotics, to cow, sheep, or goat milk and allowing it to ferment for eight to ten hours. This fermentation process changes the milk sugar, called lactose, into lactic acid, imparting a tart, sour flavor and a thick, custard-like consistency. The original Turkish name for yogurt, *yoghurmak,* means "to thicken." Whether yogurt first originated in the Middle East is unclear, but what is known is that with the domestication of animals came the process of fermenting their milk. Yogurt and other fermented foods have been a staple in the diets of Asian, Russian, Middle Eastern, and Eastern European countries for centuries. However, it is only as recent as the twentieth century that research carried out by Dr. Elie Metchnikoff identified the benefits of eating lactic-acid producing bacteria found in yogurt, thus increasing longevity in people from cultures that eat fermented dairy products. Today, yogurt plays an important role not only in a variety of different world cuisines, but also in the diets of vegetarians who depend on yogurt as an important source of protein.

Yogurt's Nutrient Content

Eating freshly made yogurt is especially beneficial for individuals following a vegetarian diet, since one cup of yogurt provides 13 grams of protein, along with a nice dose of B complex, calcium, potassium, iodine, phosphorus, and folate. When you have to take antibiotics (which can destroy the beneficial intestinal flora), it is best to eat freshly made yogurt to help replace the good bacteria. This will help prevent any future digestive problems due to a lack of healthy bacterial cultures. Because these live organisms supply plenty of enzymatic action, fresh yogurt can be digested in approximately one hour, as compared to the three hours it can take to digest other milk products. If you have trouble digesting milk, you may find that fresh yogurt, especially made from goat or sheep's milk, may be easier to digest and will actually aid in your digestion.

Fresh yogurt is a very good source of calcium, phosphorus, riboflavin, iodine, vitamin B12, pantothenic acid, zinc, potassium, protein, and molybdenum.

Nutritionally, 8 ounces of low-fat yogurt provides:

CALORIES	155	ZINC	2.18 mg
FAT	4 g	PROTEIN	13 g
CHOLESTEROL	14.95 mg	CALCIUM	450 mg
SODIUM	104 mg	MAGNESIUM	42.75
CARBOHYDRATES	17.25 g	POTASSIUM	572.8 mg
SUGAR	17.25 g		

As you can see, yogurt provides protein, carbohydrate, and fat in a balanced proportion, which makes for a good breakfast or snack with some added fiber in the form of muesli, flax meal, or fresh fruit.

In a study of women volunteers, it was found that consuming 3 ounces of probiotic yogurt daily significantly lowered their LDL cholesterol, while raising their HDL cholesterol because probiotic yogurt contains the beneficial bacteria *Lactobacillus casei*.

Healing Properties of Yogurt

Yogurt has a long history of therapeutic benefits for the gastrointestinal tract, particularly the large intestine. Research studies have shown that individuals with a compromised immune system, such as the elderly and the very ill, may enhance their immune response to immune-related diseases by increasing their yogurt consumption to three times per week.

The beneficial bacteria in yogurt, *Lactobacillus acidophilus*, binds to cholesterol in the intestine and prevents it from being absorbed into the bloodstream. The reduction of blood cholesterol lowers the risk for heart disease. Consuming probiotic yogurt may decrease your risk of heart disease by 7–10 percent.

The many scientific studies on yogurt have revealed some wonderful ways in which this fermented milk can help with certain health issues. For example:

- Eating yogurt may help prevent vaginal yeast infections. In one study, women who had frequent yeast infections ate 8 ounces of yogurt daily for six months. Researchers reported that a threefold decrease in infections was seen in these women.
- Eating 1 cup of yogurt daily that contains the active *Lactobacillus acidophilus* has been shown to lower total cholesterol by more than 3 percent.
- Probiotic yogurt can be beneficial for individuals whose appetite is diminished, as in the case of cancer patients undergoing chemotherapy.
- Probiotic yogurt also helps stop chronic diarrhea, by binding the lactobacillus to the walls of the large intestine to fight off any harmful bacteria.
- According to French research studies, consuming yogurt is similar to eating adequate amounts of fiber, showing that yogurt containing the active bifidophilus bacteria can act as a substitute for fiber and help to relieve constipation.
- Probiotic yogurt benefits intestinal issues and helps relieve symptoms pertaining to Irritable Bowel Syndrome by increasing the number of friendly bacteria and preventing the growth of harmful bacteria. Individuals who are lactose-intolerant should avoid cow-milk yogurt, and test their tolerance of goat- or sheep-milk yogurt instead.
- Probiotic yogurt is used to successfully treat *Helicobacter pylori,* the bacterium responsible for most ulcers.
- A study published in the *International Journal of Obesity* indicates that including yogurt in your daily diet can help reduce body fat and minimize loss of muscle, good news for those on a weight-loss diet. It is thought that the calcium in yogurt reduces fat cells' ability to store fat, so your cells burn more and less is produced in the liver.
- A study published in the *American Journal of Clinical Nutrition* indicates that enjoying full-fat yogurt may significantly reduce risk for

colorectal cancer. Although high in saturated fat, the full-fat yogurt contains a number of potentially cancer-preventive factors, including a protective fat called conjugated linoleic acid (CLA), which has also been shown to be cardio-protective.

- Consuming just 3.2 ounces (90 grams) of yogurt twice a day can help with bad breath by lowering levels of hydrogen sulfide and other volatile sulfide compounds, and helping to eliminate tongue-coating bacteria and reduce dental plaque formation, cavities, and risk for gingivitis.

You can save 46 grams of fat per cup by using plain, low-fat yogurt in place of full-fat mayonnaise or sour cream, in equal amounts, for dips and dressings. The flavor and consistency will be similar, and you will be doing your heart and hips a big favor.

Buying and Storage Tips

Freshly made yogurt is very different from the commercial, store-bought yogurt that has been sitting on grocery shelves, and is loaded with sugar and flavorings. According to The Council of Maharishi Ayurveda Physicians, store-bought yogurt no longer contains the fresh, active bacteria that homemade yogurt has. The best yogurt to buy is made from organic milk and contains the friendly bacteria from live, active cultures. Avoid buying yogurt products that may have been pasteurized, as the high heat kills the beneficial lactic-acid bacteria in the yogurt, rendering it useless for health purposes.

Any yogurt that you eat should contain the live organisms *Lactobacillus Bulgaricus* and *Streptococcus Thermopholis*. These are the lactic-acid bacteria usually used to make yogurt in the United States. Store-bought yogurt more than likely has traveled thousands of miles to its destination, then is stacked on refrigerated shelves to await your purchase. Also be sure to check the container's expiration date to ensure that it is still fresh. Avoid yogurts that have artificial colors, flavorings, or sweeteners, and fruit-filled yogurts that can contain too much refined sugar to make it a healthy product. Keep yogurt in the refrigerator, and if unopened, it will stay fresh for about one week past the expiration date.

Yogurt in Your Diet

There are numerous ways to include yogurt in your recipes. Here are a few tips to consider:

- Sweeten plain yogurt with maple syrup and use to top a serving of warm spice cake.
- Add plain yogurt to grains after cooking to make them easier to digest.
- Use plain yogurt in combination with sweet vegetables such as beets or carrots to make delicious cream soups that can be served either hot or cold (see recipe at the end of this chapter).
- Combine plain yogurt with minced cucumber and dill and serve as a side dish with spicy foods.
- Layer plain or sweetened yogurt with ripe fruit and jam in a tall parfait glass and serve as a light dessert (see recipe at the end of this chapter).
- Whisk plain yogurt together with extra-virgin olive oil, white-wine vinegar, a pinch of sweetener, and your favorite dried herb and serve as a salad dressing or over steamed vegetables.
- Substitute plain yogurt for milk and serve over your favorite cold cereal or granola mixture. Top with fresh berries or sliced ripe banana for a real breakfast treat.
- Replace full-fat sour cream with low-fat creamy yogurt as a topping for baked potatoes. Sprinkle with chives or chopped green onions, a dash of your favorite dried herb, and some salt and pepper to taste.
- Use yogurt to replace heavy cream to thicken sauces. Add the yogurt at the end of the cooking process and remove from the heat, letting the sauce sit for a moment while the yogurt absorbs the flavors.
- Due to yogurt's high acidity content, it makes an excellent tenderizing marinade for meat, lamb, and poultry.
- Try using yogurt in your baked goods, to help keep the flour moist with a firm texture.

To create the type of yogurt known as Greek-style yogurt, all you need to do is line a strainer with cheesecloth and set it in a medium-size bowl. Pour the yogurt into the cheesecloth and place the bowl with strainer in the refrigerator. Let the yogurt drain overnight, and in the morning you will have the most wonderful thick, creamy yogurt to use as a sour cream substitute or simply enjoy with fruit for your breakfast.

ALERT!

Purchase organic yogurt when possible, as the commercial milk produced today comes from cows treated with recombinant bovine growth hormone (rBGH). This hormone has been shown to raise the levels of insulin-like growth factor 1 (IGF-1), possibly leading to breast cancer in women.

Homemade Yogurt

Making yogurt at home is a simple and easy process resulting in rich, delicious yogurt that is high in the bacteria beneficial for your digestive system. It is also far less expensive to make your own yogurt than to purchase prepackaged yogurt from a store. You can make the yogurt without an electric yogurt maker, but they are relatively inexpensive and make the whole process much easier. You can put it all together before going to bed at night, and in the morning you can wake up to a batch of fresh yogurt.

The tools you will need to make your own yogurt include:

- Kitchen thermometer
- Yogurt maker with glass or ceramic cups
- 1–2 quarts organic cow or goat milk (you can use either low-fat, skim, or whole milk but in general the higher the milk-fat level the creamier the yogurt will be)
- Small container plain, unsweetened yogurt with live cultures or a yogurt starter you can purchase from your local health food store

Begin by heating the milk in a ceramic saucepan to about 170°F–180°F. Use your thermometer to check the temperature. This is done to kill any harmful bacteria that might be in the milk, and to change the milk protein in a way that allows it to culture and firm up.

Stir the milk continuously and watch carefully so the temperature does not exceed 180°F. You will need to sterilize your containers by pouring boiling water into them, letting them sit for five minutes, then discarding the hot water.

When the temperature in the milk reaches 170°F–180°F, turn off the burner and continue to stir it until it cools. Stirring the milk for another 2–3 minutes will prevent the milk from scorching the bottom of your pan.

ALERT!

Avoid using aluminum pans and bowls when working with yogurt, since its high acid content reacts negatively with aluminum. Best not to use aluminum for cooking at all, as it is known to leach into the food and cause possible health problems—one suspected, but not yet proven to be, Alzheimer's disease.

When the milk has cooled to 105°F–110°F, first mix the plain yogurt in its container to a smooth consistency, then add it to the pot of warm milk. Stir it for a few minutes while the yogurt dissolves into the milk. This will allow the beneficial bacteria to spread throughout the milk and begin to grow. Now pour the inoculated milk into the sterilized containers and place the containers into the yogurt maker. Follow the maker's instructions for fermentation time, but normally it takes about six hours to set up. After about six hours the yogurt should be firm. You can test it by gently turning the container to see if it keeps its shape. There will be some whey liquid on the top that you can either pour off or just mix into the yogurt before you eat it. Cap each yogurt container and refrigerate. They will keep in the fridge for up to two weeks. You can use one of these live yogurts as a starter for your next batch, but you must do so within five to seven days. You can also freeze a container of the fresh yogurt, then let it thaw before inoculating your next batch of the sterilized milk.

660 calories
27 g fat
81 g carbohydrates
25 g protein
56 g sugars
9 g fiber

INGREDIENTS

1 cup plain yogurt
½ teaspoon vanilla extract
1 tablespoon maple syrup
6 walnut halves
1 cup fresh sliced peaches
½ cup granola

Crunchy Peach Parfait

For the most health benefits, make sure to use organic yogurt containing live cultures of bacteria. Using organic for this delicious dessert can extend to the other ingredients as well.

1. Spoon yogurt into a small bowl; add vanilla and maple syrup; mix well.

2. Lightly chop walnuts into large pieces; set aside.

3. In a long-stemmed parfait glass, begin with a layer of yogurt, then sliced peaches, and finally the granola. Repeat layering to top of glass.

4. Sprinkle walnuts on top and serve chilled.

Working with Yogurt

Mixing yogurt in a blender can cause it to break down and become liquefied. Instead, either whisk it gently or fold the yogurt into the mixture when incorporating it into most recipes.

Carrot Yogurt Soup

To shorten your cooking time, consider using a pressure cooker, or if you have time to spare, follow steps 1–5 and add to a slow cooker, allowing the carrots to cook on low for 4 hours. When tender, purée the ingredients, then add the yogurt, dill, honey, and pepper.

1. Chop onion; mince garlic. In a large soup pot, sauté onion and garlic in oil until soft.

2. Add mustard seed, tumeric, ginger, cumin, sea salt, cayenne, and cinnamon.

3. Cook for several minutes over medium heat, stirring constantly.

4. Slice carrots; add to soup pot with lemon juice and water.

5. Cover tightly; simmer until carrots are tender, about 30 minutes.

6. Purée cooked carrots and cooking liquid using a blender wand, or purée in batches in a blender; return to cooking pot.

7. Add a small amount of carrot purée to yogurt, warming it slowly; whisk yogurt, dill, honey, and black pepper into carrot purée.

8. Heat mixture on low, but do not boil. Ladle into soup bowls and add a fresh dollop of yogurt and a sprinkle of dill for color.

Cooking with Yogurt

The beneficial bacteria in yogurt can be destroyed by high temperatures. When cooking with yogurt, do not add to a boiling mixture. Instead, stir a small amount of the hot ingredients into the yogurt in small increments, allowing the yogurt to warm gradually. To complete, gently stir the warmed yogurt into the hot mixture.

SERVES 8

140 calories
8 g fat
14 g carbohydrates
4 g protein
10 g sugars
2 g fiber

INGREDIENTS

1 medium onion
1 clove garlic
4 tablespoons vegetable oil
½ teaspoon mustard seed
½ teaspoon turmeric
½ teaspoon dried ginger
½ teaspoon cumin
½ teaspoon sea salt
¼ teaspoon cayenne
¼ teaspoon cinnamon
1 pound carrots
1 tablespoon fresh lemon juice
2 cups water
2 cups low-fat plain yogurt
2 tablespoons fresh dill, or 1 teaspoon dried
1 tablespoon honey
¼ teaspoon black pepper

CHAPTER 21

Fermented Foods: Essential Digestive Aids

In the previous chapter, you learned how important it was to include a fermented food like yogurt in your diet, and that every culture in the world eats some form of fermented foods to aid in digestion. That's how important these foods are for our overall health and well-being. In this chapter, you will discover how important and necessary fermented (also known as cultured) foods are for supporting your digestive and immune systems, while enhancing the flavor of food and preserving food for long periods of time.

What Makes Them Super

A serving size for cultured foods is just enough to provide the proper enzymes to break down the food and make the nutrients available for absorption in the small intestine. Sweet, sour, and salty pickles are common in Indian, Korean, Chinese, and Japanese cuisine; in North and Central Europe you will find sauerkraut as well as pickles; the Mediterranean countries serve a small glass of red wine, cider, or beer with meals to provide digestive enzymes; and in America we eat and drink all of those foods, and have no idea why we are doing so.

When foods are fermented, the bacteria, yeasts, or molds used in the process predigest the food, meaning they break down the carbohydrates, fats, and proteins to create probiotics, friendly, life-giving bacteria beneficial to the gastrointestinal system. Your body needs these super probiotics in order to function properly; they help keep your immune system strong and support your overall digestive health. Fermented foods are enzyme-rich and alive with microorganisms, known as friendly microflora. These colonize your intestines and work to keep the unfriendly intestinal organisms under control, such as yeast, parasites, viruses, and unfriendly bacteria. With a healthy, well-supported internal ecology, your immune system isn't being overworked by trying to keep the unfriendly organisms under control. Instead, it can take care of fighting infection and monitoring diseased cells in the body.

FACT

A healthy gastrointestinal tract (GI) is critical to a strong immune system. Diets rich in fermented foods work together with whole grains, fruits, vegetables, nuts, seeds, beans, and legumes to maintain a strong and healthy body.

In a brief overview, fermented foods:

- Aid in digestion
- Promote healthy flora in your digestive tract
- Produce beneficial enzymes

- Help your body absorb vitamins (C and B12 in particular), minerals, and omega-3 fatty acids
- Regulate the level of acidity in the digestive tract
- Act as antioxidants
- Contain the same isothiocyanates found in cruciferous vegetables, and therefore fight and prevent cancer

Fermented foods can be purchased in the refrigerated section of your local natural-foods store or you can easily make a batch in your own kitchen.

Healing Foods

Fermented foods come in many guises: Some you might eat on a regular basis, such as aged cheese, beer, and wine; while others can have medicinal qualities that aid in the healing process, such as raw sauerkraut, pickles, kefir, and acidophilus.

FACT

The fermented condiment known as kimchi can be traced back as much as 3,000 years ago, when it consisted of simple salted vegetables. It wasn't until the twelfth century that Koreans began to include spices and other flavors for taste, and chili peppers were added sometime in the early seventeenth century.

Let's take a look at a few foods considered beneficial for healing the intestines and helping to maintain your health:

- **Acidophilus.** *Lactobacillus acidophilus* is a microflora commonly found in dairy products and fermented vegetables. *Lactobacillus planatarum* and *Lactobacillus brevis* are also helpful microflora found in fermented or cultured vegetables. These bacteria are destroyed when heated. Acidophilus is alive with microflora to aid your digestive system, so for a healthy gut, and therefore a healthy body, take acidophilus capsules each morning on an empty stomach.

- **Cultured vegetables.** Cultured vegetables are made with a base of shredded cabbage and a few other grated vegetables, such as carrots and beets. Packed tightly into an airtight ceramic, glass, or stainless steel container, they are left to ferment at room temperature for a week or more. The process pickles the vegetables, creating a more acidic environment for the friendly bacteria to reproduce.

- **Coconut-water kefir.** Made from the water of young, green coconuts and kefir starter, this is used by Donna Gates, author of *The Body Ecology Diet,* for her clients to stop cravings for sugar; aid digestion of foods; tonify the intestines; cleanse the liver, endocrine system, adrenals, thyroid, pituitary, and ovaries; and increase energy.

- **Kefir.** A fermented milk product similar to, but considered more nutritious and medicinally beneficial than yogurt, kefir has more friendly bacteria, including *Lactobacillus caucasus, leuconostoc, acetobacter,* and *strepococcus.* It can be used to restore the inner ecology of the digestive system following antibiotic treatment. It may be difficult to find kefir in your local natural-foods store. Because kefir needs to be made from kefir grains and not a powdered starter (often done commercially), it is best to make your own at home.

- **Kimchi.** A traditional Korean dish made by fermenting vegetables such as Chinese cabbage, ginger, garlic, and hot chili peppers. High in fiber yet low in calories, it provides 80 percent of the daily requirement of vitamin C and carotene. Also rich in enzymes, vitamin A, thiamine (B1), riboflavin (B2), calcium, and iron and loaded with friendly *lactobacilli* bacterial cultures.

- **Kombucha.** Considered to be a fountain of youth elixir, kombucha dates back to the Chinese Tsin Dynasty of 221 B.C. It is a colony of yeast and bacteria embedded in a pure cellulose "pancake" made up of beneficial microorganisms and usually fermented for thirty days. During this time, essential nutrients form, such as enzymes, probiotics, amino acids, antioxidants, and polyphenols. Together they work to create balance and vitality in the body.

- **Miso.** A powerful and nutritious food, miso is a Japanese staple made from rice, soybeans, barley, or chickpeas. It is a fermented paste aged in wooden kegs for specific lengths of time. A light-colored miso is aged for one to two months, while the darker varieties are aged for up to two years. It is loaded with beneficial enzymes, with traces of B12 and antioxidants. It is said to be helpful in removing radiation from the body.

- **Pickles.** Pickles contain large amounts of *lactobacilli* bacteria, which are important to the digestion of grains and vegetables. Scientific research has shown that these friendly bacteria survive the trip through the acidic juices of the stomach to the small intestine. In the small intestine, they aid pancreatic enzymes in the transformation of dextrin (a carbohydrate found in grains) into simple sugars that can be readily used by the body. Other benefits of pickles relate to specific types, such as the alkalinizing properties of ume plum and the high niacin content of bran pickles. One property common to all pickles is high fiber, which is important to proper intestinal cleansing and function.

- **Sauerkraut.** Consists mostly of fermented green or red cabbage seasoned with herbs and salt. An excellent source of enzymes and *lactobacillus* bacteria.

- **Tempeh.** A staple food in Indonesia, where it is traditionally prepared with soy beans or a certain variety of peanut fermented with the mold *Rhizopus oligosporus*. The culturing process binds the soybeans or nuts together with a thick, white myselium of new mold growth to form a cake. It has an earthy aroma, with a taste resembling a cross between mushrooms and fresh yeast. One delicious way to prepare tempeh is to slice small cubes, marinate it in a small amount of ume plum vinegar, then fry the cubes in unrefined coconut oil.

- **Umeboshi plums.** Japanese plums pickled in salt to create a powerful alkalinizing food. Umeboshi plums help to neutralize fatigue, stimulate digestion, help detoxify the body, and balance a sweet tooth. Taken the morning after, it is an effective hangover remedy, and helps to purify water and help with dysentery issues such as food poisoning or E. coli exposure.

- **Vinegar.** Specifically, apple cider vinegar, which is a legend in its own time. Rich in beneficial enzymes and used medicinally for centuries, apple cider vinegar helps strengthen the immune system, control weight, promote good digestion, balance blood pH levels, and remove toxic sludge from the body. Externally, it can be used to soothe irritated skin and relieve tired, sore muscles.

All the pickles and sauerkraut you've eaten over the years have been much more than just a taste addition to a meal; they have actually helped you digest the hot dog or hamburger you ordered with "the works." Try to always include some form of fermented food with your meal, and your digestive system will thank you.

FACT

Nobel prize–winner Alexander Solzhenitsyn wrote in his autobiography that drinking the fermented liquid kombucha helped him survive the Siberian slave camps of the former Soviet Union.

The History of Fermented Foods

Humans have been fermenting foods as far back as can be traced. Primarily, they were fermented to improve holding and storing properties of foods. Foods like the milk from camels, buffalo, goats, sheep, or cows, were fermented naturally to produce an acidic-tasting food drink. This is how some of the first yogurts were produced in goat bags, dropped over the back of camels in the hot deserts of North Africa. Temperatures reaching 40°C or 110°F were ideal for lactic acid-producing bacteria to go to work. Since this period, many cultures have fermented a wide variety of foods in the need to develop new tastes and improving shelf life.

Food historians have attempted to trace the pickling process (preserving foods in a salt-brine solution) back to ancient Egypt. Herodotus wrote that the Babylonians and Egyptians pickled fish, poultry, and geese in the fifth century B.C.; and one cannot dismiss the pickling of fruits and vegetables originating in India, where limes and lemons were pickled whole.

Finding the origins of fermented foods is not an easy trail to follow, but suffice it to say, fermenting and pickling of foods has been a long and essential part of the history of humankind.

Discovering the Health Benefits

In 1910, Nobel prize-winning Russian bacteriologist Elie Metchnikoff noticed that Bulgarians had an average lifespan of eighty-seven years, exceptional for the early 1900s, and that 4 out of every 1,000 lived past 100 years of age. His curiosity aroused, Metchnikoff researched the Bulgarian lifestyle and found the one significant difference in their lifestyle was their large consumption of fermented milks. Later, it was noted by other researchers that the Hunzas of Kashmir and the Georgians of the former Soviet Union also lived long and healthy lives due to fermented milk products. Males would commonly live to 100-plus years and still be able to participate in events such as polo, and women were working in the farm fields at 100 years or greater. Both these cultures were very active, with sound, basic diets; but significant elements in their diets were yogurt, buttermilk, and kefir, all rich in active *lactobacilli* bacteria.

FACT

The use of vinegar was mentioned in the writings of the Assyrians, Greeks, and Romans as an important medicine recommended to aid digestion and promote a healthy liver and gallbladder. Also, Hippocrates, the "father of all medicine," frequently recommended a blend of vinegar and honey called oxymel, used for its healing benefits.

Fermented Foods Today

The group of bacteria from the *lactobacilli* family, *Lactobacillus acidophilus* and *bifido* bacterium, have been extensively researched, revealing that together the activity of these two bacteria appear to play a role in balancing the intestinal flora of the digestive tract and contributing to good health. Today, fermented foods are recommended by nutritionists and many doctors, to be eaten on a daily basis to ensure a balanced intestinal ecology. With so many factors contributing to gastrointestinal problems, including the taking of antibiotics, birth control pills, contaminated water, artificial sweeteners, alcohol, and the abundant consumption of refined sugar and high-fructose corn syrup, it's a wonder the digestive system can function at all. Fermented foods are truly the antidote to our modern refined and processed diet.

> The Georgian people of the former Soviet Union are particularly strong believers that health is very dependent on fermented milk consumption. A famous Georgian saying goes, "If you want to live long, drink more sour milk," meaning yogurt, kefir, and certain cheese products.

Fermented Foods' Nutrient Content

There are many trace nutrients in fermented foods, but what is most important are the beneficial cultures and probiotics that they contain. Rather than try to list the nutrient content for so many different foods, here is a list of the many contributing organisms that make up fermented foods:

- **Beneficial probiotics:** Due to the prolific presence of pesticides, antibiotics, and preservative in our foods, the beneficial microorganisms present in your body are being destroyed and killed off on a regular basis. These friendly microbes play a huge role in our digestive and immune systems' abilities to function properly. It is crucial that they are replenished from natural sources like kefir, yogurt, cultured vegetables, and apple cider vinegar .
- **Live active enzymes:** Active enzymes are generally only found in foods that have not been cooked, processed, or refined. They are the "spark plugs" for the body's cells because they put life back in your body. They are available in live and fermented foods and help in the digestion of foods and the absorption of nutrients.
- **L-theanine:** This is an amino acid that is known to promote relaxation and decrease mental and physical stress without inducing drowsiness.
- **Polyphenols:** These are antioxidants that fight off the free radicals that stress the body and cause disease to occur.

- **Organic acids**: These nutrients can help promote tissue and blood alkalinity and help normalize the natural process of homeostasis throughout the body.
- **Lactic acid:** This acid helps maintain healthy digestive action (through the probiotic *lactobacilli*) and with glycogen production by the liver.
- **Acetic acid:** This is an antiseptic and inhibitor of pathogenic bacteria.
- **Glucuronic acid:** This acid is normally produced by a healthy liver, is a powerful detoxifier, and can be readily converted into glucosamines, the foundation of our skeletal system.
- **Usnic acid:** This acid has selective antibiotic qualities which can partly deactivate viruses.
- **Oxalic acid:** This acid encourages the intercellular production of energy, and is a preservative.
- **Malic acid:** Malic acid helps detoxify the liver.
- **Butyric acid:** This acid protects human cellular membranes, and combined with gluconic acid, strengthens the walls of the gut in order to combat yeast infections such as candida.
- **Nucleic acids:** These acids are like RNA and DNA, that transmit information to the cells on how to perform correctly and regenerate.

Remember, it doesn't take much to be effective. A few slices of pickle, a small amount of sauerkraut or kimchi, a dollop of yogurt, or a salad dressing with unrefined apple cider vinegar is all you will need to get the job done properly. Just have those small amounts on a daily basis with each meal.

Healing Properties of Fermented Foods

The beneficial probiotics found in fermented foods are essential for your digestive health, especially when you are sick and taking antibiotics. Antibiotics are designed to kill off all bacteria, both the good and the bad. You want the bad that is making you sick to be destroyed, but you don't want to lose the good *lactobacilli* bacteria. The reason many women get yeast infections when they take antibiotics is due to the killing off of these good bacteria. Fermented foods containing live probiotics reintroduce the good bacteria into your intestines, so that while the bad bacteria is being destroyed by the antibiotics, you are making sure the friendly bacteria is being repopulated.

Buying and Storage Tips

Often, what you will find in the food stores has been pasteurized, such as commercial sauerkraut or pickles, which kills the beneficial bacteria. When buying fermented foods, look in the refrigerated section and make sure the label states that they contain live or active cultures. When storing fermented foods, keep them in the refrigerator and use within one month of purchase to ensure the live cultures. However, if the fermented cabbage or kombucha drink loses its carbonated zing, do not be concerned; they may go a bit flat, but the probiotics are still alive and well.

FACT

Lactobacilli have other functions in the digestive system. In the large intestine, they help synthesize B and K vitamins and inhibit the growth of putrefying bacteria. Dr. Phillip Evans, author of *The Biochemical Basis for Disease and Disorders,* feels that an overall sense of well-being cannot be experienced without a healthy population of intestinal flora.

Commercial Versus Homemade

Culturing your own vegetables is really your best option, even though it could take some time and effort. This gives you total control over what you are eating, and ensures the foods used in the process are of the highest quality. Most commercial products are created with taste in mind, and not their medicinal effectiveness. In the case of yogurt, this means that commercial yogurt usually has a high lactose content and is loaded with sugar. Homemade yogurt can be made to eliminate a great deal of lactose and will be much fresher than anything you can buy in a store. If the taste isn't to your liking, you can add fresh fruit and or honey to sweeten it. Store-bought kefir has the same problems: You have no control over the lactose content in the end product. As for fermented vegetables, such as sauerkraut, most commercial products have been pasteurized and do not contain live cultures.

The pasteurization process not only kills the beneficial bacteria, it may also destroy many of the enzymes and nutrients. Commercial sauerkraut may also contain a fair amount of unnatural preservatives. Fermenting your own foods at home is a healthier, less expensive, and more enjoyable option and produces a far superior product to anything you could purchase in a store.

1450 calories
14 g fat
322 g carbohydrates
33 g protein
31 g sugars
36 g fiber

INGREDIENTS

4 pounds ginger root
1 tablespoon sea or pickling salt
    (no iodine)
1 cup distilled water
½ package yogurt starter

Ginger Pickles

Ginger is a wonderful root often used medicinally for digestive issues, nausea, and seasickness. The Japanese serve it alongside raw sushi to aid in digestion. Try including a few pieces with your meals for best effect.

1. Peel and cut ginger into very thin slices.

2. Using a wooden mallet or the flat side of a large knife, pound ginger slices to expel juices.

3. Place juices and pounded ginger into a glass jar; mix with salt and water.

4. Add yogurt starter; seal jar.

5. Let it sit at room temperature 3–5 days, then store in refrigerator.

Fermenting Tips

When fermenting foods, avoid using a plastic or aluminum crock. This goes for your utensils as well. Instead, be sure to use glass or enamel pottery specifically meant for making sauerkraut and pickles.

Traditional Sauerkraut

You can chop the cabbage in a food processor or grind it in a juicer that has a grinding attachment. Another way is to pound the cabbage with a wooden mallet to release the juices.

1. Chop cabbage; set aside 5–6 whole leaves.

2. Place in a ceramic or glass crock or a stainless steel container, filling to just three-quarters full. (This leaves room for the fermentation to cause expansion.)

3. Add salt and herbs; mix well.

4. Place whole leaves across top of cabbage to cover.

5. Gently press down on cabbage leaves to compress; place a plate on cabbage leaves and add a weight such as a few canned goods on top of plate.

6. Place crock or bowl in a room with a temperature of 59°F–71°F for one week.

7. At the end of the week, remove weights and cabbage leaves, as well as any moldy vegetables under the leaves.

8. Spoon sauerkraut into glass jars and place in refrigerator.

Serving Sauerkraut

Take a few tablespoons of the fermented cabbage with your meals to aid in digestion and the reimplantation of friendly microflora. Do not heat or cook the sauerkraut, which will only destroy the live organisms you need.

MAKES 3 CUPS

220 calories
1 g fat
51 g carbohydrates
13 g protein
30 g sugars
20 g fiber

INGREDIENTS
1 medium cabbage (red or green)
2 tablespoons pickling or sea salt
2 tablespoons pickling herbs such as juniper berries

CHAPTER 22

Ten Super-Duper Recipes

Hopefully, you have read through this book and tried some of the recipes at the end of each chapter. To continue eating these high-quality foods, this chapter brings together the twenty Superfoods in recipes sure to please your discerning palate. Quick and easy to make, here are ten meals you can serve to your family, friends, or bring along to a potluck dinner. Loaded with nutrition and full of taste, you can't go wrong including these recipes as part of your daily diet.

quinoa, apples, and walnuts

A soft grain with a touch of sweetness from the dressing makes this dish a surprise to your taste buds. Protein, antioxidants, and omega-3 fatty acids provide your body with a daily dose of certain vitamins, minerals, and fiber. Although it may seem like a lot of ingredients, this recipe comes together quickly and easily, without much effort for the chef.

SERVES 8

230 calories
17 g fat
18 g carbohydrates
4 g protein
8 g sugars
4 g fiber

INGREDIENTS

⅓ cup quinoa
1 cup water
1 bunch mesclun greens, rinsed
2 apples, cut into pieces
1 red pepper, chopped
¼ cup olive oil
⅛ cup apple cider vinegar
2 cloves garlic
1 tablespoon agave syrup
2 pitted dates
⅛ teaspoon cinnamon
2 tablespoons water
1 cup chopped walnuts

Quinoa Apple Salad

Although you may not think to combine fruits and vegetables, in this instance the combination of tastes works perfectly together.

1. Rinse quinoa in cool running water.

2. Combine water and quinoa in a saucepan.

3. Cover, bring to a boil, and simmer on low heat until all water is absorbed.

4. Meanwhile, rinse and dry greens and set aside.

5. Core and chop apple. Remove seeds from pepper and chop; set aside.

6. In a food processor, purée oil, vinegar, garlic, agave, dates, and cinnamon.

7. Add water; thin to dressing consistency.

8. Pour dressing around bottom of a large salad bowl.

9. Place mesclun in bowl. Add peppers, apples, cooled quinoa, and walnuts.

10. Toss well before serving.

Agave Syrup

Agave syrup is a low-glycemic sweetener made from the sap of the blue agave plant. Blue agave is higher in fructose-producing carbohydrates than other types of agave and is considered to be the finest in the world. Quality-brand tequilas are also produced from the blue agave plant.

garlic, beans, parsley, and avocado

What you'll get in this recipe is a good serving of plant-based protein, vitamins C and A, copper, iodine, iron, magnesium, sodium, chlorophyll, calcium, sulfur, and quality fat to keep all your parts well lubricated. You don't really need the tortillas, just layer the chili onto the cooked brown rice then top it with some cheese and avocado. A dollop of plain yogurt would take this nutrient-rich dish over the top.

Two-Bean Chili Wraps

Here is a vegetarian chili that tastes great and introduces you to the soy food called tempeh. Made from fermented soybeans, tempeh is high in B vitamins and is an excellent protein substitute for saturated fatty meats.

1. In a large saucepan, heat oil; sauté garlic and onion until soft.

2. Add cumin, turmeric, and cayenne; cook until roasted, 1 minute.

3. Add tempeh; cook 3 minutes.

4. Add zucchini, red pepper, and diced tomatoes; stir well.

5. Add beans and olives; stir well.

6. Add stevia and salt.

7. Cover, reduce heat, and simmer 20 minutes.

8. Lightly heat tortillas and spoon rice along center of each. Top with chili, avocado, and cheese.

9. Sprinkle with parsley, roll, and serve.

What Is Stevia?

No more worries about the devastating side effects of artificial sweeteners! Finally, there is an herbal sweetener 300 times sweeter than sugar without any side effects. Stevia helps regulate blood-sugar levels and is safe for diabetics and those of you needing a safe alternative sweetener. Add a little at a time, tasting as you go to determine the right level of sweetness.

SERVES 6

590 calories
25 g fat
77 g carbohydrates
28 g protein
6 g sugars
14 g fiber

INGREDIENTS

2 tablespoons olive oil
6 cloves garlic, chopped
1 onion, chopped
2 teaspoons cumin powder
1 teaspoon turmeric
1 teaspoon cayenne pepper
16 ounces tempeh, minced
1 zucchini, chopped
1 red pepper, chopped
1 can (14-ounce) diced tomatoes
1 can (15-ounce) kidney beans, drained and rinsed
1 can (15-ounce) cannellini beans, drained and rinsed
½ cup kalamata olives, diced
Pinch of stevia
Sea salt to taste
6 whole-grain tortillas
2 cups cooked brown rice
1 avocado, diced
Grated Romano or goat cheese (optional)
½ cup parsley, chopped

broccoli with sea vegetables

The distinctive taste of broccoli, coupled with the mild-tasting arame sea vegetable, is tied together in a cream sauce made from silken tofu. The perfect complement of flavors, East meets West in this mineral-rich vegetable dish. Silken tofu used in this way is the perfect substitute for heavy cream sauces loaded with heart-stopping saturated fat.

SERVES 8

80 calories
3.5 g fat
8 g carbohydrates
7 g protein
2 g sugars
3 g fiber

INGREDIENTS

1 pound broccoli
¼ cup dry arame
1 tablespoon olive oil
½ onion, chopped
½ cup fresh basil leaves
2 cloves garlic, minced
1 (14-ounce) package silken tofu
3 tablespoons mellow white miso
2 green onions, chopped
½ cup fresh parsley
Juice of ½ lemon

Broccoli and Arame in Tofu Cream Sauce

Miso is fermented soybean paste loaded with beneficial digestive enzymes, instrumental in moving low levels of radiation out of the body. When not using it to make sauces, have a teaspoon each day in a bowl of vegetable or chicken broth and top with chopped green onions.

1. Cut the florets off broccoli stems; cut into smaller florets and set aside.

2. Soak arame in hot water 10 minutes; drain and set aside.

3. Steam broccoli florets until tender; rinse under cold water, and set aside.

4. In a large skillet, heat oil; add onion, basil, and garlic; sauté until tender. Add broccoli and arame; stir well. Remove from heat.

5. In a blender or food processor, purée tofu, miso, green onions, parsley, and lemon juice until creamy.

6. Pour tofu mixture over broccoli; mix well. Reheat gently if necessary, but do not boil.

7. Adjust seasonings and serve as a side dish.

Simple, Easy Arame

Soak arame in hot water until tender, about 10 minutes, then drain and toss with cooked grains, soba noodles, or into a raw salad. High in calcium and other minerals, it is the most versatile of the sea vegetables and one everyone can enjoy.

oats and walnuts

Not too sweet, but with plenty of chew, this combination of cholesterol-lowering oats and heart-healthy walnuts makes a great snack food. Take them to work to munch on your break and pack them into your kid's lunchbox. Either way, these two Superfoods provide calm, sustainable energy and nutrients for your brain.

Oatmeal Raisin Chewies

Spelt flour is an excellent substitute for wheat flour, and can be tolerated by some people with allergies or an intolerance to wheat, but still problematic for those with a gluten allergy, such as celiac disease.

1. Preheat oven to 375°F.
2. In a large bowl, mix oats, flour, salt, walnuts, raisins, and cinnamon. Add coconut oil slowly, making sure to coat oats well with oil.
3. Slowly stir in syrup and vanilla. Add water; mix until batter becomes thick.
4. Oil baking sheets with 1 teaspoon of coconut oil. Using a tablespoon, spoon batter onto an oiled baking sheet.
5. Pat down each spoonful into patties about 2" across and ¼" thick and ½" apart. The cookies will not spread, because there is no leavening agent.
6. Place cookies in oven and bake 25 minutes, or until golden brown.
7. Cool cookies slightly before removing from pan with a spatula. Cool completely before serving.

Sweet Additions
You can play with the ingredients, adding some of your or your children's favorite treats. Try adding ½ cup of carob chips or organic chocolate chips in place of the raisins, or ¼ cup of unsweetened coconut flakes with some dried cranberries.

SERVES 6–8

250 calories
10 g fat
37 g carbohydrates
5 g protein
8 g sugars
4 g fiber

INGREDIENTS
1½ cups rolled oats
¾ cup spelt flour
⅛ teaspoon sea salt
½ cup chopped walnuts
½ cup raisins
1 teaspoon cinnamon
2 tablespoons coconut oil
⅓ cup agave or maple syrup
½ teaspoon vanilla extract
1 cup cold spring water

garlic, parsley, and yogurt

This refreshing combination of foods is the perfect summer brunch recipe. Cleansing cucumbers, blood-purifying parsley, bacteria-fighting garlic, and gut-soothing yogurt restore balance to your internal organs, refresh your palate, cool the heat, and delight the taste buds. Best served chilled, with the suggested condiments on top.

SERVES 6–8

310 calories
29 g fat
10 g carbohydrates
5 g protein
6 g sugars
2 g fiber

INGREDIENTS

5 medium cucumbers
1 medium sweet onion
2 large red peppers
1 medium jalapeño pepper, seeded and chopped
4 medium cloves garlic, smashed and peeled
¾ cup fresh mint leaves, chopped
½ cup parsley, chopped
2 cups plain, organic yogurt
1 teaspoon sea salt (or to taste)
3 tablespoons white-wine vinegar
¾ cup extra-virgin olive oil
1 cup vegetable stock
1 cup water
½ cup pine nuts, toasted

Cucumber Gazpacho

Chop the vegetables in the food processor according to your preference for texture. Some may want a smoother soup, while others will want it with bigger chunks. This is where you can make this dish to suit your individual tastes and desires.

1. Peel, trim, quarter lengthwise, seed, and chop cucumbers. Hold back a cup of chopped cucumber for garnish.

2. In a food processor, process remaining cucumber in batches, scraping sides. Remove cucumbers to a bowl and set next to food processor.

3. Core, seed, and chop onion, red pepper, and jalapeño; pulse chop in food processor. Add to cucumbers.

4. In processor, purée garlic, mint, parsley, yogurt, sea salt, and vinegar. While machine is running, add oil slowly through feed slot.

5. Fold into cucumber mixture; add stock and water, stirring to combine.

6. Adjust seasonings. Refrigerate until chilled. Serve topped with toasted pine nuts, chopped cucumber, and minced parsley.

Toasting Pine Nuts

Heat a small, heavy skillet over medium-low heat and add the pine nuts. Spread them out and keep them moving with a wooden utensil or by giving the pan a shake from time to time. The nuts will release enough of their own oil, so you won't have to add any. When browned, remove to a ceramic bowl and allow to cool.

good fats come together

Whether rubbing fresh avocado onto your skin or eating it in a salad, this is close to the perfect food. Teamed with walnuts, these two Superfoods help lower your bad cholesterol and help protect you from free-radical damage. A one-two punch of vitamins C and E strengthens your immune system and gives your skin a youthful glow.

Avocado Plum Salad

This is a lovely looking salad with a sweet and sour sharpness to complement the crunch of the radish. Red grapes can be substituted for the plums if desired. Try not to over-stir the ingredients or the avocado will break down and lose its shape.

1. In a medium-size bowl, whisk together lemon juice, vinegar, agave, and olive oil.
2. Add radish, walnuts, and baby plums to dressing; toss to cover.
3. Add avocado; toss gently to cover with dressing.
4. Place in refrigerator for 10 minutes to chill before serving.

Ume Plum Vinegar
Cherry pink in color, ume plum vinegar is made from the Japanese pickled umeboshi plums. It has a salty, sour flavor with light, citrus undertones. It is a great substitute to use in salad dressings and sauces where salt is called for.

SERVES 8

190 calories
16 g fat
12 g carbohydrates
3 g protein
5 g sugars
5 g fiber

INGREDIENTS
Juice of 1 lemon
1 teaspoon Ume plum vinegar
1 tablespoon agave syrup
2 tablespoons extra-virgin olive oil
2 cups red radish, quartered
½ cup toasted walnuts, chopped
2 cups baby plums, pitted and halved
2 ripe Haas avocados, diced

superfoods unite!

Broccoli and other nutritious vegetables are tossed with olive oil and roasted until just tender. What a treat! Roasted vegetables are everyone's favorite dish, and you can change the vegetables to suit your tastes. Top them with a simple Walnut Parsley Sauce and you have a stunning gourmet dish that will surprise you with its rich, complex flavors.

SERVES 8

360 calories
23 g fat
34 g carbohydrates
7 g protein
5 g sugars
7 g fiber

INGREDIENTS

1 onion
1 large zucchini
2 cups broccoli florets
2 cups cauliflower florets
7 small red skin potatoes
1 pound green beans
½ cup extra-virgin olive oil or roasted walnut oil
1 cup raw walnuts
3 cloves garlic
1 cup parsley
Sea salt to taste

Roasted Vegetables with Walnut Parsley Sauce

Make extra sauce and toss with your favorite pasta or roasted potatoes.

1. Preheat oven to 400°F.

2. Chop onion, zucchini, broccoli, cauliflower, and potatoes into medium-size pieces. Trim green beans, but leave long.

3. Place vegetables in a large bowl; toss with ¼ cup olive oil to lightly coat.

4. Spread vegetables out on a baking sheet; roast uncovered 20 minutes, or until potatoes are tender.

5. Meanwhile, grind walnuts in a mortar and pestle; add garlic, parsley, and sea salt and continue to grind. Add remaining olive oil a bit at a time to moisten ingredients. (You can use a food processor, but use the pulsing action.) Sauce should be thick with walnuts, but wet with oil. To use on pasta, thin sauce with warm water before adding.

6. Spoon sauce into an attractive ceramic serving bowl.

7. When vegetables are done, move them to a platter and top each serving with a dollop of Walnut Parsley Sauce.

What's a Mortar and Pestle?

A mortar is a heavy, round bowl that, when used with a grinding tool, or, pestle, can mash food or grind it to a paste. When not available, use a food processor, but with a gentle pulsing-action effect for chopping, rather than a smooth purée.

super-duper fruit dessert

A quick and easy dessert or healthy snack, this combination of apples, blueberries, and walnuts provides just the right amount of antioxidants and omega-3 fatty acids and none of the guilt most desserts leave you with.

Blueberries and Apples with Walnut Cream

When making the Walnut Cream, use just enough water to cover the walnuts. Let the blender run to ensure the sauce thickens and there are no lumps or pieces of nut remaining. This sauce is an excellent substitute for dairy whipped cream and can be served over cake, such as strawberry shortcake.

1. Place the water, cinnamon, and honey in a large saucepan; bring to a simmer.

2. Reduce heat to low, add apples; stir well and simmer for 1 minute.

3. Add blueberries and continue to cook until apples are just tender and blueberries have begun to release their juice, about 7–10 minutes.

4. Meanwhile, combine walnuts, maple syrup, vanilla extract, and enough water to cover walnuts in a blender; purée until thick and creamy.

5. Serve the fruit in a small bowl topped with the walnut cream.

Walnut Substitute
Cashews can be used in place of walnuts, and make a rich and creamy sauce as well. For something more savory, leave out the sweetener and add some favorite herbs and sea salt. This makes a great protein-rich sauce to serve over grains and vegetables.

SERVES 8

200 calories
8 g fat
33 g carbohydrates
2 g protein
27 g sugars
3 g fiber

INGREDIENTS
½ cup water
½ teaspoon cinnamon
⅓ cup honey or agave syrup
4 apples, cored and chopped, skins intact
1 pint fresh blueberries or 10-ounce bag frozen
1 cup raw walnuts
3 tablespoons pure maple syrup
1 teaspoon vanilla extract
Water to cover walnuts in blender

an omega-3 rich salad

When the warmth of summer has ripened the tomatoes and the deep green parsley is full and plentiful, the wild salmon are making their annual run upstream to the spawning grounds. All good news for putting this vitamin-rich salad together with seasonal fresh ingredients.

SERVES 4

470 calories
22 g fat
40 g carbohydrates
29 g protein
6 g sugars
3 g fiber

INGREDIENTS

1 large beefsteak tomato
½ cup fresh parsley
⅓ cup fresh basil
1 shallot
12 walnut halves
2 slices thick sour dough bread
1 (10-ounce) can wild sockeye salmon
Juice of ½ a lemon
2 tablespoons extra-virgin olive oil
½ cup orange juice
1 teaspoon orange zest
½ teaspoon honey
2 tablespoons white-wine vinegar
½ teaspoon Ume plum vinegar
1 clove minced garlic
½ cup grated Romano cheese

Summer Salmon Salad

This salad is reminiscent of a Tuscan bread salad and needs a little time to marinate before serving. Allow the bread to soak up some of the dressing, but not get too soggy.

1. Slice tomato into bite-size pieces; place in a medium-size ceramic bowl.

2. Mince parsley and basil until very fine; add to tomatoes.

3. Slice shallot into thin half moons; add to tomatoes.

4. Break walnuts into pieces with your hands; add to tomatoes.

5. Lightly toast bread; slice into bite-size cubes; add to tomatoes.

6. Open can of salmon and separate out skin and visible bones; place in a bowl and squeeze some lemon over salmon. Set aside.

7. In a small bowl, whisk together oil, orange juice, zest, honey, vinegars, and garlic. Pour dressing over salad ingredients; toss well to cover. Set aside to marinate for 15 minutes.

8. Serve the salad on individual plates topped first with the salmon and then with the grated Romano cheese.

Salmon Choices

As a substitute for canned salmon, poach some fresh salmon in vegetable broth and serve chilled on top of the tomato salad. If there is no salmon to be found, canned or fresh, seared tuna fish will do, or try a piece of halibut or sea bass. The beauty of this salad is that it works no matter what protein you use.

nutrient-rich grain salad

The quinoa only takes twenty minutes to cook; meanwhile, you can have everything chopped and ready to go. If you can't wait for the grain to cool, go ahead and mix everything together. The heat from the grain will soften the vegetables and absorb the dressing more quickly. Either way, this salad is a Superfoods winner.

Quinoa Black Bean Salad

For grain salads, the longer it marinates the better the flavors are absorbed by the ingredients. Make it the night before and take some to work for lunch the next day. Bring this salad along for a potluck meal, and watch how your friends enjoy something new and delicious.

1. In a medium saucepan, combine quinoa, water, and ½ teaspoon sea salt. Cover, bring to a boil, reduce heat to low, and simmer until all water is absorbed, about 20 minutes.

2. When done, spoon into a large bowl and allow to cool.

3. Meanwhile, grate carrots, slice onions, toast pumpkin seeds, mince parsley, and rinse canned beans.

4. When quinoa is cool, add carrots, green onions, pumpkin seeds, black beans, and parsley; mix well.

5. In a small bowl, whisk together lemon, garlic, vinegar, oil, and salt.

6. Add vinaigrette; mix completely and allow to marinate a few minutes before serving.

Toasting Pumpkin Seeds

Just a reminder that raw pumpkin seeds can be toasted in a dry skillet over medium-low heat. Keep them moving around by shaking the pan from time to time or stirring them with a wooden spoon. You'll know they are done when they've stopped popping or turned a golden brown.

SERVES 8

190 calories
7 g fat
26 g carbohydrates
6 g protein
1 g sugars
5 g fiber

INGREDIENTS
1 cup quinoa
2 cups water
½ teaspoon sea salt
1 carrot
2 green onions
⅓ cup pumpkin seeds
½ cup parsley leaves
1 (14-ounce) can black beans
Juice of 1 lemon
1 clove minced garlic
2 tablespoons apple cider vinegar
3 tablespoons extra-virgin olive oil
½ teaspoon salt

APPENDIX A

Glossary

Allicin: a sulfur element, found in garlic and known for its ability to cleanse and purify the body.

Anthocyanins: any of various soluble glycoside pigments producing blue-to-red coloring in flowers and plants.

Antioxidants: any of various substances (beta carotene, vitamin C, and alpha-tocopherol) that inhibit oxidation or reactions promoted by oxygen and peroxides, and help to protect the body from free-radical damage.

Ayurveda: an ancient Indian understanding of life, considered the "mother of all medicines." It is based on preventing disease and enhancing health, longevity, and vitality.

Beano: a particular enzyme product that helps to digest the carbohydrates that feed intestinal bacteria-causing gas in the intestines.

Beta carotene: a member of the carotenoids, highly pigmented fat-soluble compounds naturally present in many fruits, grains, oils, and vegetables that can be converted to active vitamin A.

Beta glucans: polysaccharides that occur in the outer layer, or bran, of cereal grains.

Beta-sitosterol: the plant equivalent of cholesterol in animals, found in avocados; helps lower the amounts of cholesterol in the bloodstream.

Bioflavonoids: a group of naturally occurring plant compounds that act primarily as plant pigments and antioxidants.

Caffeic acid: a naturally occurring compound shown to be a carcinogenic inhibitor.

Catechins: a type of flavanoid and strong antioxidant that combats harmful free radicals and protects DNA.

Chitinases: a substance in avocados, bananas, and chestnuts associated with latex-fruit syndrome.

Chlorophyll: a molecule specifically designed to absorb sunlight and use this energy to synthesize carbohydrates from CO_2 and water.

Collagen: the most abundant protein in the body, needed to form bone, cartilage, skin, and tendons.

Cruciferous vegetable: a family of vegetables that includes, kale, collards, Brussels sprouts, broccoli, and cauliflower; high in cancer-fighting sulforaphane compounds.

Diuretic: food or herbs that help to dispel fluids from the body.

Enzymes: proteins that speed up chemical reactions in the body, such as the breakdown and assimilation of food in the digestive system.

Epicatechin: a group of chemicals called flavonols, shown to improve cardiovascular function and increase blood flow to the brain.

Essential fatty acids: omega-3 and omega-6; these are essential fats needed by the body to protect against inflammation and other factors.

Ferulic acid: a potent antioxidant that is able to scavenge free radicals and protect against oxidative damage.

Flavonoids: known for their antioxidant activity, they can help prevent free-radical damage to the body's cells. This results in protection against cancer and heart disease.

Folate: the natural form of folic acid; is known as vitamin B9, and required for DNA synthesis and cell growth. It is important for red blood cell formation and energy production, as well as the forming of amino acids.

Free radicals: specially reactive atom or group of atoms that has one or more unpaired electrons, produced in the body by natural biological processes or introduced from outside (as in tobacco smoke, toxins, or pollutants). Can damage cells, proteins, and DNA by altering their chemical structure.

Glucosinolate: a phytonutrient that actually boosts your body's detoxification enzymes, clearing potentially carcinogenic substances more quickly from your body.

Indole-3-carbinol: a compound that helps deactivate a potent estrogen metabolite (4-hydroxyestrone) that promotes tumor growth; shown to suppress not only breast-tumor cell growth, but also the movement of cancerous cells to other parts of the body.

Lactobacillus acidophilus: one of the most important friendly intestinal bacteria (microflora) and necessary for gastrointestinal health.

Lutein and zeaxanthin: compounds called xanthophylls or carotenoids related to beta carotene. They give vegetables like carrots their orange color and add yellow pigment to plants. They are also found in large amounts in the lens and retina of the eyes, where they function as antioxidants to protect the eyes from free-radical damage.

Lycopene: an antioxidant and open-chain unsaturated carotenoid that gives the red color to tomatoes and other fruits.

Lysine: an amino acid essential for tissue growth and repair.

Macronutrients: include carbohydrates, fats, and proteins. These are the foods the body uses for energy and growth.

Micronutrients: include vitamins and minerals.

Moles: a form of measurement, measuring the actual number of atoms or molecules in an object.

Monounsaturated fats: containing one double or triple bond per molecule. Canola and olive oils are rich in monounsaturated fatty acids.

Nucleic acids: RNA/DNA responsible for the renewal, repair, and growth of the cells.

Oleic acid: a form of monounsaturated fat, found in avocado and shown to help lower cholesterol in the body.

Phenylethylamine: a strong stimulant related to the amphetamine family, known to increase the activity of neurotransmitters in parts of the brain that control your ability to pay attention and stay alert.

Phytic acid: present in the bran and hulls of all seeds, it can block the uptake of essential minerals in the digestive tract.

Phytonutrients: antioxidants that disarm free radicals before they can damage DNA, cell membranes, and fat-containing molecules such as cholesterol.

Phytosterol: plant sterols structurally similar to cholesterol that act in the intestine to lower cholesterol absorption.

Polyphenols: an antioxidant phytochemical that tends to prevent or neutralize the damaging effects of free radicals.

Polyunsaturated fats: having in each molecule many chemical bonds, in which two or three pairs of electrons are shared by two atoms.

Probiotics: beneficial microflora (good bacteria) found in the intestines.

Quercetin: a yellow crystalline pigment, usually occurring in the form of glycosides, in various plants and proven to prevent unstable oxygen molecules, or free radicals, from damaging cells.

Rajasic: referring to Ayurvedic principles of a food that causes overstimulation to the body.

Saponins: a bitter substance found in plants' seed coats, that repels birds and insects.

Saturated fats: animal and dairy fats that remain solid at room temperatures.

Sofrito: a method of adding sautéed onions, garlic, herbs, and spices to enhance a soup or bean dish.

Sulforaphane: a phytonutrient compound found in broccoli and shown to prevent the development of tumors.

Theanine: an amino acid present in the tea plant. Absorbed by the small intestine, it crosses the blood-brain barrier, where it affects the brain's neurotransmitters and increases alpha brain-wave activity.

Theobromine: a caffeine-like substance found in chocolate. When taken in excess, can inhibit the body's ability to absorb minerals.

Resource Guide

B

Natural Food Supplies

Nature's Harvest
P.O. 291, 28 Main Street, Blairstown, NJ 07825
Contact Michelle St. Andre: 908-362-6766
Harvest6766@embarqmail.com

Organic Produce
www.diamondorganics.com

Whole Grains and Sea Vegetables
www.kushistore.com/acatalog/welcome.html

Organic foods and products
www.diamondorganics.com

Vegetables, Earthbound Farm
www.ebfarm.com

Cascadian Farms, frozen fruits and vegetables
www.cfarm.com

Seeds of Change, organic tomato sauces and salsas
www.seedsofchange.com

Green Mountain Coffee Roasters
(organic, sustainably grown, fair trade)
www.greenmountaincoffee.com

Health Education Web Sites

Dr. Joseph Mercola

www.mercola.com

Organic Consumers Association

www.organicconsumers.org

Energy Consumption Statistics

Energy Information Administration Web site

www.eia.doe.gov/kids/classactivities/CrunchTheNumbersIntermediat-eDec2002.pdf

USGS Web site

http://energy.cr.usgs.gov/energy/stats_ctry/Stat1.htmla

U.S. Department of Energy's division of energy efficiency and renewable energy

www.eere.gov

Saving with Recycling, NRDC Web site

www.nrdc.org/land/forests/gtissue.asp

Saving with Compact Fluorescents, Environmental Defense Web site

www.environmentaldefense.org/article.cfm?contentid=5215

Sustainable Building and Retrofitting

Bob Swain's Web site

www.bobswain.com

General building information

www.greenbuilder.com

Alternative energy systems, products, and installation

www.utilityfree.com

Saline Pool Systems

www.salinepoolsystems.com

Sick Building Syndrome

www.wellbuilding.com

Renewable Resources

www.green-e.org
www.greenfacts.org
www.greentagusa.org

Other Resources

Cleaning Chemicals

www.restoreproducts.com

Tom Foerstel's Web site for organic products

www.organic.org
www.organiclinks.com

Daliya Robson's Web site for nontoxic household furnishings

www.nontoxic.com

For sustainably harvested household products

www.seventhgeneration.com

Teflon

www.tuberose.com/Teflon.html

Chemical-free home products

www.EnvironProducts.com

Measuring your environmental footprint

www.carbonfootprint.com

What the labels really say

truthinlabeling.org

Index of
Recipes and Ingredients

THE EVERYTHING SERIES!

BUSINESS & PERSONAL FINANCE

Everything® Accounting Book
Everything® Budgeting Book, 2nd Ed.
Everything® Business Planning Book
Everything® Coaching and Mentoring Book, 2nd Ed.
Everything® Fundraising Book
Everything® Get Out of Debt Book
Everything® Grant Writing Book, 2nd Ed.
Everything® Guide to Buying Foreclosures
Everything® Guide to Fundraising, $15.95
Everything® Guide to Mortgages
Everything® Guide to Personal Finance for Single Mothers
Everything® Home-Based Business Book, 2nd Ed.
Everything® Homebuying Book, 3rd Ed., $15.95
Everything® Homeselling Book, 2nd Ed.
Everything® Human Resource Management Book
Everything® Improve Your Credit Book
Everything® Investing Book, 2nd Ed.
Everything® Landlording Book
Everything® Leadership Book, 2nd Ed.
Everything® Managing People Book, 2nd Ed.
Everything® Negotiating Book
Everything® Online Auctions Book
Everything® Online Business Book
Everything® Personal Finance Book
Everything® Personal Finance in Your 20s & 30s Book, 2nd Ed.
Everything® Personal Finance in Your 40s & 50s Book, $15.95
Everything® Project Management Book, 2nd Ed.
Everything® Real Estate Investing Book
Everything® Retirement Planning Book
Everything® Robert's Rules Book, $7.95
Everything® Selling Book
Everything® Start Your Own Business Book, 2nd Ed.
Everything® Wills & Estate Planning Book

COOKING

Everything® Barbecue Cookbook
Everything® Bartender's Book, 2nd Ed., $9.95
Everything® Calorie Counting Cookbook
Everything® Cheese Book
Everything® Chinese Cookbook
Everything® Classic Recipes Book
Everything® Cocktail Parties & Drinks Book
Everything® College Cookbook
Everything® Cooking for Baby and Toddler Book
Everything® Diabetes Cookbook
Everything® Easy Gourmet Cookbook
Everything® Fondue Cookbook
Everything® Food Allergy Cookbook, $15.95
Everything® Fondue Party Book
Everything® Gluten-Free Cookbook
Everything® Glycemic Index Cookbook
Everything® Grilling Cookbook
Everything® Healthy Cooking for Parties Book, $15.95
Everything® Holiday Cookbook
Everything® Indian Cookbook
Everything® Lactose-Free Cookbook
Everything® Low-Cholesterol Cookbook

Everything® Low-Fat High-Flavor Cookbook, 2nd Ed., $15.95
Everything® Low-Salt Cookbook
Everything® Meals for a Month Cookbook
Everything® Meals on a Budget Cookbook
Everything® Mediterranean Cookbook
Everything® Mexican Cookbook
Everything® No Trans Fat Cookbook
Everything® One-Pot Cookbook, 2nd Ed., $15.95
Everything® Organic Cooking for Baby & Toddler Book, $15.95
Everything® Pizza Cookbook
Everything® Quick Meals Cookbook, 2nd Ed., $15.95
Everything® Slow Cooker Cookbook
Everything® Slow Cooking for a Crowd Cookbook
Everything® Soup Cookbook
Everything® Stir-Fry Cookbook
Everything® Sugar-Free Cookbook
Everything® Tapas and Small Plates Cookbook
Everything® Tex-Mex Cookbook
Everything® Thai Cookbook
Everything® Vegetarian Cookbook
Everything® Whole-Grain, High-Fiber Cookbook
Everything® Wild Game Cookbook
Everything® Wine Book, 2nd Ed.

GAMES

Everything® 15-Minute Sudoku Book, $9.95
Everything® 30-Minute Sudoku Book, $9.95
Everything® Bible Crosswords Book, $9.95
Everything® Blackjack Strategy Book
Everything® Brain Strain Book, $9.95
Everything® Bridge Book
Everything® Card Games Book
Everything® Card Tricks Book, $9.95
Everything® Casino Gambling Book, 2nd Ed.
Everything® Chess Basics Book
Everything® Christmas Crosswords Book, $9.95
Everything® Craps Strategy Book
Everything® Crossword and Puzzle Book
Everything® Crosswords and Puzzles for Quote Lovers Book, $9.95
Everything® Crossword Challenge Book
Everything® Crosswords for the Beach Book, $9.95
Everything® Cryptic Crosswords Book, $9.95
Everything® Cryptograms Book, $9.95
Everything® Easy Crosswords Book
Everything® Easy Kakuro Book, $9.95
Everything® Easy Large-Print Crosswords Book
Everything® Games Book, 2nd Ed.
Everything® Giant Book of Crosswords
Everything® Giant Sudoku Book, $9.95
Everything® Giant Word Search Book
Everything® Kakuro Challenge Book, $9.95
Everything® Large-Print Crossword Challenge Book
Everything® Large-Print Crosswords Book
Everything® Large-Print Travel Crosswords Book
Everything® Lateral Thinking Puzzles Book, $9.95
Everything® Literary Crosswords Book, $9.95
Everything® Mazes Book
Everything® Memory Booster Puzzles Book, $9.95

Everything® Movie Crosswords Book, $9.95
Everything® Music Crosswords Book, $9.95
Everything® Online Poker Book
Everything® Pencil Puzzles Book, $9.95
Everything® Poker Strategy Book
Everything® Pool & Billiards Book
Everything® Puzzles for Commuters Book, $9.95
Everything® Puzzles for Dog Lovers Book, $9.95
Everything® Sports Crosswords Book, $9.95
Everything® Test Your IQ Book, $9.95
Everything® Texas Hold 'Em Book, $9.95
Everything® Travel Crosswords Book, $9.95
Everything® Travel Mazes Book, $9.95
Everything® Travel Word Search Book, $9.95
Everything® TV Crosswords Book, $9.95
Everything® Word Games Challenge Book
Everything® Word Scramble Book
Everything® Word Search Book

HEALTH

Everything® Alzheimer's Book
Everything® Diabetes Book
Everything® First Aid Book, $9.95
Everything® Green Living Book
Everything® Health Guide to Addiction and Recovery
Everything® Health Guide to Adult Bipolar Disorder
Everything® Health Guide to Arthritis
Everything® Health Guide to Controlling Anxiety
Everything® Health Guide to Depression
Everything® Health Guide to Diabetes, 2nd Ed.
Everything® Health Guide to Fibromyalgia
Everything® Health Guide to Menopause, 2nd Ed.
Everything® Health Guide to Migraines
Everything® Health Guide to Multiple Sclerosis
Everything® Health Guide to OCD
Everything® Health Guide to PMS
Everything® Health Guide to Postpartum Care
Everything® Health Guide to Thyroid Disease
Everything® Hypnosis Book
Everything® Low Cholesterol Book
Everything® Menopause Book
Everything® Nutrition Book
Everything® Reflexology Book
Everything® Stress Management Book
Everything® Superfoods Book, $15.95

HISTORY

Everything® American Government Book
Everything® American History Book, 2nd Ed.
Everything® American Revolution Book, $15.95
Everything® Civil War Book
Everything® Freemasons Book
Everything® Irish History & Heritage Book
Everything® World War II Book, 2nd Ed.

HOBBIES

Everything® Candlemaking Book
Everything® Cartooning Book
Everything® Coin Collecting Book
Everything® Digital Photography Book, 2nd Ed.

Everything® Drawing Book
Everything® Family Tree Book, 2nd Ed.
Everything® Guide to Online Genealogy, $15.95
Everything® Knitting Book
Everything® Knots Book
Everything® Photography Book
Everything® Quilting Book
Everything® Sewing Book
Everything® Soapmaking Book, 2nd Ed.
Everything® Woodworking Book

HOME IMPROVEMENT

Everything® Feng Shui Book
Everything® Feng Shui Decluttering Book, $9.95
Everything® Fix-It Book
Everything® Green Living Book
Everything® Home Decorating Book
Everything® Home Storage Solutions Book
Everything® Homebuilding Book
Everything® Organize Your Home Book, 2nd Ed.

KIDS' BOOKS

All titles are $7.95
Everything® Fairy Tales Book, $14.95
Everything® Kids' Animal Puzzle & Activity Book
Everything® Kids' Astronomy Book
Everything® Kids' Baseball Book, 5th Ed.
Everything® Kids' Bible Trivia Book
Everything® Kids' Bugs Book
Everything® Kids' Cars and Trucks Puzzle and Activity Book
Everything® Kids' Christmas Puzzle & Activity Book
Everything® Kids' Connect the Dots
    Puzzle and Activity Book
Everything® Kids' Cookbook, 2nd Ed.
Everything® Kids' Crazy Puzzles Book
Everything® Kids' Dinosaurs Book
Everything® Kids' Dragons Puzzle and Activity Book
Everything® Kids' Environment Book $7.95
Everything® Kids' Fairies Puzzle and Activity Book
Everything® Kids' First Spanish Puzzle and Activity Book
Everything® Kids' Football Book
Everything® Kids' Geography Book
Everything® Kids' Gross Cookbook
Everything® Kids' Gross Hidden Pictures Book
Everything® Kids' Gross Jokes Book
Everything® Kids' Gross Mazes Book
Everything® Kids' Gross Puzzle & Activity Book
Everything® Kids' Halloween Puzzle & Activity Book
Everything® Kids' Hanukkah Puzzle and Activity Book
Everything® Kids' Hidden Pictures Book
Everything® Kids' Horses Book
Everything® Kids' Joke Book
Everything® Kids' Knock Knock Book
Everything® Kids' Learning French Book
Everything® Kids' Learning Spanish Book
Everything® Kids' Magical Science Experiments Book
Everything® Kids' Math Puzzles Book
Everything® Kids' Mazes Book
Everything® Kids' Money Book, 2nd Ed.
Everything® Kids' Mummies, Pharaoh's, and Pyramids Puzzle and Activity Book
Everything® Kids' Nature Book
Everything® Kids' Pirates Puzzle and Activity Book
Everything® Kids' Presidents Book
Everything® Kids' Princess Puzzle and Activity Book
Everything® Kids' Puzzle Book

Everything® Kids' Racecars Puzzle and Activity Book
Everything® Kids' Riddles & Brain Teasers Book
Everything® Kids' Science Experiments Book
Everything® Kids' Sharks Book
Everything® Kids' Soccer Book
Everything® Kids' Spelling Book
Everything® Kids' Spies Puzzle and Activity Book
Everything® Kids' States Book
Everything® Kids' Travel Activity Book
Everything® Kids' Word Search Puzzle and Activity Book

LANGUAGE

Everything® Conversational Japanese Book with CD, $19.95
Everything® French Grammar Book
Everything® French Phrase Book, $9.95
Everything® French Verb Book, $9.95
Everything® German Phrase Book, $9.95
Everything® German Practice Book with CD, $19.95
Everything® Inglés Book
Everything® Intermediate Spanish Book with CD, $19.95
Everything® Italian Phrase Book, $9.95
Everything® Italian Practice Book with CD, $19.95
Everything® Learning Brazilian Portuguese Book with CD, $19.95
Everything® Learning French Book with CD, 2nd Ed., $19.95
Everything® Learning German Book
Everything® Learning Italian Book
Everything® Learning Latin Book
Everything® Learning Russian Book with CD, $19.95
Everything® Learning Spanish Book
Everything® Learning Spanish Book with CD, 2nd Ed., $19.95
Everything® Russian Practice Book with CD, $19.95
Everything® Sign Language Book, $15.95
Everything® Spanish Grammar Book
Everything® Spanish Phrase Book, $9.95
Everything® Spanish Practice Book with CD, $19.95
Everything® Spanish Verb Book, $9.95
Everything® Speaking Mandarin Chinese Book with CD, $19.95

MUSIC

Everything® Bass Guitar Book with CD, $19.95
Everything® Drums Book with CD, $19.95
Everything® Guitar Book with CD, 2nd Ed., $19.95
Everything® Guitar Chords Book with CD, $19.95
Everything® Guitar Scales Book with CD, $19.95
Everything® Harmonica Book with CD, $15.95
Everything® Home Recording Book
Everything® Music Theory Book with CD, $19.95
Everything® Reading Music Book with CD, $19.95
Everything® Rock & Blues Guitar Book with CD, $19.95
Everything® Rock & Blues Piano Book with CD, $19.95
Everything® Rock Drums Book with CD, $19.95
Everything® Singing Book with CD, $19.95
Everything® Songwriting Book

NEW AGE

Everything® Astrology Book, 2nd Ed.
Everything® Birthday Personology Book
Everything® Celtic Wisdom Book, $15.95
Everything® Dreams Book, 2nd Ed.
Everything® Law of Attraction Book, $15.95
Everything® Love Signs Book, $9.95
Everything® Love Spells Book, $9.95
Everything® Palmistry Book
Everything® Psychic Book
Everything® Reiki Book

Everything® Sex Signs Book, $9.95
Everything® Spells & Charms Book, 2nd Ed.
Everything® Tarot Book, 2nd Ed.
Everything® Toltec Wisdom Book
Everything® Wicca & Witchcraft Book, 2nd Ed.

PARENTING

Everything® Baby Names Book, 2nd Ed.
Everything® Baby Shower Book, 2nd Ed.
Everything® Baby Sign Language Book with DVD
Everything® Baby's First Year Book
Everything® Birthing Book
Everything® Breastfeeding Book
Everything® Father-to-Be Book
Everything® Father's First Year Book
Everything® Get Ready for Baby Book, 2nd Ed.
Everything® Get Your Baby to Sleep Book, $9.95
Everything® Getting Pregnant Book
Everything® Guide to Pregnancy Over 35
Everything® Guide to Raising a One-Year-Old
Everything® Guide to Raising a Two-Year-Old
Everything® Guide to Raising Adolescent Boys
Everything® Guide to Raising Adolescent Girls
Everything® Mother's First Year Book
Everything® Parent's Guide to Childhood Illnesses
Everything® Parent's Guide to Children and Divorce
Everything® Parent's Guide to Children with ADD/ADHD
Everything® Parent's Guide to Children with Asperger's Syndrome
Everything® Parent's Guide to Children with Anxiety
Everything® Parent's Guide to Children with Asthma
Everything® Parent's Guide to Children with Autism
Everything® Parent's Guide to Children with Bipolar Disorder
Everything® Parent's Guide to Children with Depression
Everything® Parent's Guide to Children with Dyslexia
Everything® Parent's Guide to Children with Juvenile Diabetes
Everything® Parent's Guide to Children with OCD
Everything® Parent's Guide to Positive Discipline
Everything® Parent's Guide to Raising Boys
Everything® Parent's Guide to Raising Girls
Everything® Parent's Guide to Raising Siblings
Everything® Parent's Guide to Raising Your Adopted Child
Everything® Parent's Guide to Sensory Integration Disorder
Everything® Parent's Guide to Tantrums
Everything® Parent's Guide to the Strong-Willed Child
Everything® Parenting a Teenager Book
Everything® Potty Training Book, $9.95
Everything® Pregnancy Book, 3rd Ed.
Everything® Pregnancy Fitness Book
Everything® Pregnancy Nutrition Book
Everything® Pregnancy Organizer, 2nd Ed., $16.95
Everything® Toddler Activities Book
Everything® Toddler Book
Everything® Tween Book
Everything® Twins, Triplets, and More Book

PETS

Everything® Aquarium Book
Everything® Boxer Book
Everything® Cat Book, 2nd Ed.
Everything® Chihuahua Book
Everything® Cooking for Dogs Book
Everything® Dachshund Book
Everything® Dog Book, 2nd Ed.
Everything® Dog Grooming Book

Everything® Dog Obedience Book
Everything® Dog Owner's Organizer, $16.95
Everything® Dog Training and Tricks Book
Everything® German Shepherd Book
Everything® Golden Retriever Book
Everything® Horse Book, 2nd Ed., $15.95
Everything® Horse Care Book
Everything® Horseback Riding Book
Everything® Labrador Retriever Book
Everything® Poodle Book
Everything® Pug Book
Everything® Puppy Book
Everything® Small Dogs Book
Everything® Tropical Fish Book
Everything® Yorkshire Terrier Book

REFERENCE

Everything® American Presidents Book
Everything® Blogging Book
Everything® Build Your Vocabulary Book, $9.95
Everything® Car Care Book
Everything® Classical Mythology Book
Everything® Da Vinci Book
Everything® Einstein Book
Everything® Enneagram Book
Everything® Etiquette Book, 2nd Ed.
Everything® Family Christmas Book, $15.95
Everything® Guide to C. S. Lewis & Narnia
Everything® Guide to Divorce, 2nd Ed., $15.95
Everything® Guide to Edgar Allan Poe
Everything® Guide to Understanding Philosophy
Everything® Inventions and Patents Book
Everything® Jacqueline Kennedy Onassis Book
Everything® John F. Kennedy Book
Everything® Mafia Book
Everything® Martin Luther King Jr. Book
Everything® Pirates Book
Everything® Private Investigation Book
Everything® Psychology Book
Everything® Public Speaking Book, $9.95
Everything® Shakespeare Book, 2nd Ed.

RELIGION

Everything® Angels Book
Everything® Bible Book
Everything® Bible Study Book with CD, $19.95
Everything® Buddhism Book
Everything® Catholicism Book
Everything® Christianity Book
Everything® Gnostic Gospels Book
Everything® Hinduism Book, $15.95
Everything® History of the Bible Book
Everything® Jesus Book
Everything® Jewish History & Heritage Book
Everything® Judaism Book
Everything® Kabbalah Book
Everything® Koran Book
Everything® Mary Book
Everything® Mary Magdalene Book
Everything® Prayer Book

Everything® Saints Book, 2nd Ed.
Everything® Torah Book
Everything® Understanding Islam Book
Everything® Women of the Bible Book
Everything® World's Religions Book

SCHOOL & CAREERS

Everything® Career Tests Book
Everything® College Major Test Book
Everything® College Survival Book, 2nd Ed.
Everything® Cover Letter Book, 2nd Ed.
Everything® Filmmaking Book
Everything® Get-a-Job Book, 2nd Ed.
Everything® Guide to Being a Paralegal
Everything® Guide to Being a Personal Trainer
Everything® Guide to Being a Real Estate Agent
Everything® Guide to Being a Sales Rep
Everything® Guide to Being an Event Planner
Everything® Guide to Careers in Health Care
Everything® Guide to Careers in Law Enforcement
Everything® Guide to Government Jobs
Everything® Guide to Starting and Running a Catering
    Business
Everything® Guide to Starting and Running a Restaurant
**Everything® Guide to Starting and Running
    a Retail Store**
Everything® Job Interview Book, 2nd Ed.
Everything® New Nurse Book
Everything® New Teacher Book
Everything® Paying for College Book
Everything® Practice Interview Book
Everything® Resume Book, 3rd Ed.
Everything® Study Book

SELF-HELP

Everything® Body Language Book
Everything® Dating Book, 2nd Ed.
Everything® Great Sex Book
**Everything® Guide to Caring for Aging Parents,
    $15.95**
Everything® Self-Esteem Book
Everything® Self-Hypnosis Book, $9.95
Everything® Tantric Sex Book

SPORTS & FITNESS

Everything® Easy Fitness Book
Everything® Fishing Book
Everything® Guide to Weight Training, $15.95
Everything® Krav Maga for Fitness Book
Everything® Running Book, 2nd Ed.
Everything® Triathlon Training Book, $15.95

TRAVEL

Everything® Family Guide to Coastal Florida
Everything® Family Guide to Cruise Vacations
Everything® Family Guide to Hawaii
Everything® Family Guide to Las Vegas, 2nd Ed.
Everything® Family Guide to Mexico
Everything® Family Guide to New England, 2nd Ed.

Everything® Family Guide to New York City, 3rd Ed.
**Everything® Family Guide to Northern California
    and Lake Tahoe**
Everything® Family Guide to RV Travel & Campgrounds
Everything® Family Guide to the Caribbean
Everything® Family Guide to the Disneyland® Resort, California
    Adventure®, Universal Studios®, and the Anaheim
    Area, 2nd Ed.
Everything® Family Guide to the Walt Disney World Resort®,
    Universal Studios®, and Greater Orlando, 5th Ed.
Everything® Family Guide to Timeshares
Everything® Family Guide to Washington D.C., 2nd Ed.

WEDDINGS

Everything® Bachelorette Party Book, $9.95
Everything® Bridesmaid Book, $9.95
Everything® Destination Wedding Book
Everything® Father of the Bride Book, $9.95
Everything® Green Wedding Book, $15.95
Everything® Groom Book, $9.95
Everything® Jewish Wedding Book, 2nd Ed., $15.95
Everything® Mother of the Bride Book, $9.95
Everything® Outdoor Wedding Book
Everything® Wedding Book, 3rd Ed.
Everything® Wedding Checklist, $9.95
Everything® Wedding Etiquette Book, $9.95
Everything® Wedding Organizer, 2nd Ed., $16.95
Everything® Wedding Shower Book, $9.95
Everything® Wedding Vows Book, 3rd Ed., $9.95
Everything® Wedding Workout Book
Everything® Weddings on a Budget Book, 2nd Ed., $9.95

WRITING

Everything® Creative Writing Book
Everything® Get Published Book, 2nd Ed.
Everything® Grammar and Style Book, 2nd Ed.
Everything® Guide to Magazine Writing
Everything® Guide to Writing a Book Proposal
Everything® Guide to Writing a Novel
Everything® Guide to Writing Children's Books
Everything® Guide to Writing Copy
Everything® Guide to Writing Graphic Novels
Everything® Guide to Writing Research Papers
Everything® Guide to Writing a Romance Novel, $15.95
Everything® Improve Your Writing Book, 2nd Ed.
Everything® Writing Poetry Book